M *from the* ainland

M from the ainland

An Anthology of
South Island Writing

Edited by

Lawrence Jones &

Heather Murray

Published by Godwit Publishing Ltd
P.O. Box 4325, Auckland 1
New Zealand

First published 1995

ISBN 0 908877 50 1

Cover design: Christine Hansen
Cover illustration: Rita Angus, 'Cass', c. 1936/7, oil
on canvas on board, collection Robert McDougall Art
Gallery, Christchurch
Typeset by ORCA Publishing Services
Printed by GP Print

Contents

Introduction

An anthology is not a natural object but a human construct, and the criteria of the selection should be made explicit by the selectors. This anthology is first of all a personal one: each selection is there because one or both of the editors liked it, and there has been no attempt at complete coverage (all significant South Island writers since 1980, for example). That personal taste has operated within the parameters set out by our subtitle, 'An Anthology of South Island Writing'. However, the meaning of those terms is not self-evident. 'Writing' is defined relatively inclusively. We include not only short fiction and poems but also excerpts from novels, autobiographies and travel writing. Excerpts are selected to fit into the anthology, interacting with the other texts around them, and thus would appear different in the context of the books from which they are taken; but then the short stories and poems would also look different in the context of individual collections or of the writer's work as a whole.

In interpreting 'writing' we made several self-imposed restrictions. One is that there should be no more than one longer piece from any one writer. Another was time of origin. We wanted relatively recent writing, for a historical anthology of all writing about the South Island would have been a very different and much larger sort of undertaking. In practice we restricted ourselves to writing published since the early 1980s. This still made for a pretty inclusive representation, for our writers range from Allen Curnow, who first began publishing in the 1930s, to Kate Flannery, whose first book appeared in 1994, and they encompass something like four literary 'generations'. 'Recent', of course, does not at all refer to the temporal focus of the selections, for that varies widely. In some selections it is the nineteenth-century past, as in Ian Wedde, Rachel McAlpine, Graham Billing and Rob Allan. In Keri Hulme this is extended back to the family, tribal and cultural past, including myth. In Stevan Eldred-Grigg, on the other hand, the focus is on the recent historical past, while in many other writers it is on the personal past of their childhood and adolescence. The personal past is, of course, central to the autobiographers — Janet Frame, Toss Woollaston, Alistair Campbell and Ruth Dallas — but there is a strong sense of personal memory in writers as diverse as Curnow, Dan Davin, Flannery, Christine Johnston and Marion Jones. In contrast, Maurice Gee, Graham Lindsay and Owen Marshall situate their works in a closely observed immediate present.

The crucial descriptor is 'South Island'. We did not interpret this as restricting the selections to works written by writers born in or presently resident in the South Island. Rather, we were looking for works that evoke a strong sense of South Island places, people and/or history. The writers themselves have a variety of relationships to the South Island. Many are born and bred South Islanders, living here now (although perhaps after some time away) and are consciously regionalistic in their writing: Brian Turner, Dallas, Billing, Eldred-Grigg, Michael Henderson, Johnston, Hulme, among others. Others were not born here but have long been resident here and identify in much of their work with South Island places, as Woollaston and Marshall. Others were born here but left and established themselves elsewhere: Davin, Curnow, Wedde, Frame, Bill Manhire. Conversely, some were born overseas but have settled themselves here as writers: Cilla McQueen, Rob Jackaman, Michael Harlow, Jones, Allan. Others have stayed awhile and left, as Campbell, Gee and Bill Sewell. All are represented here by writing with a strong feel of South Island life.

Such a regionalist criterion of selection might be expected to privilege realism, the usual mode of regionalist writing, and some of the selections do present themselves as traditional realism, as the fiction by Gee, Marshall or Joy Cowley, or the autobiography by Campbell. In other selections the writing has been personalised and internalised by the focus on memory, as in Dallas, Frame, Flannery, Wedde, Jones, Curnow, McQueen, Manhire and Eldred-Grigg; or it has been heightened by being filtered through the consciousness of a character in an extreme state, as in Billing or Henderson. Some of the most striking selections move into magic realism and metafiction, as in Farrell and Johnston, or, in a slightly different way, Margaret Mahy, or, in a different way again, in Philip Temple or in the playful surrealism of Harlow. And while one would not expect international postmodernism to figure strongly in such a regional anthology, nonetheless postmodern techniques are used for regionalist purposes in writers such as Allan, Hulme, Lindsay, McQueen and Manhire.

The arrangement of the selections is roughly geographical, moving from north to south. The anthology begins with Henderson's Golden Bay and Gee's Nelson. Then there are the Marlborough fishing and outdoor stories and poems: Cowley dealing with Pelorus Sound, Wedde with Queen Charlotte Sound and Newton with the Wairau Valley. The West Coast selections are next, put in a single group, with Flannery, Woollaston and Eggleston all dealing with the Greymouth area, and Hulme with Okarito further south. The next group are all from Canterbury: Curnow's North Canterbury and Lyttelton, Mahy's Banks Peninsula, and McAlpine's and Eldred-Grigg's Christchurch. Then comes an east coast group dealing with the strip between Christchurch and Dunedin. Marshall's Chatterton covers the whole area in his journey, while Jackaman, Frame and Farrell all focus on the archetypal South Island provincial town, Oamaru. Bernadette Hall's poem takes to the road on Highway 1 south from Oamaru. Hulme focuses on Moeraki, and then, like Chatterton, Allan leaves Highway 1 and Hall's Kilmog for the Coast Road and Karitane. Iain Lonie takes us further into the back coastal roads with Purakanui, then it is over the hill to Otago Harbour and David Eggleton's Port Chalmers, and across the Harbour to the Otago Peninsula with Billing near Otakou, and McQueen's Charles Brasch and Rodney Kennedy up on the peninsular spine. Forbes Williams and Lindsay engage with Dunedin guidebooks with different kinds of irony, Hone Tuwhare and McQueen evoke a Dunedin winter, and Harlow, Jones, Johnston and Campbell show something of the unexpected diversity of Dunedin life. Lindsay takes Highway 1 to the first stop south, Green Island. Then the road divides to go to inland Otago. Sewell and Neville Peat take Highway 87 north and west to Sutton and Middlemarch and the Strath Taieri, while Turner and Temple take Highway 8 through Lawrence and into Central Otago, Temple probably heading further south again, towards Lake Te Anau. The anthology then returns to Highway 1, following it south through Manhire's Balclutha and Davin's Gore to Dallas's Invercargill, ending the book with 'Hell'.

Most of these places are explicitly named in the selections. Some have been fictionalised, at least in name: Gee's 'Saxton' is the 'misshapen twin' of the actual Nelson, Mahy's 'Carnival's Beach' seems to be near Akaroa and Billing's 'Port Paradise' conflates Port Chalmers and Dunedin. Other writers mythologise place, so that Farrell's unnamed town both is and is not Oamaru, and Temple's trampers' hut has been mythologised by the keas who observe it (and taste its contents). Some places are unnamed but seem identifiable from the descriptions and from their contexts in the writer's work and life: Eggleston's unnamed West Coast valley (with its 'barber', as distinctively Greymouth as the 'girl of Bunz' locution in Flannery's story), Curnow's Canterbury locations, Tuwhare's Dunedin, Henderson's Takaka Hill farm, the location of so many of his stories. The expected places are portrayed: Christchurch, Dunedin, Central Otago, the Canterbury Plains, although perhaps unexpected was the predominance of writing about Dunedin and the coastal area to the north of it. Notable also is that where an anthology of nineteenth-century South Island writing would have accounts of Mount Cook, the glaciers, the Southern Lakes, these writers often focus on places where the tourist buses do not necessarily stop: Newton's Wairau Valley, Peat's Strath Taieri, Lonie's Purakanui, Allan's Karitane, Manhire's Balclutha.

While the anthology can make no claim to historical or sociological completeness, certain aspects of South Island life emerge repeatedly, indicating significant images or concerns. A repeated natural image is that of the hawk or kea — central to Peat, Newton and Temple, strikingly there in Farrell, and an indicative image for Marshall and Turner. Historically, there are references to Wakefield and colonial origins in Gee, Lindsay, Williams and Wedde (central to the novel as a whole, and thus our title for the selection from *Symmes Hole*). The pre-settlement whaling days and the Maori past figure in Wedde, Billing, Jackaman, Hulme and, by implication, Allan. The sense of historical decline is evident in the focus on cemeteries and monuments, in Farrell, Turner, Lindsay, Hulme (Maori rather than colonial decline), Jones, Jackaman and, in a more personally elegiac way, Frame. The outdoor nature of South Island culture is evident in all those fishing stories (not restricted to Marlborough, as in the Frame and Hulme selections), and in the references to tramping in McQueen, Temple and Peat, and to various sports in Henderson, Turner, Campbell, Manhire and Farrell, while beaches figure in a number of selections, most strikingly in Mahy. Religion is there frequently: a surprisingly large number of depictions of Irish Catholicism (Flannery, Johnston, Woollaston, Davin, Farrell); a perhaps more expected number of critical views of evangelical Protestantism (Henderson, Billing, Manhire, Eldred-Grigg). The secular puritanism of authoritarian schooling is there in Cowley, Eldred-Grigg, Dallas and Campbell. Politics does not figure as much, but the political past is there in McAlpine and Eldred-Grigg (a strong Christchurch concern), and there are disenchanted not to say angry views of the present in Gee and Turner.

Variety and quality within defined temporal and regional limits — that was our aim. We hope that the pleasure in reading is commensurate with the pleasure in choosing. We have been impressed with the quantity of good, intensely realised writing about the South Island, and our only regret is that space limitations have forced us to leave out pieces that we would like to have included.

Finally, a word about editorial procedures. The source for each selection is included in the acknowledgements, while the notes at the end mention other writings by each author. The title is the author's for all except a few selections; when we have supplied a title it is placed in square brackets.

Lawrence Jones & Heather Murray
Dunedin 1994

Michael Henderson

The Two-Tooth in the Thicket

The day he dragged me gagging from the dip, he found a sheep caught in a briar. Bending it snorting back, he did his knife work. Blood geysered like the water I retched.

As the slaughtered stray bucked and shuddered, he said, 'An offering, you understand, not mine but Abraham's. A dead loss cack-hander you are, but you've been spared, one of the chosen ones, see? If there were twenty days in the week, all of them disasters, you'd still sit pretty. Goddermighty preserve me as He preserves the hopeless!'

'Mr Katene has crossbreds like that,' I said, seeing the earmark plain as day. 'What'll the Katenes say?'

'That hooa's got no comeback. Should fix his fences, I'd say.'

'It's got balls, he was keeping it for a ram — '

'Hogging our grass, eating our ewes out of house and home. Nothing hungrier'n a ram hogget!' Swabbing his knife on the fleece.

'It's only a two-tooth — '

'Cook up good, good as any lamb!'

'We could've put it back, back over the fence — '

'A lot you've got to say for a kid what was fished out half-way to his maker and not half-an-hour gone! Too much for one drowning, I'd say!'

He stamped on the forequarter, the twitching muscle, and wrenched the skin down the back. 'Time you learnt. Old enough to hone a knife, ugly enough to fend for yourself, I'd say. To skin, and butcher too.'

He sliced the belly and grass spilled out greener than it ever grew, gassy as Brindle's cud.

'There, we got our grass back!' wiping his boot on the wool, green and red.

He scraped the skin flesh-up on the bush. He chucked the carcass up and wired it on Milo's twitching rump.

'There's room for you, oodles of.'

'I'll walk,' I said, 'my own two legs — '

'*Walk*! Last I saw, you thought you could walk on water! Only thing was, it was way too thick to drink and way too thin to walk along!' Slapping the horse. 'You'll ride, I say.'

I got up. The carcass stuck to my back. Sticky hot through his coat. Dip-water welled and I spat.

He rolled the skin, wool out. 'Hold this,' he said.

The vomit swelled back.

'Say after me,' he said. '*They were stoned, they were sawn asunder, were tempted, were slain with the sword; they wandered about in sheepskins and —* '

I retched and heaved on Milo's back.

'Told you you couldn't walk to save yourself!' he said. 'Drank where it was too thick, and walked where it was too thin! Your own two feet! Rank!'

Boss slunk out from the fuchsias and licked my bile off a rock.

'The Lordgoddermighty is casting the poison out, even as you'll vomit evil and riches.'

I hugged Milo, holding his mane with the two-tooth's skin. 'I'm all right now,' I said. 'Right as rain.'

'If He chooses,' he said.

All I prayed to be chosen for was to be Sutcliffe on Saturday.

In bed that night, postponing the verses, I said, 'That skin was crawling, lousier'n a hedgehog — '

'Hooas don't dip. Now you'll understand what a Katene straggler can do to my clip!'

'Mr Katene chose it for a ram, one he'd — '

'It was Abraham's! Forfeit to Abraham, you understand? Now you'll get this off pat, or I'll skin you alive!' Shoving the book at me, black, heavy as a boulder, hinged and clasped like a chest to bury me. 'Word for word, or I'll flay and flog you until you wish you were a dog, you'll envy them so!'

Sutcliffe flayed the leather off the ball, and Sinbad got flogged for eyeing whores and ogling Princesses —

'Twenty minutes,' he said. 'In twenty minutes, I'll be back. There's no other choosing, not for them that's chosen!'

On the edge of my bed in the cold, bare room, every book but the one book being an abomination — the Arabian Nights most abominable of all, holding the one that excluded all others like a suicide's boulder dragging on my neck as I recited *Take now thy son, thine only son, whom thou lovest, and get thee into the land, and offer him for a burnt offering* as I heard him wedging the wood, then the handle of the milk bucket and his hobnails were back steamy with the froth of Brindle's milk as I cried, 'That wasn't twenty minutes, it couldn't of been!'

'*Have* been,' he said. 'Say have been.'

'Have been,' I said, watching the bubbles pop, thinking if only they don't all burst I'll stay safe, he won't, not today —

'No,' he said, 'I doubled your portion. It was forty, forty minutes you had, a microcosm of the time your heavenly father stayed in the Wilderness for your own sake, to save you from being a dead loss, a total flop on earth, so now you'll know twice your lot, won't you? Give me the Bible.'

I gave him the book, but I could not free my neck from the boulder or my ears from the echo, *buy-bull, buy-bull* — I was drowning in the dip. Brindle's froth bubbled like the ram lamb's blood on his boot and I began half in hope and half in hopelessness, '*And it came to pass after these things, that God tempted Abraham, and said unto him, "Abraham," and he said, "Behold, here I am." And he said, "Take now thy son, thine only son Isaac, and get thee into the land"* — '

'*WHOM THOU LOVEST*!' he shouted, slamming the book into his palm, then the clasp into my ear before I got my hand up —

'You forgot *whom thou lovest*! How could you forget whom thou lovest? Where's your mind at? What there is of it between those lugs of yours! I'd elastoplast them down, only they'd cross over at the back! *And keep your hand down*, the hand that reeks of Onan!' Grabbing my hands while he bashed my chilblains once for *whom*! twice for *thou*! and three times for *lovest*!

'Begin again,' he said.

Sutcliffe facing up again after Adcock had felled him, returning to the middle despite doctor's orders, the bandage like Sinbad's turban, blood showing through over his stitched-up ear, taking guard once more on that suicidal Port Elizabeth pitch, Adcock with the wind, Heine from the other end, the meanest pair on the veldt, in the world —

' . . . And Sut — *Abraham, Abraham rose up and strapped on his* — saddled! *saddled his ass, and took two* — two of his men — young men — *and Isaac* — Isaac his son, *and cleaved the wood* — '

'Clave!'

' — *and clave the wood for burning* — the burnt offering, *and went on* — *unto the place* — '

'And rose up!'

'I said rose up, I said it!'

'It is repeated, dumbcluck! Dunderhead! Blockhead!' Belting the side of my head, the tasselled marker flicking, Sutcliffe's bandage unwinding, blood dropping to the popping crease, Sutcliffe taking centre with his own blood —

'I said it, I said it!' I cried.

'Once, not twice, you said it, dope! Take the book. Once you may omit the Word, once maybe, but twice — stop your dreaming!'

'I said it! I said it!'

But he was the one who rose up shouting *you did not say the other rose up!*, pulling his belt from its loops, the skinning knife dropping to the floor, yanking at my pants even while his own slipped as he heaved to turn me and Mum filled the door, blood beating in her temples, her throat, 'Harold! Harold!'

'Come in! Come on in!'

'Harry, no Harry!'

'I'll give you the buckle too, there'd be not a man worth manhood if born of feebleness like yours we always had to be! If Goddermighty had a second son he'd not be made of woman!'

Sutcliffe could not hear, he could not hear the yelling for the dinning in his ear and the bloody dressing, still he stepped back and pulled the lifting ball high and hard over square, flaying the attack —

'I'll flay you alive and not suffer a woman, a bleating ewe on hind-legs, to teach me the power and potency it takes to be a man worthy of the Word!'

My mother's scream, '*For the love of* —'

My father's reply as he shoved her back and turned the key, 'Love? Weasel piss, you mean!'

Brindle's froth gone as his unbelted trousers fell about his boots, black hairs on milk-white skin, his legs never saw the light of day, one kneecap in a spasm. I kicked out, hoping to dismember him worse than Adcock in the cods.

Sutcliffe adjusted his thigh pad, his box, useless to prod the pitch, the ball dug in wherever it pitched, lifting into the groin, the ribs, the head —

He pinned me with his mad kneecap *and Abraham built an altar — and laid the wood in order, and bound Isaac his son, and laid him — laid him on the altar* —

'I remember!' I shouted, 'I remember it!'

'You'll remember it alright,' he said.

'But I do!' I cried. 'The words, all of them!'

'You're no son of mine until you do!' he said, binding me in the sheets *And Abraham took*, no, *stretched out — stretched forth his hand, and took his* his sheath-knife *his knife to slay his son* and lammed and lamed me with the belt, the baldric my Granpa brought back from the Ardennes, until the blood showed through.

'Take the book,' he said, pulling on his trousers, threading the sheath back onto the belt as he backed away. 'By the morning, you'll have it forever. You shan't come out till you do.' Locking the door from the outside, then shouting in the kitchen, 'As for you, you'll keep to your pikelets and plates, woman!'

With Adcock hit out of the firing line, and Tayfield the offie on, I knew Sutcliffe flayed the attack unbowed, nothing would stop him now. Behind the locked door I knew it as I took the boulder *take the book*! and got out the window, putting my bare foot on the garden tap to get down, feeling the duck cack like plasticine between my toes as I ran my fingertips along the friendly grooves until I got to the bearded palm where the lawn was clear and frothy with dew under the stars, they leaked like the tits of the sow I swilled with Brindie's skim.

I took the book and told the dogs to shut up and they did except for Boss. I bashed him with the book until he cowered on his chain at the back of his kennel and would not move his tongue against any of the chosen because of the boulder. I knelt and put my head inside his lopsided house and told him that I should not bring the price of a kelpie, nay, I shalt not, anymore than the hire of a whore into the kennel of Boss my Dog, I shalt not, for I knew these were abominations abominable to Boss my kelpie Dog.

Then I took the boulder as I had been told except that I ran it along the barbs on top of the fence and it ran with me except for bits that stuck to the barbs like licorice in teeth. I took the boulder and I went with it to keep me from hired whores and Sinbad's sins to the dag heap where my own two feet slipped and I lost the boulder until the embers under the offal pot flared and I saw it embossed, four crosses encircled with the words *Family Circle* which I had not taken in before. I pulled it by its tassel. In thanks for the light, I tore at it and fed the flame plentifully until the ram's organs boiled dry and the fire made me think one thought, *water*, and then like a dog returning to lick its spew I took the boulder through the yards, out of the cow paddock where Brindle lay obscurely churning her cud, through the horse paddock into the holding paddock, down the ridge, through the macrocarpas dense on the nob, onto the bridle track into the valley where the dip reflected yellowly, the night was too milky to be black, the boulder was black.

I took the boulder as I had been told, past the briar that had clasped the ram lamb, the briar where my father, my earthly father, had collected rosehips all through the shortage because I was a War baby, he was proud of gathering the rosehips, it was his war effort. In the milky light the bush had a dense shadow, but the shadow was blood as though all the rosehip had drained into the pitch the ram had dug up with its dying kicks.

I took the boulder as I had been told except that now I flung it, flung it into the poisonous dip, the trough full of sheep piss and Cooper's yellow chemical to kill the parasites. The tassel floated in a noose.

I climbed the hill without the boulder. I came back past the bush, there was wool in it but I left it there. I came back up the bridle path and through the trees into the horse paddock. Milo slept facing the east, waiting for the sun, standing with his right rear hoof showing the shoe that had to be replaced. I called *Brindie sook, buxy Brindie*! but she lay unmoving, a tawny whore with her rump in the hollow stump. Except for Boss, the dogs huffed and then whimpered and settled when I got to the yards.

Without the Family Circle leaves, the embers under the offal vat hardly glowed. I saw my outline in the dag heap.

I picked up a paling and played a cack-handed shot. Sutcliffe sailed serenely to his century. I swept Tayfield backward of square and Sutcliffe called me through. Boss cowered in his kennel.

I went into the meat-house. The ram's carcass hung milky-white on a hook. I poked slits in the flap under its ribs and pushed my arms through until the carcass sat on my back. It felt cold and then it felt hot as I came out of the shed, past the offal pot, past the dogs, the hungry dogs, and up to the lawn where I saw the track my feet had limped in the dew.

Everything milky-white in the night, the house, even my bed. I took the ram off my back and pushed it ahead of me through the window. I put a foot on the tap and I didn't care about the cack. I climbed into my room and turned back the sheet. I placed the neck on my pillow. Then I covered the rest of the carcass with the sheet. Blood showed but it was mine.

For the third time I got through the window and this time I closed it.

Empty-handed, I re-crossed the lawn. My wickets were standing there.

Boss yipped as I tugged him out and slipped his collar off. Then I took the other collars too, setting free the huntaway, the beardie and the eyedog. I scraped the offal out of the pot and as the dogs gobbled and scoffed I poked the collars one by one into the last of the embers and left the burnt offering there.

I did not stop to close the gates. I kept walking. The milky-whiteness turned to rosehip. Collar-free, the dogs gambolled around me, nudging my elbows and chin, their shadows darkening, lengthening, shortening. Bert Sutcliffe and I drove Heine through the covers and flayed Adcock mercilessly. Effortlessly, I ducked and swayed under his bumpers. They flew harmlessly by, as harmless as the fernbirds. Each time I played a shot the dogs cringed. Then they saw it was a game and hared off as though I was throwing them sticks.

When I stopped and sat they licked my welts, my ears, the hand that reeked.

We came to the source and I sucked as they lapped.

They licked the ram off and showered me with icy water.

Maurice Gee

[Saxton]

from *The Burning Boy*

The distance between the Birtles's house in Spargo Street, Duckham Square, and the 'toasty warm' Round house above the river and golf course in Coppermine Valley can be measured socially. I won't attempt it; will drive you through Saxton instead. First though, a bit of history.

Saxton was a Wakefield town. A vertical slice of old England was meant to take root there. When the settlers came ashore in 1841 they marked out sites for a jail and a courthouse, a magistrate's house, a church and a school. Agriculture and commerce did not need marking out.

The town had bad times but good times followed, social distinctions became blurred, Saxton grew into an egalitarian New Zealand town. There are people here descended from first-ship settlers and, in the minds of some, a Saxton aristocracy, but most of our citizens are not impressed by such things. Climate, topography, hard work and ambition and greed and commercial chance determined the town's shape more than social theory and distinctions.

The gap between rich and poor is widening again but that isn't peculiar to Saxton.

Geography has been a determining factor. Hills and sea cut us off from other places. We're not on a direct route except to smaller towns. The nearest city is forty minutes by air but if you go by car and ferry you must travel all day. Some people like this. A visiting Classics professor said that Saxton reminded him of a Greek city-state. He said, jokingly, that it should secede from New Zealand and was kind enough to suggest Athens not Sparta as a model.

Fishing, timber, horticulture, pip-fruit sustain us. One mustn't forget tourism. American and continental English are heard in the streets. Japanese honeymooners ask locals to photograph them on the cathedral steps — focus and timing pre-set. Dutch and Swedish travellers pick apples in the season. Saxton is remote, but the world passes through.

Things you may be shown or come across: the cathedral, which gave us the status of city when in fact we were still a town (we still are a town); the art gallery, founded by a bishop and bearing his name (it is funded, not too willingly, by the city council, and has recently been enlarged in a style most people, though not Tom Round, find very tasteful); Queens Gardens (Victoria was the queen) and the duckpond, lying just away from the town's main street (beautiful roses, filthy pond where ducks wait out the shooting season, squabbling for bits of bread lunching shop-assistants throw); Founders Park, where a pioneer town has been set up, using old buildings saved from demolition; the waterfront drive, named for, opened by, the present queen. The list could go on but there's no need. There's nothing here that simply must be seen, though one or two things are unique: a plaque marking the field where the first rugby match in New Zealand was played; a hill known as the Centre of New Zealand; a boulder bank enclosing mudflats and the port. It's a geological phenomenon found nowhere else in the world. (That, at least, is what we are told.) And there are three or four lovely wooden churches.

Saxton is comfortable for the visitor. There's a Quality Inn and plenty of hotels and motels and boarding houses, and three camping grounds, one at the beach, and a youth hostel and several private hostels. The sunshine hours are the highest in New Zealand. You can swim at the beach or in the rivers (the rivers now, those out of town, can make you feel in a world new-born), or go north into the maritime park and find yellow beaches, clean blue sea, tramping tracks through unspoiled bush (the world new-born again), or south to the lakes and ski-fields. You can fish for trout. You can visit the potters and weavers and print-makers and silversmiths and glass-blowers (Saxton attracts them), and set off round the vineyards on the wine trail and pick your own tree-ripened apples and peaches. You might easily decide Saxton is a place free from troubles.

Look harder.

Stay around a while and keep your eyes open. Walk in the back streets. Go up river if you prefer. Only a hundred yards past the Arts Society ladies sketching willows and toi-toi by the footbridge you'll find a concrete bridge with 'Donovan Sux' spray-painted on a pier — Donovan is our mayor. In a dark cave underneath, kids are sniffing solvents from plastic bags. There are street-kids squatting in an empty corner-dairy by Duckham Square. That house-truck at the swimming hole — rather picturesque, with the young woman sitting on the step breast-feeding her baby and the man with the carburettor spread out on a sack, and shirts and towels and underpants drying on the grass — is there because there's nowhere else to go. Police will move it on before long. And while we're up the river, and speaking of police, that helicopter rattling your teeth is making a marijuana sweep. Back in town school's out and schoolboys and girls are smoking the stuff while their older siblings, unemployed, are drinking in the pubs.

Let's not worry about time of day. That drunk fellow who falls over by the streetlamp and takes five minutes climbing to his feet is a Russian sailor from a tuna boat. He's lost his liquor-store bag of whisky and gin and his two pairs of jeans and his Lada parts. He won't make it back to his ship. Local goons (one of them's a mate of Neil Chote) roll him in an alley and kick him senseless. He'll be three months in hospital and then will be flown home and will never really understand what happened to him in Saxton.

Go down to the courthouse on a Tuesday. Sit in the waiting room with the butt-scorched floor, with young fellows in boots and broken sneakers and jeans and bush singlets and leather jackets, listen to them speak, listen to the girls, with their nicotine-stained fingers and red-rimmed eyes. It's not the same language used by those lawyers who go by — young fellows, young women too. See how they dress. You can illustrate a two nations argument here. What are the charges when the accused, those in here, those brought in from the cells, face the judge? Cultivating cannabis. Possession for supply. Driving with excess breath alcohol, blood alcohol. They've pissed in a doorway, punched the neighbour or the *de facto*, kicked in the window of a menswear store. They've stolen from a container lorry parked up for the night. Threatened a constable with *numchukkas*. Threatened a chemist with a knife and got away with a pocketful of prescription drugs. They've kicked a Russian sailor half to death. They're mill-hands, knife-hands, labourers, bushmen, fish-splitters, sickness beneficiaries, solo mothers, unemployed. The judge sentences them to prison or periodic detention, puts them under supervision, orders reparation. He fines them and disqualifies them (the shop manager too, the estate agent, the retired shoe salesman). Every Tuesday there's a new batch. Shelley Birtles has passed through (theft of a chequebook and a credit card). Shelley is under six months' supervision.

Meanwhile, in plush offices — no, that won't do. But Saxton does have what John Toft calls its 'little millionaires and clever bankrupts'. No, he says, New Zealand doesn't belong to the big foreign boys, not yet. It's the little guy who's got it, inflation millionaires, there are more than a dozen in this town, mostly land agents. They buy and sell, buy and sell, and produce nothing along the way. (John gets angry.) They take the money and other people take the debt. You try and buy a bit of land at the edge of town, for a fair price, you can't do it. They own it all, these fat fellows, these little boys. You don't believe me? Look at the registration of properties. They sit there waiting for the value — ah, not the value, the price — to rise. (But the spirit goes out of John, he seems to die one of his little deaths. Says to Norma, 'Don't ask me, ask your friend Tom Round. He plays their little game with them.')

We've moved away from history and seem to be back with the Rounds, so let's do without that drive I mentioned and stay with them. It's half past seven. They have their dinner later than the Birtleses.

Ian Wedde

[A Pre-Wakefield Pastoral]
from *Symmes Hole*

Though there'd been times every bit as quiet as time at sea could be, when he'd lain abed off-season at sunrise, awake out of mere habit and because the cocks were singing out at each other up by the edge of the bush; because he could hear the dawn racket of birds from the big timber, and because his biggest little chap was rattling the top of the pot on the fire, getting a cold spud and a bit of fish. And he'd lain there with his whiskers pressed between her strong shoulders, early light beginning to come through the sack drape across the wide bunk. She'd be breathing long and steady, with a little snore as the breath went out . . . smell of woodsmoke in her hair, bit of a piddle smell where the little feller had come for a cuddle before she put him back in his bunk with the girl. Creak of the door as the biggest little chap went outside . . . he'd hear him working up a bit of a cough out there, not wanting to risk a clout by making a racket inside: *agh agh ahem*! — like the tobacco rattle of the big men, and a monstrous spit. *Dingaling* of his pee against the bit of tank-iron by the smokehouse . . . *agh agh ahem*! — little bugger's left the door open. He'd hear the calm tumble of little waves on the ramp of the beach, distant halloo and woody rattle of oars through the still air, faint bark and yelp of a dog from down the beach. Biggest little chap going past the door, whistling very quietly . . . going past again whistling louder. . . .

He'd gentle one hand round between her big soft breasts, feel her pretend to be more asleep than she was . . . climb over from his inside half of the bunk and push out through the sacking and there'd be the boy in the doorway, quick as a flash, and him standing with a straight-out spar under his shirt-tail. One big Pa-step toward the door, hand raised . . . and the boy'd skip outside . . . dawn light up the eastern sky above the hogback. 'You want this, boy?' advancing with his open hand, '. . . making all that racket?'

'Ka haere e matou ki te mahi ika . . . e Pa, you said . . . !' pretending to be scared, and half-way scared in case he'd guessed his Pa wrong. '. . . Pa, you said?'

Inside for a dip in the pot, mouthful of cold tea from the can . . . he'd wrap a doughboy in his handkerchief and get his tobacco, pull on some slops, fetch his knife. By the time he got to the beach the boy would have the lines from the tackle shed. Stink was strongest there where the oil soaked down into the sand, where the scraps and fritter and bits of butchered meat and tongue got tramped across the beach — about time to get across to Anaho, clear out Ngarewa's mob. . . .

Cool water at his knees . . . sunlight shooting up behind the hogback, some high heaps of cloud, wind might come up later . . . tide soon turning to flood, time to get across by the bit of reef off Whekenui, take some of those big cod. Pulling over to the rocks across the bay, little chap's face all peaceful with pleasure . . . whip in some bait with doughboy on the hooks . . . they'd leave a few fingers of water in the bottom of the boat, let the sprats flap in that and stay fresh.

And there'd be a couple more wakes spreading across the calm roadstead . . . echo of shouts in the quiet . . . flop of water where Jackson was sculling to his set-line . . . rattle from across the bay when Logan stepped his mast and pulled up a bit of limp sack for a lug, man wouldn't row if he thought there was any chance of air, he'd sit creaking his tiller back and forth, whistling for wind. . . .

. . . and he'd bend his back into the oars, he'd have his feet braced against the stern thwart of the little dory, he'd take a sight astern on the big pohutukawa tree on the point and keep it behind the little chap's head. He'd watch the wake lengthen straight astern with the flanking lines of oar-dips, and the little connecting trails between dips where water had run off the oars as he leaned forward and drew the oar-blades back, dripping, over the glassy surface. A black shag would clap up off the water, big slick wings beating behind its outstretched neck on a flight along the surface of the bay, and when it landed to fish the ripples would spread across the wide channel. Back at the bay smoke would have begun to rise from fires . . . tiny in the distance, couple of kids running along the beach . . . canoe shooting out from behind the headland and making for Onapua . . . few puffs of breeze ending the dawn calm.

Where his course took him inshore he'd hear the big pigeons and the tuis thrashing about in the branches of the early berry trees. The tui'd be watering up his song, getting the trickle of it right. And he'd hear the pipping of warblers, and big hoarse blackback gulls checking the dory. The peaceful morning would move in on his senses, he'd hear how the calm was a net of sounds . . . and the low-water reek of seaweeds and washed-up bush wrack — tart savours that spread his nostrils jaded from the greasy beach, like a drink of spring-water amber with leafmould cutting through the stale aniseed of the arrack rum.

. . . there'd be terns and blackbacks crashing the channel ahead, maybe a few pairs of gannet, though they were usually gone by early spring . . . a few shags ducking, little penguins bobbing back up — he'd know that barracouta maybe were driving the shoal-fish to the surface. Sometimes he'd pull out to the shoal and take a heave or two with a barracouta-nail, the long crazy fish would snap at the red manuka lure, he'd let Hemi haul them to the side of the dory and then he'd club them with the busted mattock he kept in the boat. If they'd been feeding well they made a good groundbait, bloody and oily with a big gut. They'd pull mussels from the reef off Whekenui, he'd put some in a sack with the opened barracouta and pound it all to a pulp with the mattock against the gunwale of the dory, and let it down with his grapple for a groundbait.

. . . they'd anchor themselves off the reef with plenty of slack in the warp, and fish the flood. And although it wasn't a good deep off the reef, not like the big holes out past the heads, he'd sometimes feel the great shovel snatch of a hapuku, he'd stand with his feet braced apart, delicately hauling the line at the limit of its breaking strain, knowing he'd be lucky to hold the groper on a cod hook near the surface, but sometimes he did, with patience. He'd ease the great fish up, and gaff it deep as he could, under the bony plating near the gills. There was a custom that the hapuku went to the Maoris at the beach — they used the same word as the fish's name for stuffing yourself with tucker, a big hapuku was a special feed. But he always kept the throat and what they called the tongue, and the cheeks.

Once or twice close in by the reef he'd snagged an octopus, they'd go limp if they were free of the rock, but then they'd grab on to the boat and squirt water and black muck everywhere . . . they were good cooked underground in the Maori ovens — sweet, like fowl.

It was easy to fill the boat . . . half the time he lay across his thwart looking over at where the nikau palms and treeferns grew above the water on the steep walls of the Sound, or down-channel at the salt-blasted seaward limit of the passage, or up-country at the big timber and the blue inland heights.

. . . when the pohutukawa flowers had fallen and it was calm, the surface of the water was sometimes filmed with the dingy, spent crimson of the blooms. He'd seen a broad scum of pink krill drift in on the tide too. After big rains the sea would carry bobbing rafts of bush wrack, pods and sticks and washed-down leaves. In the few places where creek-flats and lower gullies had been cleared, the run-off would carry a clay stain out at the mouth . . . at its edges you'd see the silt dropping deeper like an unsteady waving curtain where the clear current ran. Once, sculling at night with a muffled oar and a pitch flare, netting guarfish above the shallow seagrass flats, he'd looked down through water so clear he'd thought, I could *breathe* that — shrimps and nodding seahorses came to the light, and the shoals of long-snouted guarfish flashing with blue phosphorescence.

If there was a breeze coming up-channel he'd sometimes dip his fingers in the sea and wet his nostrils and in the air that he then breathed he'd imagine he could smell the salt haze of distance way past Koamaru out into the Tasman, or from the Pacific south past Rerunder Point — or from points east of south, where the immense Pacific horizon would be stacked with its towers of early summer windstorms, those three- and four-day gales that heaved a twenty-foot swell up the Straits, like the one that capsized the schooner *Shamrock* back in '34. . . .

. . . he'd been on the lookout at the Heads . . . back up the Sound everything was in ruins, the Ngati Tahu had burned the place out. They'd been living off fern root and fish and Guard hadn't come down from Sydney — he was on the barque *Harriet* but no one knew where she was. It was blowing hard from the south-east when the *Shamrock* showed from Port Nicholson with a relief supply of potatoes and pigs. She went in stays at the Heads but before she could gather way a squall capsized her. There'd been thirty Maori from Port Nick on board, all drowned — that had put a tapu on fishing . . . for six weeks they'd lived on the lip of a Right whale, on fern root, birds. Guard had showed up in a whaleboat from Taranaki — the *Harriet* had wrecked on Cape Egmont right where the *Tory* was now . . . the Waikato there had captured Betty Guard and her little boy, and they'd killed her brother and cooked him and offered him to her. . . .

And if the breeze was anywhere in the west, you'd sometimes pick up the station stink, even out at the Heads . . . and you'd get the waterway weed and reef, guano rocks, and the sweet airs of the forest.

If she'd set nice and the breeze was good, he'd stick up the stub mast and the lug, he'd scull an oar at the stern, or he'd give it to the boy to swing on while he cleaned cod, as much as the household needed — the rest he'd leave at the beach, the folk could come for it.

. . . even with a following breeze somewhere in the east, the authentic reek of the beach would find them before they sighted the smoke of the house-fires. Swinging the lug across and bearing in from the channel, or pulling around the headland, they'd make the bay. He'd string his share on flax loops and toss the rest above the high-water mark. He'd tip the dory on her beam ends in the shallows and the boy would sluice her out. If it was clear the sun would just be getting warm . . . he'd eat a breakfast of fresh cod outside the whare . . . he'd split some to dry, some to smoke.

They'd eat cod-head stew that night . . . rich gelatinous reservoirs of the great skulls . . . potatoes . . . flax-root dumplings. And her mouth would smell of the sweet jellies of the stew, her hands of the oil . . . and the rich smell of her sex, that he'd haul up his shirt-tails to lunge for in the dark behind the sack drape of the wide box-bunk. 'E, e, Whata. . . . !' Heave of her strong familiar haunch, the tilt of her warm belly, greased with her flow and loosened by childbearing.

Joy Cowley

The Cleaning of Windows

When he cut down the tree she came flapping at him like a ship in full sail, hair flying, arms tilting. He'd never seen her so mad.

'It's only an old manuka,' he said, trying to match his voice to hers. 'Gee, Aunty Magda, you said good burning wood.'

'I said driftwood!' she roared. 'There's plenty along the beach!'

'Some of it's waterlogged. It's full of salt. It'll burn your chimney out.'

'Thank you, Sam, but I've been burning driftwood for forty years. I haven't lost a chimney yet, or a good healthy tree. What got into your skull?'

'I read it somewhere. You're not supposed to burn wood that's been in the sea.'

She crouched right down to touch the edge of the manuka stump. He saw the way she wiped her hand across the wet red wood and he thought, she can take a running jump, the silly old chook.

She looked up at him. 'Your trouble, Sam, is you believe every flipping thing you're told. Open your eyes, boy. Think for yourself. You got to in that house of yours or you'll end up with your brain in a matchbox.' She stood up slowly, her hands in the middle of her back. 'Get in the habit of questioning bloody everything.'

'But it's common sense, Aunty Magda. The salts in the driftwood burn hotter —'

'Salts, my backside! Get out the tractor and go down to the beach. I'll give you a hand.'

Strong with anger, he went into the shed, took the battery off the charger and carried it in his arms to the old David Brown. Like everything else on the farm, the tractor ran on patches. The wiring was bandaged with sticking plaster, strips of plastic shopping bags and bits of sacking. A hole in the inlet manifold had a jam-jar lid glued on it. A cracked head meant that the engine could only be run cold but it went all right. Like her, it was a bit rusty but it still had a lot of go.

While he was connecting the battery, she came and heaved the trailer on to the drawbar and then she got up and stood there in her gumboots and brown coat done up with safety pins. He didn't look except from the edge of his eye but he could feel her stare on him, waiting for him to do one more wrong thing.

He knew what he was about and he showed her, firing up the old David Brown and swinging the trailer in a wide arc through the gateway and down the track to the beach. Only when he hit the rough patch did he look back. She was still standing on the trailer, hands on hips, grey hair bouncing out of the woollen cap, still trying to stare him out. His father was right. She was as crazy as a cock-eyed cow.

He stopped the tractor down the beach a bit and she helped him gather up the grey bones of trees which had been stacked along the stones by flood tides, some of them wet and too heavy to move, some laced up with kelp. It was hard work. They didn't talk much until the trailer was near enough to loaded and she needed a rest. Then, leaning back against the tractor wheel, she pointed across the bay.

'Sam, you ever notice something about those hills? They're all female.'

He shaded his eyes with his hand. The sea was as flat as green oil except for patches fired by the sun. The land was the same as always, dark green bush to the water's edge, a few birds flying, a couple of holiday baches white in the distance, a yacht moored off Weka Point.

'Every bit of land in the Marlborough Sounds,' she said. 'Thighs, shoulders, breasts and bellies, all ways you look. See? There and there? Shapes of women —'

He looked and looked away again.

'— lying in the water. Look at the crease in that bottom. Look at the elbow raised like she was pushing herself out of the sea.'

'Yeah,' he said, uncoiling the rope from under the trailer.

'You ever notice that before, Sam?'

'No.'

'You see it now?'

'Yeah. Kind of.' He threw the rope over the trailer and looked back over his shoulder at the hills squatting on their own reflections. 'I suppose they're lady shapes, all right.'

'All wrong!' She pounced on him, jabbing her finger at his chest. 'They're just hills. That's all. The rest I made up. See what I mean, Sam boy? You got to look at things the way they are. Don't just take anybody's old say-so. Those aren't women. Those aren't any nonsense excepting hills.'

'I know that,' he said, but it was already too late. The mask of the hills had been removed, showing the contours he had seen on forbidden late movies. The shapes shifted as he looked and dared him to possess them by giving them names. He licked his top lip, pulled the rope tight and knotted it, tested the tension to make sure the wood couldn't slide off, and all the while his eyes were furtively touching hollows thick with manuka scrub and peaks tilted up to the sun. 'I know they're just hills,' he said, hating her.

No matter what he felt at times, or what was said at home, he didn't like other people talking about her. When the kids at school called her names, he could do something about it. He was bigger than they were. But with adults it was different.

The day the new dental nurse came, he was sitting outside the staffroom eating his lunch when through the window, clear as a bell, came Mr Pruitt's voice.

'It's a queer set-up. Brother and sister can't stand each other. Never could, I'm told. The farm was left to them both but they cut it in two. Harry's got one side of the peninsula, Magdalena the other. There's an eight-foot-high deer fence running along the spur of the hill between the two properties, real Colditz stuff. The brother farms his side but hers has gone back to bush, a pity really. She's as mad as a meat-axe and just as tough. Spends most of her time out fishing.'

For as long as he could remember, her back porch had been littered with useless things, broken machinery, burnt-out toasters and irons, knives without handles, sick hens, orphaned lambs. A one-legged pukeko lived there. She fed it every day because it couldn't scratch for a living, she said. At night the possums came in to eat the leftovers. He had learned to watch where he put his feet.

He took his gumboots into the wash-house, and in the cool dark he turned on a tap to wash his hands. The window had been broken and sealed with cardboard so that only a rim of light shone past the cobwebs and dead blowflies. It was a while before he saw that the tub under the tap was already half-full of water and in it was a large drowned crayfish.

'Gee, that's big!' he yelled.

'Lunch!' she called back.

'Where'd you get it?'

'In one of the cray pots.'

'Yeah, but where?'

She came into the wash-house and lifted the crayfish from the tub. Her hand was fair stretched to hold it. 'I found me a new spot at the back of the Chetwodes. You know the reef where we get the big cod? Half a chain north of that.'

'What's a chain in metres?'

'How would I know? No one asked me if the country could go metric. That's dead enough. I can't abide the cruelty of dropping living creatures into boiling water. Come on, wash your hands.' Still in her coat and woollen cap, she stoked up the wood stove and filled the big preserving pan. 'It's a bit deep out there. That's why the divers have missed it, I reckon. Must be dozens of the beasties. You cut us some bread, eh? This is the fourth big one in three days. Think you can manage half?'

They ate the hot crayfish with butter, salt and pepper, sucking the meat out of the legs and scooping out the coral with their fingers. Afterwards, he offered to wash the dishes.

But she'd got up from the table and was settling herself in the big chair. 'You don't get paid for doing dishes,' she said, putting a cushion on the wooden box. She took off her woollen socks, one grey, one brown, while he poured olive oil from a bottle into a tin mug.

'Your hands warm?' she said.

'Warm enough.' He sat on the floor beside her and she put her feet up on the box.

'I might go to sleep before the hour is up but don't stop,' she said. 'If you hear me snore just go gentle like.'

He tipped oil into the palm of his hand and allowed it to warm there.

'You'll get five bucks today.'

'Five!'

'The rate's going up because you're good.' She closed her eyes. 'But you get nothing for cutting down that poor bloody tree,' she said.

'What do you do over there?' his mother asked.

'Oh — things.'

'What sort of things?'

'All sorts.' He gave his dinner full attention but she wasn't going away.

'Like what?'

Now his father was focused too. He had eyes the same colour as Aunty Magda's, a sort of washed-out grey.

'Like —' He noticed that on the bench there was a bit of scrunched-up newspaper which his mother had used for cleaning the kitchen windows. 'I clean windows for her.'

His mother's mouth opened but it was a while before the laugh came. 'Magda clean windows?'

He shook his head. 'Uh-uh. I told you. She gets me to do them.'

'Harry, did you hear that? She's getting Sam to do her housework, for heaven's sake!'

'What's she paying you?' his father asked.

'Five dollars an hour.'

'Five? So who's complaining? Listen, when I was his age I'd have shovelled shit with my mouth for five bucks an hour.'

'She's never cleaned windows,' his mother said. 'Why should she start now?'

'Maybe she likes to see out. I dunno. Five bucks is five bucks, eh Sam?'

'Yeah.' He laughed.

'How do you clean them?' his mother asked.

'Newspaper. I rub them with wet newspaper and then with dry.'

'Well, all I can say is it's a pity you don't get in some practice at home,' she replied.

'You don't give him the right incentive,' his father laughed, rubbing his thumb and forefinger together.

'What else do you do over there?' his mother asked.

'We had crayfish for lunch,' he said. 'It was huge.'

'You're kidding!' His father leaned forward. 'A real pack-horse?'

'Just about. Aunty Magda's found a new place for her cray pots. She says there are hundreds.'

'Where?'

'Back of the Chetwodes. That place I showed you where we get the big cod — a bit north of there. How far is half a chain?'

'About here to the clothesline. Is she still setting her pots?'

'Every night. It's deep. She says the divers have missed it.'

Then he caught the shine in his father's eyes and said, 'You can't set any pots in her place, Dad.'

His father laughed. 'Don't worry. I wouldn't dream of it.'

Aunty Magda had long cold feet as hard as boards, white in the middle and yellow where the skin was thick. He knew her feet so well that he could have drawn maps of them with his eyes closed. In fact, any time he shut his eyes he could see them, the toes which curled under nails as thick as sheep's hooves, the flat plains criss-crossed by lines, the dry cracked areas of the heels, the bumps and lumps along the sides. He wondered if people ever read fortunes from the soles of feet.

When he'd warmed the oil, he'd spread it over the entire foot, then, with one hand under her heel and the other round her toes, he'd move the foot in circles to loosen her ankle joint. That made her relax, she said. Next would come the toes, one at a time, rubbing and squeezing each cold little hill of flesh and massaging down into the valleys which separated them.

He couldn't bear to have anyone touch the soles of his feet. When he was a little kid and his mother had tried to wash the soles of his feet in the bath, he'd squirmed out of control, his head going back under the water.

Aunty Magda didn't move. He could tickle, he could scratch, he could press his fingernails into the skin until they left marks, but her feet stayed dead still. Her head was still too, resting back on the chair, eyes closed, although sometimes she'd moan softly down her nose.

While she was taking off her socks, she said, 'You didn't tell your father about my crayfish possie.'

He shrugged the question away.

'Did you?'

'Did I what?'

'Tell your father where I'm getting crays?'

'No, course I didn't.' He felt bad about lying.

'Good. This is one thing he's not getting his thieving hands on.'

He poured the oil into the mug. 'Aunty Magda, why can't you and Dad be friends?'

'Friends?' She looked surprised. Then she lay back in the chair. 'Too much blood under the bridge.'

'What do you mean?'

'You don't get paid for asking questions,' she said.

He heard his parents talking in bed, his mother saying, 'I don't like him going over there every week.'

'It doesn't do any harm.'

'Don't be so sure. She's got a strong influence on him.'

'Sam's a sensible kid.'

'He's only twelve. She fills his head with nutty ideas.'

'Yeah, yeah, but he knows they're nutty. Look, you should encourage him. One day she's going to leave him that farm. She's got no one else to leave it to.'

At school, Miss Tolley had them out in the football paddock, drawing pictures of trees and the bike shed. Craig did some drawings which set the kids laughing, and when Miss Tolley asked to see he screwed the paper up and shoved it in his pocket. She made him take it out and show her the pictures.

Craig protested, 'It wasn't my idea, Miss Tolley. It was Sam. He reckoned hills are tits.'

The other kids laughed and yelled.

Miss Tolley turned her head. 'Did you say that, Sam?'

He didn't answer. His face was hot as fire.

'I'm very disappointed, Sam,' Miss Tolley said.

Some of the others were adding fire to his burning. 'He said bums, too, Miss Tolley. Some hills are bums and some are tits.'

Miss Tolley sighed. 'To the impure all things are impure. You may go inside, Sam, and work at your desk.'

He woke suddenly, some time before light, hearing the scrape of the dinghy on the beach outside his window. He couldn't see anything for the garden trees, but in a while he heard the splash of oars and then the sound of a diesel engine. On the dark grey water, the dark shape of his father's boat moved, without lights, beyond the trees, and disappeared round the point.

He went into his parents' room and switched on the light. 'Where's Dad going?' he asked his mother. 'Mum?' She rolled over, flinging her arm across the empty space in the bed. 'What's Dad doing with the boat?'

'Sam, for goodness sake! It's only half-past four!'

'I heard Dad go out in the boat.'

'He's putting out a set line. Go back to bed.'

'Why didn't he wake me?'

'You've got school. Please, Sam! Put out the light. It's killing me!'

When he came home that afternoon, he discovered that his father had gone to town. He'd got a case of snapper, his mother said, and he'd taken them into the restaurant.

'Snapper? How big?'

'Oh, so-so.'

'Where'd he get them?'

'Beatrix Bay. He said they're running well.'

'That's good.'

But he immediately went out to look in the back of the garage. He saw that his father's diving gear was dry in the cupboard and hanging from the rafters were the cray pots, strung with cobwebs and dust.

On Sunday morning he helped her set up the smokehouse for six silver-belly eels.

The smokehouse was an old fridge with the bottom knocked out, planted up the hill by the back of the house. There was a chimney dug in the earth and covered with sheets of iron, a hole for a fire at the other end. While he hung the salted eels on hooks, she lit the fire. He noticed that she was using twigs from the manuka tree he'd cut down, but he didn't say anything. He closed the smokehouse door.

'Dad's been catching a lot of snapper lately. You been getting any?'

'No. Is he smoking them?'

'Uh-uh. Takes them to a restaurant in town. Only we're not supposed to say, because he hasn't got a licence.'

'What restaurant?'

'I don't know.'

She blew on the fire. The twigs flared and crackled. 'It's nice someone's lucky. I haven't had a cray all week. Think I might just have a poacher.' She threw a handful of sawdust over the flames. 'You sure you didn't tell your father about my possie?'

'He hasn't been near it. He puts his lines out in Beatrix Bay.'

'So you did tell him.'

'I think —' He struggled. 'I don't remember. I might of.' She was looking at him, waiting for more. 'It definitely isn't Dad. I looked. His cray pots are hanging in the shed, all dusty. Maybe there just aren't any more crayfish there.'

'Maybe so.' She got up slowly, unwinding her back. 'You're a good boy, Sam. Dopey but worthy.' She put her hand on his head. 'You should hear the way my feet talk about you.'

He woke suddenly Monday morning, thinking the house was on fire. Why fire, he didn't know, except that his mother had set off screaming like that once before when a pan of fat had gone up in flames.

'Oh my God, oh my God, oh my God!'

He stumbled and bumped down the hall and into the kitchen doorway. It was his father who was hurt. He was sitting in a chair near the table and he had teatowels wrapped round both his hands like huge red-soaked boxing gloves. His face was white as bone and there was blood everywhere, on the floor, on

Mum's nightgown, on the table, blood dripping down his wet fishing clothes.

His mother was screaming, 'My God, Harry! I've got to get you to a hospital!'

They left him to get ready for school on his own, but he didn't. He went down to the beach, launched the blood-spattered dinghy and rowed round the point to Aunty Magda's.

She wasn't outside anywhere that he could see. Her boat was on the mooring, nothing in it but oars; her hens still hadn't been fed and her gumboots were on the back porch. He pushed the back door open, not bothering to take his own boots off.

She was sitting at the table wearing her woollen cap and her coat over her nightgown, and drinking tea out of a saucer. The room smelled of wood smoke and toast.

'You spliced in razor blades!' he shouted at her. She stopped drinking but didn't say anything. 'You put razor blades in the buoy ropes on your cray pots!'

She looked at him as though she could see right through to the bench behind him, a dead stare without a blink.

'Mum's taken him to the hospital. His hands are cut to bits!'

She turned back to her saucer and sucked her tea. 'Don't bother me with that,' she said.

'Razor blades!' he was bawling. 'All your stupid talk! Cutting down trees! Boiling crayfish! He's your brother, you crazy old looney liar! You cut his hands to bits!'

She went on drinking her tea while he went on calling her the worst names he could think of.

'How could you do that?' he yelled.

She flapped her hand at him. 'Open your eyes, boy!' she said.

John Newton

Sparrowhawk

1
That being bush country
autumn tends to be still
and clear. Round the house
the yellowing poplars
and silver birches in the shelterbelts
moult, but somehow those cloudless
May afternoons make
the bush itself seem even closer
and more solid.
Woodpigeons flap from gully to gully,
snowy-chested, fat with berries.

2
It was one of those breathless
autumn afternoons
I saw the sparrowhawk.
Glittering, small-eyed
bullet of a bird
strewing feathers and down,

and when the birds were gone
there were pigeon feathers
still hanging, white
against the deep screen of bush,
drifting
in weightless circles
in the clean day.

John Newton

Taylor Domain

1
When the norwest blows
nowhere is secret from it, not
the hospital   not the saleyards
not the perspex spire
of the Elim church: there is no

getting away from it
Heat drums on the iron
roof of the sawmill Trailbikes
generate clouds

of dust   Escholtzias
run wild in the creekbed
holding up their blazing orange
cups to the glare, to the dry
air whistling down off the high country

whipping the blossoming
clotheslines, withering
the small squares of garden
that nestle here under the stopbank

2
All day
the season's first forest fire
burns in the direction that the wind comes from

The wind itself is a fire which burns off
the grass. The arch

which by late afternoon
reaches in a flat curve high across the valley
is black like cloud
like shadow, like smoke

3
Only towards evening does the wind
start to ease: now

in that softening I walk looking
down the stopbank.   The sawmill

is silent. A single trailbike
shares the Domain with schoolgirls on horseback.

A goat on a dogchain
tugs at stalks on the bank above scorched

lawns and gardens reviving under
sprinklers, the last sun

lights two walls of smoky hills,
the wilting breeze shuffles through the poplars.

4
The arch spans
the valley, from one chain of hills
to the other, it spreads its black wing

over everything: sweetpeas
foxgloves, pink and white   fennel
poppies that throb in the shadowy
half-light   Coke can
condom   variegated thistle.

On the High Street bridge
headlights come on and black
from the cloud-span starts spilling into black

which is night, the sweaty
grass underfoot
rustles and once more the chattering
beetles   well up in flight

Kate Flannery

A Girl's Best Friend

from *Like You, Really*

Reen has found a photo of her old playmate, Marilyn Soper. She fingers the white plastic frame, feeling nostalgia wash over her at the sight of Marilyn. She indulges herself in the melancholy certainty that those were the best times, the times with Marilyn, the times before adulthood and what Reen thinks of as The Disappointment of Love.

Marilyn is in her wedding gown, yards of white lace and a thicket of netting. She holds a single rose. Reen thinks that now she is thirty her sense of romance should be a little chastened, but — and this is despite her recent jaundice with marriage — she still feels the old excitement at the sight of a bride.

Reen wants to explore the past. She wants to dig around, sift information and uncover clues, pinpoint the exact moments in her history that she was happy.

Actually what Reen should be doing now is packing photographs into cardboard boxes; she is helping her aunt dismantle her grandparents' living room. But she finds that all she wants to do is sit in her grandmother's hard fireside chair and stare at the photo of Marilyn, at the familiar grin, at the dark hair, oddly tamed and secured, at the made-up face and manicured nails.

'Whaddaya *staring* at?' Marilyn would say. 'You wanna take a picture?'

'Lasts longer.'

An afternoon in summer

Reen's grandmother slices tomatoes, paper-thin, onto a white plate. She pulls apart the loaf and slices off the lambswool. Reen's sister, Pip, spreads the lambswool thickly, lovingly, with butter and then with raspberry jam. Rose, Reen's mother, angles the teapot spout towards the ceiling, *showing it to the pictures,* Reen's other grandmother calls it. There is only one picture in this room, though — a framed photo of Pope John XXXIII; tucked in behind the frame is a dried stem of macrocarpa, left over from last Palm Sunday.

Tommy, Reen's father, reads the paper, reaching around for the tomato sandwich Nana has made him.

Reen watches her grandfather eat, he has no teeth and his lips suck inwards as he chews; he smiles up at Pope John, slivers of onion bobbing at the sides of his mouth.

Shafts of sunlight cut diagonally into the dark kitchen. The heat from the coal range makes Reen heavy-limbed and sleepy.

A loud staccato rapping on the window wakes her; a face pushes up against the pane, the nose and lips squashed and bloodless. The mouth grins madly and a braying voice calls out: 'GIDDAY, MRS MONDONI, GIDDAY, MR MONDONI, REEN THERE?'

'No respite for the wicked,' Rose says cryptically.

Marilyn barges through the back door and into the kitchen, smacking her hands together, her whole body humming with barely contained excitement. The spirals of her tight perm wobble like coiled springs.

'GIDDAY, EVERYBODY! Hey, Reen,' Marilyn speaks rapidly, swaying on her heels, 'you wanna come 'n' ride in Reggie's new car, it's a Valiant?'

'HEY, POPPA! HOW YOU TODAY?' Marilyn turns to Poppa, slapping him on the shoulder and bending down grinning into his face. He grins back, toothlessly.

'Keep it down to a dull roar, would you, Marilyn?' Rose says. 'There's a woman sick in Timaru.'

In Greymouth

There were two realms in Greymouth, Reen thinks; Nana and Poppa's where the principle of quiet is broken only occasionally by Reen and her sisters' loud laughing, or Rose's snapping fury at the narrowness of the kitchen; where the adults doze after lunch and Reen and Pip and EmEm might browse through the stacks of old *Reader's Digests* in the front bedroom or rearrange the First Communion photos on the chest of drawers; where on sunny days they sit in cane chairs beside the vegetable garden, reading to the sound of cicadas, or Reen and her sisters stand in front of the washhouse sink winding wet hankies through Nana's mangle, or dip stones from the beach into a bucket of water to see what colours they are when wet, whether they have any hidden deposits of silver and gold.

Over the fence at Sopers' the doors bang, Marilyn and her mother, Elsie, shout down the passage to each other, Marilyn rages at Reggie, her brother, and the radio racing commentary mingles with Elsie and Reggie's old Elvis records; all this is heard through the open windows. Standing on the Sopers' verandah or rounding the side of the house to the back door, Reen's impression is of a house bulging erratically with noise, like the squat and bouncing houses of television cartoons.

There is a surplus of belongings, too — Marilyn's old toys, clothes from other decades, piles of *Popular Mechanics* and pink *Women's Weekly* paperback romances, old paint tins, extra furniture that has never been thrown away. There is no stained wood, like Nana and Poppa's, but yellow painted walls, chipped and blotched, strangely coloured furniture, leopardskin bedspreads and rugs and pictures of Spanish ladies with large, olive breasts.

Reen tries to remember a time before she knew Marilyn

The winter she was seven Marilyn was there on the verandah with Nana and Poppa when Tommy and Reen pulled up in the Nancarrow taxi.

The Christmas after she started school, Reen remembers playing with Marilyn down at the lagoon, belly-flopping off the jetty, floating EmEm's wind-up bath toys and losing them over the other side.

Reen can recall a photograph in Marilyn's photo album: she, Reen, is two, two and a half maybe, tucked up in Marilyn's doll's pram, an elaborate vehicle raised high off the ground by big shiny wheels, like an old-fashioned carriage. Marilyn is in the photo, too, grinning at the camera, gripping the pram handle with both hands, proprietary, determined.

Reen finds that Marilyn goes back as far as her own memory.

Reen hasn't seen Marilyn for seventeen years, since Marilyn left for Nelson, fifteen and pregnant. Reen's Aunt Teresa knows a little.

'She gave up the baby,' Teresa says. 'But she married that boy, Gordon, anyway.'

'She's still in Nelson. I met Elsie up town one time. She went religious — Marilyn, that is — talking in tongues and all that.'

'*Marilyn?*' Reen can't believe it.

'Well, better than being the town bike, I say.'

Reen frowns at her aunt.

'Anyway,' says Teresa, peaceably, 'Mama had a real soft spot for that girl.'

Marilyn in charge

Marilyn comes over and takes Reen by the hand back to Sopers' to play.

'You were like a doll to her,' Rose said once.

In Marilyn's bedroom Reen gazes round at a sea of pink and fluff, a sticky sweet girlish room. Marilyn shows Reen her booty. An army of teddies and fluffy dogs, bunnies and love-mice line the pink shelves, two and three rows deep. The big dolls' pram is parked in the corner, a pile of dolls heaped up in it, clothed, unclothed, long, short-haired, sometimes headless and limbless, sometimes with the fingers of a whole hand chopped off neatly at the first joint. Marilyn has a pink plastic-quilted jewellery box, too, a ruby-encrusted gold crown on the lid; inside a ballerina in a red-spotted tulle tutu pirouettes speedily if you wind the key underneath.

Marilyn sits Reen up on the high bed, on the pink-and-white bedspread, surrounding her with a laager of treasures. She tries bead necklaces and Woolies rings on Reen, ties clumsy bows in her hair. Reen likes Marilyn's Miss Cornflower tea-set and the raccoon with the zip-up tail where you can keep hankies or shortie pyjamas. She likes her play make-up kit, the red lipstick, the gold-rimmed powder compact.

Marilyn lurches about the room, big and graceless, a golliwog in fairyland. She wears a dress and lace-fringed white socks and patent leather shoes, clothes that sit incongruously on her square, chunky body. Her socks are dirty, she has blotches of honey and toast crumbs on her bodice, and a wide milk moustache. At night Elsie wets Marilyn's hair and twists it around rags so that in the morning it hangs briefly in bunches of ringlets which she catches in wide ribbons; by mid-morning the ribbons are trailing or gone, lost outside, caught on a nail, pulled out crossly by Marilyn herself.

Outside the bedroom Marilyn pulls Reen along behind her. They play in the Memorial Park, where Marilyn likes to spin Reen fast on the merry-go-round; they go down to Buller's for packets of sherbert, which Marilyn spoons onto Reen's tongue; they go to the beach, where Marilyn holds Reen's hand tightly and tells her to stay away from the water; they go over to Dulcie Ward's, the old deaf woman at the back of Sopers', where Marilyn talks slowly to Dulcie with her hands and Reen eats soft yellow coconut biscuits from a coronation biscuit tin.

Inside Marilyn's head

Reen has heard whispers, she has seen pink pills. She asks Rose about fits. Nana says Marilyn has been like that since she was born. Rose says *fits* is not the right word, it's *epilepsy*, which is just something wrong in the brain and nothing to be afraid of, her cousin Dan Kennedy had it and as long as he took his pills he was all right.

Reen is nervous of Marilyn for a while, watching her sideways and from behind, watching her at breakfast to make sure she takes her pink pills, anxious that Marilyn isn't provoked, doesn't explode suddenly into a thousand gristly bits, which is how Reen thinks of fits.

Another afternoon

Reen is on the Sopers' verandah, rocking gently on Marilyn's swing; it has silky ropes and a frilly white seat-cover, stained and grubby now, with frayed edges and unravelling strands.

Reen watches Reggie working under the bonnet of a car. Reggie has set up his workshop — a corrugated-iron lean-to — just to the left of the verandah and has taken down the front fence so he can drive his cars onto the lawn. (Reen's aunts complain about this when they call in on Nana.)

Reen likes Reggie. She watches his hands, black with grease, and the way he wipes them carefully between jobs. Reggie is much older than Marilyn, twenty years nearly, old enough to be Marilyn's father, Reen has worked out.

'That Marilyn is a typical afterthought,' Rose has said.

'My little autumn leaf,' says Elsie, pressing Marilyn to her breast — *bosom,* really, Reen thinks, vast and spongy, though Elsie is not big all over; she has a spreading middle but shapely legs and surprisingly trim ankles.

Marilyn and Reggie have their father's build and colouring; they are solid and stocky like Frank, with tough skin and coarse black hair. Marilyn ties her hair with rubber bands now, strange skewed pigtails and rough plaits; Reggie's hair is cut long and slicked back at the sides with Brylcreem, like Elvis the Pelvis, Tommy says.

'Reggie's got a DA,' Marilyn tells Reen, smirking. Reen tries to look knowledgeable.

'That's a duck's ARSE!' Marilyn laughs her harsh, sawing laugh. She clasps Reen hard about the middle, squeezing. 'Don't be dumb all your life, kid!'

While Reggie is working on his cars and Reen is rocking, Marilyn sits on the verandah parapet, banging her heels and calling out to Reggie.

'Who's your girlfriend now, Reg? Since Mary-Rose has gone off?'

Marilyn leans back and tells Reen loudly, 'Mary-Rose went up to Nelson, she got sick of waiting for Reg. You gonna be a bachelor-boy now, eh Reggie?'

'Yeah, well you're telling the story, Podge.' Reggie is taciturn, poking about with the spanner and screwdriver, speaking only when absolutely necessary; his voice is rasping like Marilyn's but deeper. Marilyn keeps at him, a hefty pup, worrying and barking, nipping and snapping, testing Reg's humour.

'I heard Mary-Rose's got another bloke, anyway. Girl of Bunz told me.' Marilyn's heels hammer idly, an irregular, provocative beat.

'Ma says Reggie loves his old Ma too much to get married. No one's gonna cook like his Ma does. That right, Reggie, you Ma's boy?'

Reen watches Marilyn laughing, leaning forward gawking at Reggie, her yellowed teeth showing. Reggie wipes his fingers on the rag he keeps in the back pocket of his overalls.

'I've just about had enough of you, Podge.' He comes towards Marilyn, still wiping his fingers and Marilyn shouts for Elsie, sorry now.

'MA! MA! Bugger off, Reggie! MA!'

Reen can hear Rose over the fence, calling her name, calling her for lunch. She watches Reggie approaching Marilyn, curious to see what he will do; she smiles at Marilyn's snorting hysteria, her fear and laughter.

Reggie stands in front of Marilyn, rubbing his hands slowly with the cloth, pressing Marilyn's legs into the wall with his groin. Marilyn arches back, gibbering, calling out. 'Sorry! Sorry! Don't, Reggie! MA! MA!'

Reggie grins, reaching behind Marilyn and pulling her upright.

'MA! REGGIE'S GOING TO HURT ME!' Reen can hear Elsie now, banging the kitchen door, striding down the hallway. Reggie stands eyeballing Marilyn, then his hand shoots out and he twists her left nipple hard, quick and expert.

'Jesus, Reggie, you bugger,' Marilyn cries, clutching her breast, squeezing and rubbing it. Elsie appears on the verandah at the same time as Rose's head pops up over the fence.

'Reggie!'

'Are you deaf or something, Reen?' Rose says, eyeing Marilyn. 'C'mon, move it!'

Reen slides off the swing. 'See y'after,' she calls to Marilyn.

'Jesus Bloody Christ, Reggie!' Marilyn is saying, scowling down at her breast. She has a grease mark on her pink seersucker blouse.

Reen and Rose

Of course Rose doesn't like Marilyn.

When Reen is next door, Rose stalks the fence, helping Poppa pick tomatoes, but listening, listening, Reen knows, for rough talk, signs of degeneracy.

Reen would like to explain Marilyn to Rose, explain the value of her crashing boldness, her lack of ordinary restraint, her rude, shocking world.

But these are not qualities Rose has any time for.

Frank and Elsie and Reggie

Frank Soper has been laid up for fifteen years, since his accident down the mine.

Just as Reggie is years older than Marilyn, Frank is much older than Elsie — nearly as old as Poppa — so he seems more like Marilyn's grandfather.

Reen has seen Frank hobbling about in the back garden, feeding the chooks or picking gooseberries, but mostly he sits inside on the kitchen window bench, propped up against cushions, his bad leg stretched out; he listens to the racing commentaries and all the soaps.

Sometimes Marilyn orders Reen into the kitchen where Elsie kneels on a chair, singing along to the radio, leaning over the table reading the paper and smoking her special, sharp-smelling cigarettes, where Reggie is hunched in his singlet, eating ham and mustard sandwiches and wedges of fruit cake, where Frank lies on his bench, gazing out the window.

'Come 'n give your old man a kiss, princess,' Frank calls out to Marilyn, his voice high and thin, from years of disuse, Reen thinks.

'Youse kids want some lunch?' Elsie shouts. She makes egg and lettuce and Eta mayonnaise sandwiches, 'door-stops', Frank says, Reen can hardly get her mouth around them. Elsie pours milk for Reen and Marilyn, asks Reen how's Mrs Mondini, she's a great old lady, what is she now? Eighty-five, eighty-six, she must love youse coming, Rose cooking for her and Tommy mowing the lawns, nothing like kids when you're older, look at my two, Elsie beams at Reggie and Marilyn, mouths plumped out and chomping.

'Reggie's had to be the man round here since Frank's accident, my right arm.' Elsie leans over Reggie, kissing him on the shoulder and he bats her away. Reen watches Elsie find another cigarette and light it, sucking back and blowing out lustily.

'And as for this little surprise! No luck for eighteen years, then bugger me days, a little package.'

'Podge?' Reggie growls. 'Little?'

'*C'mon*, you. You loved her. Reggie *adored* her, didn'e, Frank?'

'Certn'ly did.' Frank is nodding for Elsie but looking away, raising his hand at Poppa over the fence.

'Y'know who she's named after, Reen, our Marilyn? Y'heard of Marilyn Monroe? The film star? *Gorgeous*!' Elsie is bear-hugging Marilyn from behind, burying her face in Marilyn's neck. 'Ohhh, what a doll! I saw *Gentlemen Prefer Blondes* four times. Frank used to say I looked like her, too, didn'cha, Frank?'

'Certn'ly did,' Frank says again.

Elsie starts singing in a breathy, little girl's voice, '*The French are glad to die for love . . .*' Reen watches Reggie and Frank and Marilyn staring at Elsie as she shimmies her wide hips and walks as if down steps, languidly, crossing her feet over, thrusting her breasts forward. She crooks her elbows, holding her hands up, palms forward, fingers limp; she is widening her eyes and singing:

But square-cut or pear-shaped
These rocks don't lose their shape.
DIE-MONDS ARE A GIRL'S BEST FRIEND!

Reggie leans back in his chair and gives a low whistle.

'Ma,' Marilyn wipes her hand across her mouth, 'me 'n' Reen are going down to the beach now.'

'Yeah,' Elsie starts clearing the table, her cigarette between her teeth.

'Well, no fighting with those Carmody boys, y'hear?'

Reggie and Gordon and Marilyn

Marilyn's boyfriend, Gordon, has long hair and long nails curving into the tips of his fingers, dirt underneath.

Sometimes Reggie works on Gordon's car and Reen watches from the verandah with Marilyn and Gordon. Gordon lights cigarettes two at a time, for himself and Marilyn. When the high-pitched buzz of the cicadas forces them to shout, Gordon picks the insects off the side of the house and shakes them in his cupped hands, making them drunk and sick, silencing them for a while. He throws them onto their backs; Reen watches them spinning on the concrete path, their flailing legs thin as hair.

When Gordon leaves, burning down John Street in his Falcon, Marilyn stands on top of the letterbox, yelling, waving him off.

'Gay Gordon, eh?' Reggie says, wiping his hands. 'I'm keeping my eye on him, Podge.'

'Oh shut your face, Reg.' Marilyn is happy enough, grinning down at Reggie from her narrow perch. The letterbox wobbles under her weight.

'Get down, Podge, you'll break the bloody thing.'

'STOP CALLING ME PODGE, YOU HAIRY BASTARD!' Marilyn's shout makes Reen blush. She can feel Rose's eyes over the fence, narrowed and flinty, staring a hole in her back, fixing on Marilyn's screwed-up face.

'Okay, gorilla! Let's see how strong you are.' Marilyn is laughing again, launching herself off the letterbox at Reggie whose arms shoot outwards, surprised, reflexive. He upends Marilyn, swinging her over his shoulder and back again, so that he is holding her upside down by the ankles, his face red with the effort, the muscles on his upper arm pushing outwards. Marilyn is laughing raucously, and gulping, sucking in her dress which hangs, inside out, around her face, exposing her white briefs, her fleshy hips, the soft expanse of her belly.

Strip Jack Naked

They sit in a circle, Marilyn and Reen, Gordon and Reggie. The curtains are drawn and the door shut and Reen sweats in the extra clothing Marilyn has made her put on.

It is girls against boys.

'They just wanna see your tits,' Marilyn says, baldly. 'Or your fanny. A free squizz.' She cups her breasts cockily; they are biggish and she walks with them thrust outwards. Reen's own breasts are hardly formed, though she has what Rose calls a trainer bra.

After an hour of play Reen is even hotter, though she has fewer clothes on. She is down to shorts, one T-shirt and a sock. Her face is warm from the beer she has drunk and her eyes and nose smart in the pall of cigarette smoke. How come she and Marilyn have to dish out cards so consistently? Reen wonders. Gordon and Reggie still have most of their clothes on, though they have all argued over Reggie's watch and Gordon's chain, Reen taking courage from Marilyn and loudly insisting they don't count as clothing. But Gordon and Reggie prevail and Reen feels a certain pleasure in their rough, overriding voices. They say little, drinking and smoking in a determined, businesslike way, grinning hard whenever Reen and Marilyn are obliged to strip.

Marilyn has only her shorts and bra and pants left, and Reen can feel that Gordon and Reggie are impatient now, leaning forward, waiting for the moment when Marilyn's breasts, lolling heavily inside her underwired bra, will spill forth. Reen herself feels an excitement, a tingling, a wetness.

It is just as Rose has said, alcohol makes you careless.

Reen feels pleasantly woozy, unembarrassed; she wishes Reggie would look at her, T-shirtless now, look at her trainer bra where she feels her nipples stiffening. She leans back against Marilyn's bed, the bedspread ruffle brushing the nape of her neck, making goosebumps rise. She watches Gordon and Marilyn; Marilyn is nearly naked, her head back, neck arched as she drags expertly on her cigarette. She is unconcerned, throwing cards into the middle with her usual swagger. She throws down her last four cards to Gordon's king and Gordon crows, starts tugging at her underpants. Marilyn lies back, her cigarette between her teeth, uncurling her crossed legs into the middle of the circle, sliding her pants down their stocky length.

'Dadada*DAH*!' She waves her pants above her head, then grabs a bottle from Gordon's hands.

Reen stares at Marilyn's bush of black hair, shocked at its abundance; she has only a sprinkling herself, still softish and downy.

'Okay, kid!' says Marilyn. 'Got a faceful?' Reen laughs, turning away sleepily to Reggie.

'Game's over!' says Marilyn.

Reggie is sitting hunched over, staring at Marilyn.

'Stop staring, you hairy pervert!' Marilyn shouts at her brother and stands drunkenly, lifting one leg to put on her pants. Reggie raises his face slowly as she draws on her pants. Reen watches him looking, his eyes hooded and dreamy, at Marilyn's black bush, at her heavy, swinging breasts. She watches him laughing quietly, draining his glass, licking the foam from around his lips.

Some things Reen did with Marilyn

They gave Marilyn's dolls short haircuts.

They jumped feet first off the diving board at the Centennial Pool.

They threw shells down onto the Reevetown Bowling Club green.

They rode the twenty-cent toy train at Truman's, making loud choo-choo noises.

They pierced hundreds of borer holes, finding the ragged trails beneath the friable wood in Nana and Poppa's back porch.

They sneaked into Dulcie Ward's kitchen when she was sleeping and stole Oddfellows.

They let off old firecrackers down in the sand dunes.

They drove over to Cobden with Reggie and ate fish and chips out of packets down at the Cobden tip head, watching the Bar, the choppy point between the two tip heads where the river meets the sea.

Brides of Christ

On days when Marilyn tires of her own invention, when Reggie is not there to tease, or when Elsie drives the two girls out of the house, on these days Marilyn likes to go over to Nana and Poppa's and look around. At these times Reen has a brief custodial authority, opening and closing cupboards, granting permission, demonstrating and explaining.

Marilyn likes to look at Nana's Christmas cake; she likes to check out Reen's Christmas presents; she likes to spy on Poppa, kneeling beside his bed, holding his rosary beads, muttering to the luminous blue Virgin on the chest of drawers. When Poppa is not there Reen shows Marilyn Nana's thick gold wedding ring hanging over the Virgin's clasped hands; Nana's fingers are too fat for it now.

Best of all, though, Marilyn likes to plant herself before the chest of drawers in the front bedroom, lean on her elbows and stare at the bevy of First Communicants, Reen and her girl cousins, veiled and white-robed, prayerful hands and holy expressions, pressed up against each other in a jumble of photographs. Marilyn is thrilled by these photos, asking Reen, again and again, to tell her the cousins' names and why they are dressed like miniature brides.

'Because that's what you do,' Reen says, pleased at providing something exotic for Marilyn. 'And you walk up the aisle in twos and you get the Host and afterwards you get a medal on a white ribbon and a certificate with curly writing.'

'What's a *host*?' Marilyn asks.

'The Body of Christ,' Reen says automatically, recalling Sister Maria Goretti's instructions.

'Are you Holy Rollers then?' Marilyn asks. She stares and stares at the photos. She likes the dress and veil worn by Sandra and Anna and Perina best; the dress has lacy layers and a scalloped hem, the veil is long and full and held in place by a circlet of artificial lily-of-the-valley. Marilyn always shifts these photos to the front; Reen doesn't mind, she and her sisters change the photos around every few days, giving everyone a turn at the front. Reen likes the photo of her twin cousins, Jeanie and Monica. She likes the exact sameness of the girls, their dresses, veils, rosary beads, buckled shoes, crisp white ankle socks, their long fair plaits tied with white ribbons.

'That's what I'll have when I get married,' Marilyn says, holding up Perina's photo.

'They're *not* brides.' Reen wants to correct this gap in Marilyn's understanding.

'Well, they look like brides. I'd have flowers, though. My cousin Erica, she had this massive bunch.'

'They're just wearing white, that's all that's the same,' Reen says.

'And I'd have white gloves and a really long train.' Marilyn sighs. 'You have that breakfast thing afterwards, *see*, like a wedding breakfast.'

'Yeah,' says Reen, proud, 'and I got some mother-of-pearl rosary beads from my godmother.'

'Hah!' Marilyn slaps Reen's back, laughing her strange laugh. 'Really? Those things old Pops has? Do you do what he does? Hah! Hah!'

Reen shakes her head, silenced by Marilyn's mirth, taking the back seat again after her brief period steering. She follows Marilyn out of the bedroom, out of the house and over the road to the park where they swing slowly at first, talking of wedding cakes and the kind of icing they'd have, then they pump harder and faster, belting their legs and bodies back and forth, thrashing the warm air, racing each other to go higher, to see over the pohutukawa tops into the dark-brown water of the lagoon.

Toss Woollaston

The Twenty-seventh Nun

About my third or fourth round, some of my Catholic customers asked me if I had called at the Convent yet.

No, I said, I hadn't thought of it.

I should, they told me, the nuns liked the Rawleigh products, both for their own use and to give as presents to mothers on their visits. They had their own pocket-money, it wasn't much, but they were free to spend it as they wished.

My protestant upbringing had me in silent protest. I wasn't going to call on a sinister place like a Convent. My business was with housewives, one at a time. I didn't call on businesses, or collective groups of any kind. Their powers of resistance, mutually reinforced among members, would I felt be too strong for my timid salesmanship.

But the next round, and the next after that, the women came at me again. 'Have you called at the Convent yet?'

It came to a point where I wouldn't have been able to face them again if I hadn't called.

So, one afternoon at half-past-one, I leaned my bike against the high, green painted corrugated iron fence at the back of the Convent in Alexander Street, opened the gate, and went in. I saw three gables, longest, middle-length and shortest. The longest and nearest was opposite where I came in. There was a doorbell button. I pushed it, and waited.

I waited a long time, not liking to push it again in case I offended. Perhaps they were all at prayers? What did nuns do at this time of the day? Complines? Matins? Whatever the reason, it seemed it wasn't the right time for me to call. I would go away and tell the women I had called at the Convent but no-one answered.

Just as I had decided this I heard footsteps — *pitta-pat, pitta-pat* — approaching the door. It opened and a young nun said, sweetly but very firmly, 'How d'you doo?'

It was so compelling that I answered the same, like an ape taught a trick. I had a moment of inward embarrassment, hoping she hadn't noticed my too-close imitation and ascribed it, perhaps, to impudence. Then I told her I was the Rawleigh man and had called to see if they would like any Rawleigh products.

'Oh,' she said, 'you've come to the wrong door.'

'Have I?' I said. 'Which one should I have gone to?'

'That one there,' she said, leaning out as far as her grip with her left hand on the doorpost would allow, and pointing with her right forefinger to the middle gable. My sense of humour overcame my timidity and I couldn't resist asking — 'Shall I go there now?'

'Oh no,' she said indulgently, 'it'll be all right.'

I proffered her my Rawleigh card, with the list of all their products printed on it. She disappeared into the inner fastnesses with it leaving me outside the politely closed door.

I waited. And waited. I wondered how long I would have to wait — or be able to. Before she came back I had got to the point of deciding again to abandon the call and tell those women I had tried at the Convent, but failed. Then she opened the door and presented me with my card, now marked with a very handsome order, by far the biggest I had ever had at a single call — six cartons of Violet Talc — four packets of Vegetable Oil Soap — four bottles of Ready Relief — and sundry units as well. I didn't have enough stock with me to fill such an order, I had to tell her. I would have to go home and call again with the goods. When would be a good time?

She didn't seem to know.

'Would this time tomorrow be all right?'

'Yes, that would be a good time.'

Next day when I rang the bell at the correct door it was opened — after the usual long wait — by a different nun. My arms were full of the things they had ordered, and she had on a useful-looking black work apron. I stood expectantly, hoping she would hold it out for me to put them into.

But she didn't. She just stood there, waiting. I had to ask, 'Where shall I put them?'

'Oh, you could put them there, I suppose,' she said, standing back and indicating the bare boards beside the hall runner. So I put them down — six cartons of Violet Talcum Powder, four bottles of Ready Relief, four packets of Vegetable Oil Soap — and we both got the giggles.

Then I stood up and waited, expectantly.

She twigged at last and said, 'Oh, I expect you'd like to be paid?'

I agreed I would, and she went away again. This time I waited longer than ever — so long that I again debated leaving, abandoning the goods unpaid for, recovering from the loss in time on business elsewhere and never visiting the Convent again.

Just before I won against myself she came back, wringing her hands and saying, 'I can't find the Reverend Mother *anywhere*! I think she must have gone to the Bank.'

We agreed I should come back at the same time tomorrow and be paid.

I did, rang the bell at the right door, and met still another young nun — this one red-haired. She had put her wimple on in a hurry it seemed, and left a strand of hair out, above her forehead. It was beautifully wavy.

But she greeted me with the identical 'How d'you doo' that the others had used on me. I got the impression they must have 'How-do-you-do drill' in the morning, as part of the day's discipline.

'This is becoming quite difficult,' I told the red-haired nun — 'I've been up here three times now and had to explain my business from the bottom up to a different person each time.'

'Oh,' she answered airily — 'you could come here twenty-seven times and meet a different person every time.'

About my being paid — there still seemed to be some difficulty. She invited me in and conducted me through long, long passages at right angles to one another, till we came to a dreadful dingy parlour, full of vulgar imported images of saints and a Virgin Mary. Then she closed the door and left me.

She left me a long time.

Longer than any I had waited yet, outside the door at the back.

I could look out of this parlour window at Tainui Street in front, where the traffic went up and down freely. If I went out of the front door and quickly down the path no one might see me and I could escape. I had come to the now familiar balancing point in this debate when I heard, just outside the inner door of the parlour, the loudest and most sibilant stage-whisper I had ever heard —

'How much does he want?'

Silence. Then —

'I can't hear you.'

Someone was at the other end of the passage refusing to come closer with the information sought.

'Three pounds twelve and six!'

Silence again. I waited, cringing from the presences of the oppressive saints-and-the-Virgin.

I was feeling what a thief I was, waiting to take so much money from those shocked nuns, when the door at last opened and the owner (I presumed) of the stentorian stage-whisper entered, smiling sweetly. She put a handful of all sorts of small money on the table for me to count with her — one or two ten-shilling notes, the rest in silver — half-crowns, florins, shillings, sixpences and three-pences, and even a few pennies. It was all there — three pounds twelve and six. I wrote out a receipt, we smilingly thanked each other, and she ushered me out of the front door to walk legitimately down the curving path between swelling lawns to Tainui Street — from where I had to walk round via Puetahi Street — *Pew-tic-a-high*, as the locals say — to recover my bicycle.

I called at the Convent again next round, but they didn't want anything. Nor the round after, nor the one after that. I struck them off my regular calling list. They had my card with the telephone number, they could ring if they wanted anything.

One day months — 'nay years' — years afterwards (by that time I had a car) the phone rang just after lunch and a voice announced that it was speaking from the Convent of Mercy. I asked for a minute to get a notebook so that I could take their order.

But it wasn't an order, not for Rawleigh Products at any rate. The voice went on to identify itself as that of Sister Mary Clare and to ask if I gave art lessons.

I said no, I was sorry, I couldn't afford to do that, I had to earn money at another occupation to keep myself and my family and couldn't spare time to give art lessons — not at a rate I thought people would want to pay. True, I had taken week-end schools for University Extension — but they paid more than I felt I could ask for privately. All the spare time I could get was not enough for my own painting.

Oh! the voice was devastated. It had so hoped — I heard floods of disappointment in it, a storm of despair, earthquakes dislocating long-built-up hopes.

Reluctant to be totally cruel, I asked if she knew my work. I know what I thought of the painting of nuns usually — nothing I would want to be involved in. She rallied instantly to the defence of her application. Of course she knew my work, she had seen it at the Art Society. 'Beautiful, the Woollaston work!'

Not only was flattery hard to resist, the thought arose in me whether the mercy should be all on their side, those dwelling in the Convent of it. What if some poor soul of genuine artistic sensitivity and need were incarcerated there, without access to any source of real artistic enlightenment? Would I be right to withhold my tuition in such a case?

I wavered. The voice picked up the lapse and moved in. She had so hoped — etc. etc.

I said I found the ground a bit poor for canvassing on Friday afternoons, too many people were out shopping. Perhaps I could spare a couple of hours on Friday afternoons. Would that suit?

That would be wonderful, Mr Woollaston.

Thank you so much. What would be my fee.

'No fee,' I said. At what I felt I could ask, I didn't want to set a precedent. It would have to remain an exception to my practice.

We settled on the next Friday afternoon to begin. When I arrived I was invited into the horrible parlour where I had waited, that other afternoon long ago, to be paid. Sister Mary Clare's first question was, What would be my fee?

No fee, I reiterated.

Then no lessons, she retorted. They did not take charity at the Convent of Mercy.

I prepared to leave.

Then she came up with a solution — perhaps premeditated? Had we any children in need of music lessons? They had a famously good music teacher at the Convent.

We had Anna, then about nine. We *had* thought of her having music lessons.

It was settled then, a term's art lessons for a term's music lessons. The art lessons began right there. She would realise, having seen my work, I pointed out, that I would not be interested, for instance, in helping her copy pictures of pretty scenes for her friends for Christmas?

'Yes, Mr Woollaston.'

We would study space, its construction, not the imitation of its appearance in nature.

'Yes, Mr Woollaston.'

We would set up a still-life, and consider it as an example of volumes, cubes, spheres, and so on.

'Yes, Mr Woollaston.'

Oh, she was all obedience!

But it wasn't long before it became clear she couldn't draw, let alone understand cubism. Faced with a still-life, she would collapse and say, '*You* draw it for me, Mr Woollaston.' I realised I had been duped.

But I was caught — Anna's music lessons had to be paid for. Towards Christmas she came out in her true colours. 'I thought I would ask you to help me make pictures for my friends of these scenic gems.' She produced some photo picture-cards.

'Don't you remember what I said at the beginning?' I admonished her — 'and you agreed.'

'Och!' she retorted, fully Irish now — 'you and your dry old cubes!'

From then we gave up the pretence that I was teaching her drawing and talked of literature — we both loved Gerard Manley Hopkins — but not both of us James Joyce. 'The filth, Mr Woollaston!' It wouldn't have done to tell her I didn't mind 'filth' — even enjoyed it, especially the way James Joyce presented it. She took refuge in a statement 'Music is the only art that cannot offend God.'

Delicate God and His thought defenders!

We talked of life, and people, and my fear of coming to the Convent. Miss Webster, the Librarian of Greymouth, herself a Catholic, had told her when she asked if she thought I would give her lessons that I wouldn't — I would be frightened to come to the Convent.

'Frightened to come to the Convent!' she challenged me — 'What nonsense! Why, it is our home. We are as human as any other family. You should hear the *noise* these girls can make in their free time!'

I could believe it — I still remembered that stentorian stage-whisper outside the parlour door the day I was waiting to be paid. I told her — not about that, but about my having lost my fear of the Convent long before, when I had called on Rawleigh business. I told her of the three different young nuns I had met, and of the third one telling me I could call twenty-seven times and meet a different person every time.

When she heard that, her manner suddenly changed. The humour and badinage went right out of her voice. She looked up, puzzled. 'Did she say twenty-seven?' She asked, very seriously.

Then her mind cleared. 'Oh, yes, that's right,' she said — 'there's an old one upstairs, always in bed.'

Kim Eggleston

Wednesday Afternoon in June

The whole afternoon
smells of wet beech
and damp soil
Even when I light a cigarette
the smoke swings slowly
through the air
that hasn't dried all day
Good afternoon for walking
through old sawmills
smoking Mild 10's
Washing hung on the line
for a week
and the pale sun
shines luminous
through the barber's trailing ribbons
Good afternoon
to sit and let the rusting leaves
fall and slide, slide and fall
To catch beauty
in your throat,
cross your heart
and hope to live
And after tea
in the hour
between light and dark
fetching a box of wood
I hear the dog growling
and I look up the fence
and see him
A big man in a big coat
with a hat low on his eyes
standing there
watching the dog
still and silent as the big beech tree

a gun broken over his arm
He stands there
watching me
watching the dog
then he turns and crunches
down the road
Gone hunting
and the night closes
solid and damp
behind him.

Keri Hulme

from Fishing the Olearia Tree

o my love, there are lean hammer-headed clouds
menacing us from the horizon
and red-eyed moths beating on the doors

and the kettle, snoring away on the hob

'You would not know just by looking
but under that corner of my lawn
is the corpse of a shining cuckoo
which, in ecstatic prospect of the Bismarck archipelago,
failed to notice my window — and there
lies nextdoor's cat after mauling once too long
once too often/my home fantails one May morning, and
under here I buried the remains of my heart —
o, the potatoes? Like the sunchokes they
are self-sown — well, at least I never planted *them* — yes
it is a green well-nourished lawn.'

> The house-cricket is winter-drowsy
> and the spiders are moving in
> but zitzit zitzit zitzit
> until this gig is done

Objects taken in
become intrajects.

We are all taken in.

Can I wind my voice into your ear
and around your heart? O yes
I can, because your eyes let me
let me in —

My house lies
equidistant between Antarctica and Australia:
I can't hear a call from either
but a thousand miles a thousand years away
a wave rises in Hawaiki-nui Hawaiki-pamamao
and breaks here

on the rocks in the dark, the rocks at the far end
are fat with mussels: select some dozens
and steal them away.
Young shellfish, I scrape you so easily out of your shells . . . aue!
so rich with the possibilities of life! Ka tangi ahau with tears of steam
but it's just a shame and your damnation you taste soo sweet
— and these extras,
peacrabs tucked in the soft security of mussel mantle;
peacrabs loaded
with ochre-red eggs, taste a bit gritty but taste pretty good, as
does a sea-spider
couched away here in the steamed mantle erstwhile cool home,
the little toil now still
of chitonous candy-glass legs, crunch. Ah well, we all
should make such sweetness, such douce noise at our going

'the sea hath fish for everyone'
and so it is:

What luck!
A hen-crab, in berry
and me with pot and appetite
just sitting here
ready!

A Taoist sage-of-the-beaches
supplementing the chancy gifts
with seaweed
and sad mutants that crawl ashore

. . . o they shout in chorus
stick her in the iron pot
try her out —

I go fishing with spiders
I go fishing with flies
sometimes I catch fish but
there is more to fishing than catching

the cloud of terns glitters blacks flickers glints as they wheel
foil and white wing and dark cap and reel

                    so the bush is grey, grey the lake
                    and the hills retreating greyly
                    from the eyes
                    and the rain falls unceasingly
                    from grey and sodden skies
                    while the steely bladed flax
                    flexes and shines with/unholy sparking pride

the drone of days coming
            going going

and the black brooding bulls in Flanagan's paddocks

and the still white bird at the water's edge

Allen Curnow

A Time of Day

A small charge for admission. Believers only.
Who present their tickets where a five-
barred farm gate gapes on its chain

and will file on to the thinly grassed paddock.
Out of afternoon pearl-dipped light the
dung-green biplane descended

and will return later, and later, late as
already it is. We are all born
of cloud again, in a caul

of linen lashed to the air-frame of the age,
smelling of the scorched raw castor oil
nine whirling cylinders pelt

up-country-smelling senses with, narcotic
joyrides, these helmeted barnstormers
heavier scented than hay,

harnesses, horsepiss, fleeces, phosphates and milk
under the fingernails. I'm pulling at
my father's hand *Would the little*

boy for selling the tickets? One helmet smiles
bending over yes, please yes let me,
my father hesitates, I

pull and I don't let go. Neither does the soul
of the world, whatever that is, lose
hold of the load, the bare blue

mountains and things hauled into the time of day
up that steep sky deepening from sea-
level all the way west again,

this paddock, the weight of everything, these people
waiting to be saved, without whom there's
no show, stay in place for ever.

A hand under each arm I'm held, I'm lifted
up and over and into an open
cockpit *Contact!* nome-LeRhône

fires ninefold, the chocks kicked clear, my balaclava
knits old sweat and foul oil, where tomorrow
was encloses me now.

Allen Curnow

A Busy Port

I

My turn to embark. A steep gangplank
expects me. An obedient child,
I follow my father down.

It happens that the sun will have topped
a black hill beside the time-ball tower,
and found the spot of a fresh

tear on Bob Hempstalk's cheekbone, whose wet
red eyes blink back seaward where he leans
for'ard at the wheel-house glass;

one hand wipes an eye, the other shakes
a half-hitch loose, unlashing the wheel.
A man's tears, obscene to me

caught looking. Too late now. The time-ball
drops. Quayside voices (not for my ears)
discuss the dead, bells repeat

ding-ding across the wharf. Brightwork traps
the sun in brass when I next look up,
following my father down,

who made the trip himself many years
past. The old rust-bucket gets up steam.
Frequent sailings from where we live.

II

Winched aboard still warm over the for'ard
hatch the morning's bread hangs by a breath
of its own. It smells of bed.

An enriched air. The urinal under
the wharf drip-feeds, the main steam below
sweats. Darky Adams, deckhand

engineer stoker bangs his firebox
open, slings in a shovelful, slams
the insulted flame back home,

thick acrid riddance topples the way
smoke rolls by its own weight, in an air
that barely lifts, off the stack.

One jump clear of the deck the plank dips
with a short uneasy motion, deep-
sea talk to the paddler's foot

out of my depth, deeper yet, off the Heads,
our Pillars. Pitching like a beer-can.
I'm hanging on tight, can't hear

clashes from the stokehole for the wind
yelling, crossed on the wheel he's yelling
back, 'Ay, bit of a stiff breeze'.

Eyes that last I saw in tears can read
abstruse characters of waves, on course
between them, our plunging bows.

Margaret Mahy

[Hands]
from *The Tricksters*

Jack and Anthony walked down the track followed by Harry. Anthony had the pale skin of someone who had passed straight from winter to summer with no spring in between. He had the trick of looking around him as if he were remembering things, and so he already seemed at ease with the track down to the sea. Then, beyond the orchard and the native bush, they came face to face at last with the harbour, held in a circle of craggy hills in the cone of an old volcano. Its grey spaces and reflecting films of water at low tide made it look more like a prehistoric estuary than a commercial port, even though docks and cranes, small as children's toys, could be seen directly opposite. Thin soil lay draped over the bones of the land, in long, curving folds, falling, always falling, down to the sea and ending in a ragged coastline of tiny bays and indentations. Native bush grew darkly in the gullies; the gaunt ridges were freckled with the gold of gorse and broom. The two landscapes ran into each other and made a new countryside altogether (not pretty, but desolate, beautiful and timeless). Towards the eastern end of the beach was the boathouse with Charlie's *Sunburst* drawn up on the ramp, and beyond that, just as if sand and seagrass had somehow worked themselves into a useful shape, was a little cabin propped up by flax bushes and wild yellow lupin. Harry saw Anthony notice it.

'That's the old whare,' she told him.

'What? A-a warry? You've lost me now,' said Anthony doubtfully.

'It's a Maori word for house — in this case a little, old hut,' Jack explained. 'We've got a fishing net in it, and one or two other things. And four bunks! It hasn't been used — oh, for about three years.'

'I expect it was handy in the wife-swapping days,' Anthony suggested.

'Yes, it probably was,' Jack agreed absent-mindedly. He was wrapped in his own thoughts, but Harry looked keenly at Anthony, thinking he had made a sly family joke almost without anyone noticing. The breeze lifted his hair, which was a soft, light brown with fair streaks in it, not curling so much as rippling like the sea.

He caught her eye, shrugged slightly and made a gesture that took in the sea and hills.

'An extinct volcano . . . The harbour . . . Carnival's Hide!' he said. 'Well, here I am.'

'Here you are!' Jack agreed, but Harry thought Anthony had been using the words to talk to himself. Her imagination played a trick on her by suggesting she had seen him standing here before, even though she knew it was his first visit.

Voices came sonorously over the water. To the west, Serena and Benny were established on a large, smooth rock, higher and flatter than its neighbours. Mysteriously their reflections swam in the sea below them for, though the rest of the harbour was chopped by the wind, directly under this protecting rock, within the curve of the small promontory, the water was smooth enough to form a mirror. Their images rose and fell with the sinuous breath of the sea. Serena and Benny peered intently into the water, chanting softly to their reflections.

'What are they looking at?' Anthony asked.

'Oh, it's a private ceremony!' Jack said lightly. 'Rather like a game in a graveyard. That's the very rock where Teddy Carnival dived and disappeared.'

Anthony looked fascinated.

'It must be alluring,' he remarked at last. 'There's a definite charm about frisking around the edges of doom. I've played in a few graveyards myself.'

'We've always been very happy here, ghost or not,' Jack said.

'I don't doubt it,' Anthony said. His face was pleasant rather than handsome, but as he spoke, staring over at the children, something enigmatic and imperative looked out of his mild, blue-grey eyes.

Harry, who at seventeen was the closest of them all to being a child herself, knew just what the children were doing and swam over to them, finally pulling herself up beside them. They lay on their stomachs on the wide, warm rock, saying a name over and over again like an incantation.

'Teddy Carnival! Teddy Carnival! We are here, O Teddy. You are not alone,' they murmured.

'You'd be terrified if he did come. Don't give the sea your own names whatever you do,' Harry warned them, only partly teasing them.

'He was never found,' said Serena in a sonorous, melancholy voice. 'There's a bottomless cave down there, and he was sucked into it.'

Harry lay down beside them on the rock. The wind roared and shook its hot mane over them, while her hair dripped wet freckles on to the stone, which dried almost as soon as they formed.

'It's not bottomless, nothing like!' she said. 'I've felt all over that cave and it's not much longer than an arm. It's more like a tunnel really — a tunnel left by a volcano worm.'

'Don't frighten me,' Benny cried, for he sometimes suffered from nightmares. 'I'm not scared of Teddy. But no volcano worms!'

'She's inventing, you know how she does,' Serena said.

'Anyhow, Harry Hamilton, you used to call Teddy too, and give him your name. It's just a way of remembering him, like putting flowers on his grave.' She looked intently at Harry, but all she could see was a curtain of hair and the tip of a nose.

'Christobel started it,' Benny said, as if that made it all right, while Serena stared at Harry a moment longer, then sighed deeply.

They all three stared into the water, but the only faces they saw there were their own, differently drowned, a darker green than the green sea.

'What do you want for Christmas?' Benny asked Serena, beginning another game.

'A white pony with a cream mane and tail and a scarlet saddle and bridle,' Serena said promptly, 'or a lot of tame golden pheasants that will eat out of my hand and won't come to anyone else.'

'You won't get anything like that,' he said, shaking his head.

'I know that,' Serena replied, 'but you said what did I want, not what would I get!'

'I'd like a racing car or a hang-glider — blue, so I would look as if I were hanging on to the sky,' Benny said. 'What do you want, Harry?'

Harry was about to say she couldn't think of anything she wanted and almost thought it was true, but, as her mouth was opening, her thought turned inside out and she saw plainly that what she wanted was not nothing, but everything. She was sick of feeling closed in by people above and people below, of being good old Harry, not wonderful Ariadne, for that was her real name. She was sick of being gratefully but carelessly praised for docility when she wanted to have a turn at being the difficult, brilliant one instead, and she longed to be overwhelmed by something so whirling and powerful she could never be expected to resist it.

Being the middle one of the family suddenly seemed like an illness she had suffered from all her life, which might finally kill her if things did not change. But to wish for change was like wishing for a white pony with a cream mane and tail, or a sky-blue hang-glider. She began to play with her wish a little bit, to tell it, but in such a way that its true nature was hidden.

'I'd like a book,' she said slowly, dabbling in a rock pool.

'Grunt! Grunt!' cried Benny scornfully. 'Just a book!'

His glasses made him look clever, but he was a slow reader and suspicious of the printed word.

'It's a special book, this one,' Harry said. She had just found a ring of white shell, the collar of some vanished mollusc, the rest of the shell broken off and carried away.

'As you read my book you alter the world. You read Chapter One, look up from its pages and — hey presto — things have changed.'

'Like *Alice in Wonderland*?' asked Serena, interested.

'Not that sort of change!' Harry said, peering down into the water again. 'It would be just little changes to start off with, and nothing would move while you watched it. But each time you looked up, the world would have altered more and more. Things would get brighter and brighter, and the moon would come down, inch after inch, until it broke into a thousand little moons. Mirrors would begin to cry silver and leak out rainbows, and the glass people would come out searching for the one they belonged to. You'd look up from a page and see the reflections getting about, peering into people's faces, and when they found the right one they'd hug them, and from then on that person would be seen in their true beauty.' Harry fell silent.

'Go on!' Serena said, profoundly intrigued. She stared at Harry as if Harry herself might be an unknown glass person in disguise.

'Oh, nothing more — only that, when you got to the end of the book, you'd feel there was a face watching you through the last page, and when you turned the last page, you'd find that you were a book yourself,' cried Harry, suddenly delighted with her own invention. 'You were a book, and someone else was reading you. Story and real would take it turn and turn about, you see.'

She slid the white ring on to her finger. It was rather large but looked convincing on her brown hand.

'There! I've married the sea. I'm Mrs Oceanus,' she said. 'Everything comes out of me.'

Serena pondered this all. Frowning, Benny asked, 'Suppose you were hugged by a reflection — what would it feel like?'

'It would feel like a jump,' Harry said positively. 'A jump into a high place.' She could see her water-face, blurred and misty below her, she stretched out her arm and touched it so that it broke into many different rings spreading out below her. 'My book would make something happen in the outside world by the power of its stories,' she said.

'There's no such book though,' said Serena, 'or you could get it from the library.'

'The waiting list would be too long,' Benny said gloomily, for he always wanted to read books based on television programmes and had to wait a long time to get them.

'I'll write it myself then,' Harry promised, muttering back to the muttering sea. Now, just to bring commonsense back into the world, Benny pushed Serena, who was round and rolled easily, into the water and then jumped in after her. They swam off, bubbling and shouting and their churned-up reflections swam with them, leaving Harry to watch her own piece itself patiently together again. She thought she might not wait for it to come looking at her, but embrace it first and by taking it into herself grow brighter — as bright as Christobel perhaps. Now was the time to be bright, now school was over until next year, now she was her own person for a while. Half-smiling, she slipped gently into the water, feeling cautiously for branches that might have been carried against the rocks by a forcible tide. However, she could feel nothing except for the water, like wonderful silk, cool and warm at the same time. Even though the tide was out she could not quite touch the bottom, so she turned over in a slow somersault and dived down into the sea.

The water in the harbour was never quite clear. Particularly on a nor-west day there was always some mud suspended in it, so Harry entered a semi-opaque world rather than a translucent one. The feeling of her hair streaming behind her was wonderful. She had become a current, an eddy, a part of the ocean.

The little cave appeared like a black submarine eye watching her swim towards it and then became a plug-hole through which all the oceans of the world could run and roar, emptying out between the stars. Harry had to reassure herself that it did not go on forever by putting her hand right to the back of it, as she had done many times before. But this time something different happened. For a moment she thought a red-hot wire had sliced down and severed her hand, and then she thought it was a blade of ice, and finally she knew her hand was still joined to her, for she could feel its fingertips and bending thumb. There *was* discontinuity, but it was not in her. Her hand had found an alien space there in the tunnel under Teddy Carnival's rock, so she was in one place, and somehow, her hand was in another. This was the first terrifying thing to happen to her. The second was that another chilly hand took hers and held it very lightly. There could be no mistake. She could distinctly feel the fingertips and the ball of the thumb. Then something (she thought it was a mouth) whispered against her palm and at once her palm could see. It could see the age of the rock, the volcano in which the rock had been born out of fire, and the salt water that had slowly shaped it over thousands of years. Pictures of a rambling garden, in which a spade and garden fork stood up like witnesses, formed in her mind, and Carnival's Hide could be seen beyond them, recognizable but indefinably altered. Her mind was flooded with memories not her own; she saw, not through her eyes, which were full of salt and greenness, but through her lost hand. Shouting furiously underwater, she snatched her arm back out of the tunnel with no trouble at all, though she was uncertain if her hand had actually come with it. Her cry could not be heard, but rose in silver bubbles before her eyes, just as if she were a screaming girl in a comic book. 'Eeeeeek!' would be written in the heart of each bubble, but it would stay unheard until the bubbles burst on the surface of the sea. Meanwhile, she dived upwards until her head came out. She coughed violently in the face of the wind, while salt tears, some of them from under her eyelids, poured down her cheeks. A weird, whooping sound filled her ears, but it was only her own sound, made as she struggled to get her breath again. There were screams from the beach too, but cheerful ones, for Jack was romping with Serena and Benny, and Anthony was laughing and encouraging them. Everything was as it should be.

She had vanished for a minute — maybe less. At least she knew she could hold her breath for that long. As she bobbed in the water, lungs panting, heart pounding, a great jumble of thoughts running through her head, she found herself believing that the space beyond the rock was the same space that existed behind the lines of print in her book, and she had but managed to reach through to it and had actually touched one of its inhabitants.

Somehow she had crumpled things up by wishing to be the sea's wife, with everything coming out of her so that points in time, which had once been far apart, had actually folded together. Her hand was safe, clenched on the end of her arm — but inside her she was divided, the homely, familiar world behaving in a normal way on one side, and on the other a prospect of madness.

Harry decided to climb back on to the rock until she had got over her shock and could face the world calmly. She turned in the water and got the worst fright of all. The rock was not empty. A man was sitting there. For a moment she thought it must be Anthony because, though she knew this man, he was not a member of her family. But then she heard Anthony's voice behind her, so of course it couldn't be him. Besides, this man was undergoing a crisis of a sort she had never seen or even imagined before — not a mere, nervous twitching of the skin, but a terrible seething, as if at any moment he was about to boil furiously. For fractions of a second he ceased to exist, and though Harry's eye was tricked into carrying him over these gaps, she knew he was not continuous, only an intermittent presence trying to make a place for himself in the world. He was fully dressed and soaking wet, kneeling and staring out to the horizon, his hair dragged down by the weight of the water in it. Water streamed from every part of him.

There was no reason why people should not walk around the coast to Carnival's Beach. Though the little seashore seemed to belong to the Hamiltons, it could not really be privately owned. However, she knew this man had not picked his way round the headland as people occasionally did. He was too sudden and too wet — the source of many springs — and from the side of his face that was partly visible to her, the water ran red.

Treading water and gasping, knowing him at last, Harry imagined a face eaten away by mud crabs, and then a face untouched by water or crabs or time, which might be even more frightening. Besides, he was certainly bleeding. With every moment of recognition he became more and more real and horrifying, until Harry ducked her head under the water and tried to fill her thoughts with something else. She thought desperately of characters in her own story — of winged Belen, of mocking Prince Valery; she did everything she could to deny the existence of the man on the rock. When she came up again the rock was empty. He was quite gone.

A great shouting now began from Serena and Benny, and their pleased excitement reached over to bewildered, frightened Harry. She began a lopsided, clumsy dog-paddle, one hand still clenched, away from the rock, limp with shock and astonishingly drowsy in the water, as if suffering from an after-effect of concussion. The family were looking and listening. They began moving up the hill.

'It's happened at last,' Harry said, taking a breath as she swam, but speaking with her lips under water so that words bubbled out softly. 'I've gone mad from imagining things.' Even if she spoke out clearly no one would take her seriously.

'Dreaming again, my poor old Harry!' Jack would say, rubbing her head affectionately. 'But we'd better get a bit of speed on. That's Ma's car coming down the hill. She'll need a hand.'

So Harry came out of the sea and began following her family. There was nothing else to do. The rock was empty. Her hand was still safely on the end of her arm, her ring of shell had washed back into the sea. She reared up on legs that felt as if they might yield to the strong backwards slide of the water that flung lacy wings high around her knees. Up along the track ordinary family life was going on and Harry would have to join in. But as she thought about it, it seemed no more substantial than a sea mist, which — at a given word — would dissolve into nothing, and carry her with it.

Rachel McAlpine

[Kate Awakens]

from *Farewell Speech*

I think of the ten years that followed my marriage as my great sleep. I was like a racehorse being trained and groomed and exercised — but for what? I had no idea. It all seemed rather pleasant at the time, but there was an emptiness, a pointlessness which I have never known before or since. On the surface I was leading a busy and almost an enterprising life. If I told you the things I did in those years you might even be quite impressed. But I was useless, unused, and there is no greater tragedy. Of course I had to supervise my household, but before long I found Poppy, who took all those irksome duties off my hands. Wonderful Poppy, the best housekeeper in Christchurch!

My hunger for stimulating talk was not gratified by Walter. Let me give you an example.

'Three entrance gates and one exit gate are essential.' This was when the A&P Society was creating the show grounds. 'Then people can have re-entry passes.'

'A splendid idea, Walter,' I would reply.

'And we absolutely must have shade trees, and urinals in at least two places.'

'And a place for women to lie down,' I would remind him.

Through Walter I met lawyers and politicians and clergymen and scholars, yet every social occasion tended to degenerate into gossip or talk of drains. Soon after our marriage I made a bold decision. I started my Saturday soirées to which selected gentlemen were invited for the purpose of discussing interesting topics. The Land Question, Moral Aspects of Economics, the Evolution of Marriage, that sort of thing. We enjoyed ourselves vastly, and rightly or wrongly I lived for Saturdays.

Why didn't I ask any women? Jessie, you shame me. Apart from my own family I didn't know any educated women. A few had graduated from the University of New Zealand, but they were far too busy doing serious things to attend my frivolous soirées, or so I told myself. Any other women found me too serious, my opinions too bold, that was my reasoning. The truth is that I greatly enjoyed having half a dozen intelligent men all to myself for a few hours each week. It was partly vanity, partly thoughtlessness. And remember, I was still sound asleep.

We moved from St Albans to Madras Street in the centre of Christchurch, and I decorated the house. How I fussed over all that! Then, when I was twenty-nine, Walter and I sailed for England.

'Going home, eh!' As the *Rangitikei* sailed out of Lyttelton Harbour, Walter couldn't disguise his joy.

'Just for a while,' I said, watching the green indented coastline drift past.

'You'll like Bath,' he promised.

'My family is here,' I objected.

Walter assumed his sad pug face. 'My family is your family, they'll love you.' Oh, he meant well, but imagine seriously thinking his stodgy brothers and aunts could replace my whole vivid family! 'Once you've seen the doctors our future will be clearer.'

'True,' I murmured. I see no harm in telling you that after six years of married life Walter was very keen to have children, particularly as his first marriage had been without issue. For the hundredth time I wondered why I felt half-hearted. To be fully a woman was to be a mother; no matter what thrilling hypotheses about marriage were aired at my soirées, everyone took this for granted.

'Of course, a little baby would curtail your activities,' Walter said kindly. 'No more soirées when you're a mother!'

The journey was quite beneficial for my various tiresome medical problems. I read and wrote, and missed my gentlemen. When we reached England, Walter's friends were so frightfully predictable that instead of forgetting New Zealand, I missed my life there even more.

In particular I missed Mr Alfred Saunders. He had no parallel in my acquaintance, and yet he typified what I liked most about the colonial people. You never knew him personally, did you, Jessie? How could anyone describe Alfred? He was in his late fifties then, but he could run rings around the young. He was a rogue member of Parliament, immune to party politics, a pioneer, miller, baker, farmer, educator, mesmerist, gold-digger, writer, breeder of horses and hens, trainer of wild steers . . . We met when he diverted the Ashburton River and set up a mill. He never sat still for long. As you know, Ashburton is all of fifty miles to the south of here, but unless Parliament was in session he attended most of my soirées. Did you know Walter had been a miller in the Old Country? That was one thing they had in common.

Imagine how I missed my friend as I took tea with the English gentlefolk. They were blind and deaf, locked in the past. Have you been to Bath, Jessie? It's said to be England's most beautiful city and yet it seemed dead to me.

'You must be so lonely in the colonies,' one elderly cousin sympathised. 'No kindred spirits! No history, no links!'

I began to suspect there were qualities in New Zealand that I had entirely overlooked, as I had overlooked the uniqueness of our Saturday conversations. What were they? The invisible problems, the invisible people of Christchurch? Had I been leading a Bath sort of existence there? What sort of life was a real life in Christchurch? I lay awake at night turning this over.

'I'm so proud of you, my dear,' Walter would say after every social occasion. 'They all adore you so.' I could not open my heart.

The doctors submitted me to tedious examinations but could offer no cure for my barrenness except for rest and peace of mind.

'Life is too strenuous in New Zealand,' Walter argued.

I visited my family in Liverpool and Scotland, but even there I felt curiously dislocated. Where did I belong? After a year we returned to Christchurch. Walter sulked a little but he was very kind to me.

I found Alfred fired up about a great victory: all men over twenty-one now had the right to vote in national elections. What an uproar! Not just the property-owners, mind, but every man Jack.

'Alfred, you've done it!'

'One step on the right direction,' he corrected me. We both knew that the franchise was still a tangle of privilege, with men of property having several votes. 'Helped by my friends and some of my enemies.'

'What enemies? Everybody loves Alfred Saunders!' That made him smile, for he clashed with everyone sooner or later.

'Sir John Hall was a staunch supporter of the Bill,' he said from under those curly eyebrows. 'We worked together rather well.'

'You can't tell a book by its title,' I said.

'Tory!'

'So why are you still so cross?'

'Same old story,' he growled. 'We nearly had support for a clause which would have given women the vote! And that wretched Seddon led the opposition.' He took another gulp of cold water as if it were strong drink.

I soothed him, for this was one of Alfred's running battles. Can you believe, Jessie, that during my long sleep I never thought of it as my battle? I devoutly wanted women to vote, and I agitated on our behalf with every influential man who crossed my path. Yet I couldn't see how I could involve myself more personally, so I didn't try.

My little sister Isy married Henry May, and George gave him a branch of Beath's to run in High Street. When the Deans sold some land in Riccarton our family bought a good-sized block. Isabella and Henry built a house, and our youngest brother Frank began building too, with a young lady from Ashburton in mind. I visited Isabella frequently as their house was taking shape.

'Kate, you and Walter must build here too,' Isy said as we picked our way over the rough ground and stood on her verandah. The stunning mass of the Southern Alps stared us in the face, inflamed by the setting sun. 'We'll all be within walking distance.'

But Walter was settled in Madras Street.

'The city's so bad for your health,' everyone told him. 'The air in Riccarton is clean.' He really was an old fuddy duddy but I didn't press him.

'I shall design us a house just for the fun of it,' I told him. It was seven years before we winkled him out of the city!

Meanwhile he was still eager for me to conceive, and I began to feel like a failure. Now, Jessie, I'm going to tell you something that only two other people on this earth have known. Why shouldn't I? Those who consider me a wicked woman will have the pleasure of having their bad opinion confirmed. Those who regard me with adulation will doubtless find an excuse for my behaviour. I'm eighty-five. What use are secrets to me now? This happened over fifty years ago, when I was only thirty-two.

I used to visit the Hanmer Springs in search of health, particularly at the height of summer. The establishment was comfortable, the company congenial and the waters salubrious. One January I visited with a sharper purpose in mind. Human beings are creatures of habit and a certain gentleman from Napier was taking the waters, a distinguished gentleman whose name I shall not mention. He was urbane, intelligent, dark and shiny-skinned from the sun. We liked each other. At the inevitable musical evenings, I turned the pages while he played the piano. One afternoon we walked together along a forest path, and I confronted him directly.

'I hoped you would be at Hanmer this year,' I said. 'I think you know I greatly enjoy our conversation.'

A tree fern had fallen across the path and he held out his hand, helping me over. I did not disengage my hand, but stopped and gazed into his eyes, looking for signs of revulsion. There were none, although the gentleman was confused.

'Mrs Sheppard, we all adore you, and your presence makes a joy of January.'

Phrases! Compliments such as I received every day of my life. How could I convey to this subtle gentleman my most unsubtle desire? I chose bluntness.

'Mr A, I am here in the hope of curing my state of barrenness. Yet I am almost certain that my infertility is a consequence of my husband's condition, not mine.' I paused for a long while, still holding his hand. The gentleman's face paled, then went a dark red as he absorbed what I was saying.

'If I can help you in any way,' he said at last, raising my hand to his lips, which had a faintly purple tinge.

'I want a child!'

He looked swiftly up and down the path, and, finding it empty, drew me close. As he kissed me my heart pounded so noisily that the bellbird's song faded away. I found my arms embracing him and my body greeting his most eagerly. Without words we walked through the forest to a secluded gardener's shed, and there on a dusty wooden floor I knew what I had never known before. Oh Jessie, it was not just a child I had wanted all those years!

For a week I gave myself to him utterly, although he was not the man of my heart. Our time together was precious. He had a good wife, and I a good husband. When we said goodbye we agreed we should never meet again unless by accident.

He wrote me one letter. 'My dear Mrs Sheppard, I cannot refrain from writing just once to thank you for the most beautiful days and nights of my life. I have been to Paradise and my life from now will be lived in that knowledge . . .' I should have burned it at once, but I tucked it away among my other papers.

There! Are you disgusted with me? Oh no, you simply don't understand. Or do you? In October I had the great joy of giving birth to my only son Douglas. I cannot be sure that Walter himself is not the father. Perhaps the gentleman from Napier fathered my child, or perhaps he performed a different miracle, bringing me such an excess of relaxation that at last I was able to conceive.

But again I am jumping ahead in my narrative.

When I returned from Hanmer it was to find my mother weak beyond hope. It was a frailty of spirit rather than flesh, for she was only fifty-nine. I was overwhelmed with guilt, as if I had bought my fulfilment at the cost of her life. As I grew certain of my pregnancy, she drew nearer to death, and within three months it was over.

Her death shook me. Jessie, if you think people get used to bereavement, if you think that mourning is something that grows easier with practice, you are wrong. Losing Mama was painful. Mama was vivacity and grace, she was charm and wit and loveliness. She added spice to a life in Scotland which might otherwise have sunk into mere duty. She was luxury. I had lived my life with her flavour in my mouth. She had never quite adjusted to life in Christchurch. I suspect she never got over the loss of Uncle Jamie. When Father died, she transferred to Uncle her deep reason for living, for although she was the best of mothers, she was primarily a man's woman. She loved to flutter around a strong man, luring him to greater heights; that was the way she lived her life.

Her death threw me into chaos. She was the one soul standing between me and the gates of death. Now they were yawning in front of me. If I were to live only as long as Mama, I was well over half-way through my life. I retired from all social engagements and thought long and deeply about her life and my own. For all her influence on friends and family, what had Mama achieved? For all her brilliance, what changes had she wrought in society? She had lived as a handmaiden to men, and yet she had constantly urged me to live my life in the mould of Father and Uncle Jamie. 'Make the world a better place!' was almost the last thing she said to me. It was nothing new; again she was echoing the men in her life.

Red-hot in my mind was the episode in Hanmer. I began to see my whole life as selfish and wasteful. Thanks to my birth and upbringing I had a certain power, but I never used it except at one remove, by influencing men. Perhaps I had been a toy for men, but in return I had treated them as toys or useful tools.

I had never in my life doubted that I was a person, a valuable human being. It was the gentleman from Napier who helped me understand that I was also a woman; yes, specifically female. From this understanding there emerged another devastating insight. I gradually realised that, being a woman, I suffered from all the disabilities of a woman. I was like other women, I was not a unique being in my own right as I had always unconsciously believed.

Then I came full circle in my thoughts. I grew sure that if I wished to overcome the disabilities of being a woman it was simply not enough to behave as women had always done. Now, for the sake of Mama, who would hardly have understood the issue, I swore I would do my work. No more discreet manoeuvring behind the scenes! I had regarded my soirées as a radical arrangement, potentially a force for change in society. Yet the opposite was true, for with my soirées I had been perpetuating everything I deplored. I was very like Mama. For her sake I would learn to take responsibility openly like a man.

I could not attend Frank's wedding in Ashburton because my confinement was close. Two days later Douglas squeezed his way into the world. I sobbed with relief to see my baby whole and wonderful. His timely arrival shook me out of depression and reinforced my will to work instead of play, to work in a way of my own. My long sleep was over.

Stevan Eldred-Grigg

Cinderellas Waiting for the Ball

from *Oracles and Miracles*

The Historian

The Feron view of schools was that they were prisons built by 'them' to turn working people into slaves, to tangle and trick working people with words and numbers and symbols, to let loose a noose of language and send it flying through the air to strangle you.

Kindergartens, for example.

Kindergartens, according to a pamphlet published in the 1930s by the Christchurch Kindergarten Association, had been founded by high-minded ladies intent on offering working class families a chance of getting 'advanced early childhood education' in 'light, airy buildings with pretty gardens and teachers trained in the latest methods'.

'Bunch of stuck up tarts,' Margaret Feron said, 'making themselves feel good by filling our kids with ideas.'

But the stuck up tarts were allowed to have their way because as the hard pressed mothers of Addington slogged away at their cooking, washing, scrubbing, mending, they were glad of the chance to get rid of some of their burden by sending their kids to kindergarten — even if it did mean the kids might come back home again with heads stuffed full of 'ideas'.

So Ginnie and Fag went along to kindergarten and their struggle with 'them' began.

Ginnie

Me and Fag started going to Selwyn Street kindergarten when we was four. We was really worried cause Mum had been talking about it as though it was on a par with Nazareth House, except there wasn't any nuns and they didn't lock you up and make you stay there overnight. We was worried too cause the kindergarten was about a mile from our house and we didn't know how we was going to get there. Then Eddie made us a trike. He got odd bits and pieces from the engineering works and the council dump and that, and put them all together, but unfortunately when it came to a seat he couldn't find one so he tied on a piece of sacking.

Mum didn't come with us to kindergarten, she didn't even stand and watch us go.

'All right youse kids,' she said. 'Time to git going. Make sure you don't cause trouble.'

We'd been hoping she would wave us off, we'd been whispering about it of a night. But when she just opened the kitchen door and shut it behind us we wasn't really disappointed, we hadn't really expected her to do anything different.

So off we went. We took turns pedalling while the other one stood on the back.

We knew all the streets, we'd been up and down them often enough, so we wasn't scared of getting lost. Our big worry was the dogs in the yard of a house in Burke Street. They was Scotch terriers, and we was terrified of them, they was horrible little yappy things that used to rush out at us whenever we went past. If we was with our brothers or one of our big sisters they'd give the dogs a boot, but me and Fag was terrified of having to go past them by ourselves.

Well we solved that problem by going about half a mile out of our way, sort of wending round back streets till we got past the dogs and back onto Selwyn Street.

The next problem was when we got to kindergarten, some of the better off kids started slinging off at us.

'What a latey of a trike,' one of them said. 'Hasn't even got a seat, just an old spud sack.'

Me and Fag sort of looked at each other.

'This trike's a special sort,' Fag said. 'It's um, a special racing model and there's sacking on it to protect it, cause our father thought it was going to rain heavy in the night and he put sacking over the trike to protect it.'

Fag was good at spinning a yarn. So while she cracked up our trike all the other kids started jostling round us looking at it.

'Gee,' they was saying, 'a real *racing* trike.'

The boy who'd said it was a latey, his name was Ronnie. He was a pasty little boy but his parents was well off by our standards and he was sitting on a shiny red and silver trike with a bell.

'Can I have a ride?' he said. 'I'd really like a racing model.'

'Well,' Fag said. 'I don't know. This is a really special trike, and our father said . . .'

Blah blah blah.

'As a special favour,' she said. 'And we'll keep an eye on yours for you.'

Soon all the kids was lined up for turns on our racing model, while we whizzed round on theirs. And I can still remember hearing the tinkle of the loose hub caps on our trike and thinking how queer it was that those other kids could be talked into thinking that a heap of old junk was better than what they had.

That was the way things was for the two years we went to kindergarten. I don't remember much about the actual teaching and that, though I can remember thinking the teacher was a *lady*, and feeling scared of her cause of that, but also thinking she was a bit sort of stupid too, cause she talked and dressed in a strange sort of way, like ladies did. But she wasn't important, the important thing was the other kids, and me and Fag felt we really had to battle to keep our end up with them. They all seemed so much better off than us, though when I look back at it now I don't think many of them can of been, they was all from working families like us, but some of them had a few extras we didn't have, and a lot of them had fathers. One boy whose father worked on a night shift we really envied, cause sometimes the father would walk round to the kindergarten and pick the boy up and take him home, and to us that really seemed out of this world, something really marvellous.

'Oh our father's in the building trade,' we'd say, hoping the other kids would think he was a carpenter or something and not just a labourer.

'He's away right now,' we'd say. 'He goes away to work on the Peninsula. But he'll be coming home next week and he's going to bring us a doll, he's going to bring us a watch. He's gone up north for a big job and when he comes back he's bringing bangles for us from Brighton.'

For a while our main ambition in life was to have gold bangles. It was a fad. One of the big department stores was selling these gold bangles and some of the better off girls turned up dangling them from their wrists at kindergarten. They wasn't really gold of course, they was just some trashy sort of metal with a thin coating of gilt, but they was all the go. They was called 'adjustable bracelets' cause you could make them grow as your wrist grew. So these girls sort of sauntered round the playground flashing these bangles at us, and me and Fag got *desperate*.

One day when we got home we found Mum out and the kitchen un-guarded. So we stole a piece of bread and spread some meat paste on it and hid in the dunny and had a feast.

Fag suddenly stopped chewing.

'Meat paste jars,' she said.

She stuffed the rest of the bread in her mouth, grabbed me and ran back to the kitchen.

'Notice the lids?' she said.

I hadn't, of course, so Fag got the meat paste jars down again, lifted off the lids and there, flashing at me, I saw . . .

'Gold bangles!' said Fag.

Next morning me and Fag was sauntering round the playground with brass rings from the meat paste jars on our wrists.

'Oh yes,' we said. 'Our father got us these as a little surprise.'

I don't know who we thought we was kidding, but we was certainly kidding ourselves.

Then we turned six and started school.

Ginnie

We didn't want to go to school of course. Mum had been threatening us with it for years, so it wasn't surprising we was scared when the morning came. We was all sulky and grizzly while Peggy tried to tidy us up a bit, brushing our hair and washing our faces and that. Mum didn't say anything till the last minute.

'Stop yer bloody whingeing,' she said. 'Yer going whether you like it or not and all I can say is good riddance, two less moaning bloody kids I have to put up with.'

Which she probably felt a bit sorry about, after she'd said it, but of course being Mum she'd never let on.

Hock and Peggy had the job of taking us to school. Me and Fag was sulking, with our heads stuck down in our chests and our feet dragging.

'Hurry up, come on, hurry up,' Hock and Peggy said. 'If you don't hurry up we'll be late and our teachers will give us the paddywhack.'

In the end they got really frantic, they pinched us and *dragged* us down the street, cause I think they really would of got the strap if they'd been late.

And of course when we got to school it was even more horrible than we'd imagined.

It was Sydenham School, a great big huge ugly old place with wire fences all round it. Inside the fences was grey asphalt and dirty concrete and dirty rust coloured bricks and of course kids, hundreds and hundreds of kids, rushing and shrieking and yelling.

Hock and Peggy dumped us outside a classroom and ran away.

Me and Fag looked round bewildered. A bell rang somewhere. Suddenly all the hundreds of kids hurried up onto verandahs and lined up in queues, and of course we didn't know what we was supposed to be doing, so we just stood there where Hock and Peggy had left us.

A woman came out of the classroom. A fat, dumpy woman, with a face like a clown mask all white with powder, and bright red lipstick slashed across her mouth. She sort of minced out on teetering heels and looked at the queue of kids by the door, then looked down at me and Fag.

'And what, may I ask, are you two girls doing here?' she said.

I started to cry.

'We're Daphne and Janet Feron,' Fag said.

The woman sort of whinnied.

'Oh no!' she said. 'Not more Ferons! I seem to have been teaching Ferons ever since I came to this school.'

Some of the other kids snickered a bit, but not really sure whether they was supposed to or not.

'Smarmy fat bitch,' Fag muttered.

'What did you say young lady?' the woman shrieked. 'What did I hear you say?' Etcetera, etcetera, etcetera.

So we didn't start off our scholastic career with what you might say was an ideal introduction.

The woman yelled at us for a while, calling us stupid and impertinent and sly, 'like all the Ferons'. Then she changed down gear and carried on for a while longer about the stupidity of kids in general. Then in the end she seemed to sort of lose interest in it all.

'Any child with their wits about them,' she said, 'would have seen five minutes ago that the first thing to be done in the morning is form a queue outside the classroom door.'

Me and Fag stumped up onto the verandah and joined the queue.

'Enter, class,' said the woman.

And we all shuffled through the door, out of the sun and into this big grey room crammed with desks and a big dark map of the British Empire.

'You Feron girls,' the teacher said. 'Sit here.'

She clutched us by the shoulder, steered us to a desk, then went and sat up on a sort of platform.

'Writing,' she said. 'Get out your slates please.'

Me and Fag looked round desperately as all the kids dragged slates and bottles of water out of their desks.

'Just do what everybody else does,' Fag said.

So we looked in our desks, but of course they was empty.

Fag shrugged her shoulders. Two big tears rolled down my cheeks.

'Hand up high,' the teacher said. 'Write in the air what you see on the board.'

She wrote Bb Bb Bb Bb on a blackboard.

'Easy,' Fag said. 'We can do that no trouble.'

Me and Fag spent a fair bit of time looking at newspapers and magazines at home and we'd sort of picked up some idea of letters, though we didn't understand any words. So we stuck up our hands with all the other kids and started writing Bb Bb Bb Bb in the air, feeling quite proud of ourselves.

But that was a mistake.

'What do I see?' the teacher bellowed. 'Left handed Ferons?'

Her face had gone all pink from excitement and all the other kids turned round to stare at us. Some of the kids sniggered, but most of them just looked sort of stupid, just a sort of glazed look, like they were glad it wasn't them and that was about all they could manage to think about.

The teacher seemed to burst through all the faces and pounce on us. She had a wooden ruler clutched in one hand.

'We don't use the left hand, Janet and Daphne Feron,' she said, 'we use the right hand. What do we call left handed people, children?'

'South-paws-Miss-Mitchell-son,' the kids all chanted.

'Cack handed,' Fag said.

Miss Mitchellson looked at Fag in a state of shock for a minute, then started to enjoy it even more.

'In this classroom you will not use such disgusting language, Janet and Daphne Feron,' she said. 'And in this classroom you will soon discover why I keep this ruler handy at all times.'

She whacked it down on the desk, then bounced back to the front of the room.

Fag poked out her tongue but then a little tear started to squeeze its way out of the corner of one eye. I was really scared, cause if that woman could make Fag cry then things looked black all round.

And things *was* black all round.

It turned out that after writing in the air we had to write the letters on our slates. And of course we still didn't have slates.

'Where are your slates, Janet and Daphne Feron?' the teacher shrieked.

'Haven't got any,' Fag said.

'We haven't got any, *Miss Mitchellson*,' said Miss Mitchellson.

And so on and so on.

Well that was the start of years of sitting and sitting and sitting on hard wooden benches listening to big bullying women reefing off at us. They all seemed to be big buxom creatures, those teachers, big well fed buxom women who all seemed to wear cardigans and blouses and woollen skirts. And their main job seemed to be finding ways to pick on you. Which wasn't hard to do, of course. We soon learnt that the way to survive at school was to just try not to be noticed. We would try to sort of shrink down into our benches, hoping and hoping at the start of each year that we'd be given a desk at the back of the room, where we wouldn't be so easy to see.

I can't seem to remember my teachers as individuals, they just seem to have been a procession of bullies with powder on their faces and big chunky rings on their fingers.

Mind you, I do remember what particular torture each one specialised in.

Like, with Miss Mitchellson it was the ruler. If ever you stepped out of line — whack. And the whacking started first thing each morning. Each morning we had to write letters in the air, and each morning of course me and Fag did it with our left hands and Miss Mitchellson would nag and nag us and tell us southpaws never got anywhere but Sunnyside. Then in the end, when she'd worked herself up into enough of a paddy, down would come the ruler on our knuckles.

'That is not the way to do it, Janet and Daphne Feron,' she'd say. 'We use the other hand.'

Then afterwards, the horrible slates would come out and the screeching would begin as fifty kids tried to scratch Bb Bb Bb Bb or Ff Ff Ff Ff fast enough to avoid the flying ruler.

Our next teacher kept going berserk about homework. She'd load us down with all this work to do after school, then next day the first thing was to sniff and snuffle through us all to find out who to strap.

'What do you mean, Janet Feron?' she'd say. 'You didn't finish your homework because you couldn't understand it! Well you know what happens to impertinent little misses who think they can get around me!'

I can still see her knee. I think it used to be lifted nearly as high as her face as she brought the strap down on my hand.

The next teacher loved to get a kid up in front of the class to torment and display her authority over. If you broke a slate pencil or said three times three was six, it would always be, 'Janet Feron, up to the front of the class.'

And if you tried to take your time about it she'd be down from her platform, lugging you by your shoulder.

Getting us up in front of the class was horrible in another way too, cause it was part of the humiliation of 'getting clothes through the school'. It was this scheme they had at Sydenham School, where people who had money would give their old clothes to the school and parents who was poor could ask to be given some. The school would make the clothes up into parcels and every so often would hand them out to the kids from the poor families. Mum had her name down for free clothes, of course, and of course we hated it. We'd be sitting on our bench, trying as usual to merge with all the other kids, when the school secretary would walk in with some brown paper parcels and me and Fag would look at one another and have this horrible sinking feeling.

We'd put our heads down even lower, hoping the teacher would forget we was at school that day.

But of course it was no good.

'Daphne and Janet Feron,' she'd say, 'your clothes are here.'

We wasn't the only ones getting free clothes, there must of been as many as a dozen or more kids in each class getting clothes through the school, but we only thought about ourselves as we slunk up to the teacher to be handed these lumpy parcels wrapped up in old brown paper with string. And they was always horrible clothes. I can remember once I was given a horrible pink velvet dress with a pair of red, horrible, shiny leather shoes to go with it, and I had to clitter clatter round for a year or more in those shoes with that dress and I must of looked like something from a sideshow at the A & P.

It wouldn't of been quite so bad if Mum had of been able to alter those clothes to make them fit, but she couldn't, she didn't have a sewing machine, so it would of meant hand stitching and Mum was long sighted and couldn't do hand stitching any more. She could of bought glasses I suppose, but where was the money going to come from?

Things got worse when we left the Primers.

At first we thought Standard One was going to be a real step up cause we was told we was going to be leaving slates behind and from now on was going to be writing in ink. Then we discovered we was going to be 'getting books through the school'.

It was like the hoo-ha about clothes. Kids whose parents had money could just buy their books and pens and that, on the first day of the new school year. There was a stationery shop round the corner from the school and on the first day the well off kids would turn up jingling silver coins in their pockets. The teacher would hand them a list, it was called the 'stationery requirements' list, and off those kids would go to the shop while in the meantime me and

Fag and the rest of us had to just sit writing words in the air. Then back the other kids would come, they'd slap their piles of shiny new books down on their desks and look round triumphantly.

It always took a long time for our books to 'come through'. Mum had to apply to the school in writing, saying she was poor. Then the school would check up on her to see if she really was poor. Then our names would be put on a list. And then finally, after weeks and weeks of waiting, our books would turn up.

And in the meantime the kids whose parents had money would open up their glossy new books and start to write, while we made do with what bits and pieces of paper we could find.

Mum had an old dog eared exercise book at home, it had been Eddie's when he was at school, so every morning she'd pull out a couple of pages and hand them to us.

'There's no point making a meal of it,' she'd say. 'You'll have to use this.'

Then, if the teacher had had trouble swallowing her eggs and bacon that morning, there would be the usual inquisition.

'Janet and Daphne Feron, why haven't you got your books yet?'

We'd have to stand up to answer.

'We're sorry, Miss Soandso, we're still waiting for our books to *come through the school.*'

Then when they did come through there always seemed to be one book or other missing. We'd leaf quickly through the pile, checking that everything was there. And it never was. So Mum would have to write another note and the whole business would have to start all over again.

Mum was quite good at writing notes. We found that out because school was so horrible we started to pretend we was sick. We'd tell Mum we had things wrong with us, things it was hard for her to check up on. Like earache. And if Mum did get taken in, or if it was one of the rare times we really was sick, she'd write a letter for us to take next day to the teacher. It was always the same letter, she wrote it year in year out. It went like this:

'Please excuse Janet Feron from being absent from school.

And oblige,

M. Feron.'

That was *the* letter. And it was always written on a little scrap of paper, never a whole sheet, just a corner torn off the old dog eared exercise book.

But me and Fag soon discovered that staying at home wasn't any better than going to school, cause Mum made us work.

'Lie in bed and the poison goes to yer head,' she'd say. 'Git up and about and you'll be right in no time.'

This wasn't the cure she prescribed for her own 'bad leg' of course, but Mum knew better than we did that rules was made to be broken.

So between school and home it was a case of frying pan and fire and me and Fag didn't see how we was ever going to escape back to just being kids again.

The Historian

There was no hope, according to Feron wisdom. If you hoped for anything you were kidding yourself; there wasn't any hope. You were doomed to be whatever the impersonal, eternal forces of the universe said you should be.

The universe, of course, was Christchurch.

Feron wisdom was the exact opposite of what businessmen and lawyers and landowners said in the newspapers. According to them this was the land of opportunity, the land of hope and freedom. You only had to look at Parliament, where Labour had just got hold of the Treasury benches. Or the chambers of commerce, where people like Sir Bert Pelf who'd started off life with the obligatory sixpence in their back pocket were now puffing cigars and telling everybody all about it. Or 'the comfortable cottages and bungalows' of South Christchurch where 'even working people now enjoy wages and conditions that would have astonished their parents or grandparents'.

You only had to look at the department stores and office blocks in the city, where workers 'no longer had any cause for complaint regarding the lighting, ventilation, and general comfort and convenience' of facilities. Even a Fendalton matron happening to do a pee in the staff toilets of Hallensteins or Calder Mackays or the DIC would feel at home when she found herself enthroned on a rimu seat over a flushing porcelain bowl between polychrome vitreous tiles. The bad old days had gone, workers now were 'looked after with a solicitude that was very rare indeed in the old days'. In the 'modern factories' of Christchurch the matron from Fendalton, if she peeked around the shop floor door, would see a place as clean and smart and attractive as her own kitchen, where of a morning she'd find cook busy amidst winking steel and copper. 'The day of the gloomy, poky factory has definitely passed,' the City Council observed, 'and now the workers carry out their tasks under improved conditions that add greatly to their general efficiency. Nowadays no industrial building is erected without the most careful attention being paid to the health and comfort of the working men and women to be employed within it.'

Businessmen and lawyers and the rest of them had been saying that sort of thing to people like the Ferons for generations. But it was water off a duck's back to the Ferons, they never swallowed a bar of it.

'Things will get better one day,' Margaret Feron would say, 'and pigs will fly.'

But things were different for Ginnie and Fag. They were born in the Jazz Age, the Age of Electricity, the Age of Progress. Things were changing.

Newspapers and magazines riffling their way into the Feron kitchen fell open on promises of love, money, happiness. Cinemas, enclosing Ferons in plaster and chrome, flickered dreamlike images of optimism before their eyes. Schoolteachers chanted the slogans of education. Clergymen crooned about salvation. Department stores dazzled them with shimmering plate glass, armies of slender young papier-mâché ladies drooping under voile, georgette, crêpe de Chine . . .

So Ginnie and Fag came to the knowledge that things had changed for working people; things weren't as bad as they used to be.

Cars, for example.

'Motoring is no longer the luxury of the rich,' one newspaper declared the day Ginnie and Fag were born, 'but within the reach of every industrious citizen.' Working people could save up their wages and buy themselves flivvers or baby Austins or natty little Prefects and tool about the town. There were more cars in Christchurch in proportion to population than in any other city in the world, 'with the single exception of the city of Detroit'.

And electricity. Things had really changed with electricity. Grandmother in the old days had 'puddled out in the rain to cut wood for a smoky stove and took a whole day to do the washing', the Municipal Electricity Department told the Ferons in one of its publicity brochures. But now housewives in the city got 'perfect cooking heat in a moment, on a range of cleanliness undreamt of in those far off days'. And they heated their homes with electric radiators, they swept their floors with 'electric sweepers', they found that with the help of their wonderful new electric washing machine 'modern washing hardly requires the wetting of the hands'.

Well it was true that the Ferons didn't have a car, and it was true that in Braddon Street and Kent Street none of their neighbours did either.

And it was also true that they didn't have a vacuum cleaner or an electric stove or an electric washing machine or an electric radiator, and although the Municipal Electricity Department and General Motors and the Zealandia Gramophone Manufacturing Company were telling them every day about 'Modernity Cleanliness Progress', if any of them had had the time to look at the statistics they would have found that when Ginnie and Fag were born fewer than three out of ten people in the whole of the City Beautiful had access to electricity.

But of course most working people didn't have time to look at the statistics and anyway they knew that a few years ago nobody had owned cars or vacuum cleaners or gramophones or washing machines, so it was obvious there was progress, wasn't it? And that meant it was just a matter of time before some of the progress reached the Ferons.

And it already had. After all, there were electric lights in Kent Street.

And although the lights were the only thing in Kent Street that were electric, and although the Feron women like most working women everywhere in South Christchurch continued like their grandmothers to scald their hands to a corned beef red as they boiled up their washing in the copper out the back, and burned the skin off their knuckles with lye soap as they scrubbed dirt off the linoleum in the front, and singed the tips of their fingers as they poked sticks into the cooking range in the kitchen, Ginnie and Fag knew that things were *getting better all the time*, that 'the City Beautiful at this moment, although already offering its fortunate citizenry the most advanced and most abundant goods our wonderful era can offer, is but a foretaste of the future of affluence, freedom, and opportunity that awaits us all'.

Fag

What happened was we got on a treadmill of dreams, Ginnie and I. We got talked into hoping for things, and talked into thinking we'd be happy if we got them. And of course we weren't going to get them, most of them didn't even exist, they weren't even there to be got.

School started it. Because although it was horrible and we hated it, and though we were so unhappy at school that we counted ourselves lucky when we were just sort of quietly bored, just stupefied, school made us want to 'do well'. Part of the problem was we turned out to be quite clever, Ginnie and I, so because of that, and because we were scared of the teachers, we ended up being very sort of diligent and sedulous. We learnt quickly how to do what they wanted us to do, make neat rows of numbers and words on paper and say the right things about the words and numbers at the right time. So we not only ended up wanting to 'do well', we actually *did* well, as far as they were concerned.

As far as we were concerned too. We started to get tickets on ourselves.

Once school had given us literacy it started to open up other things, it started giving us access to the whole world of words. And that was really something. That really excited us, especially me. Because before starting school when we'd looked at books and magazines and newspapers we'd thought they looked very interesting but also very esoteric, very remote. When you can't read, language on a page just seems like an endless stream of letters, but once you've been taught to look at it the 'right' way and you start to see that it can be made to form pools or lagoons of meaning, well it's dazzling.

All of a sudden we were yanking newspapers out from under the cushion of the yellow chair and reading.

The headlines, the words inside the cartoon balloons, the movie and love magazines scattered with cigarette ash on our big sisters' beds, the big fat words of the advertising posters from one end of Colombo Street to the other — Self Help Stores, YOU PICK UP THE GOODS WE PICK UP THE BILL, Come in Now and BUY BUY BUY — all these words became a bewildering promise of vicarious sensation.

Shops were wonderful places. Ginnie and I would drift down Colombo Street gazing into the windows, reading the slogans, dreaming of a universe of rayon stockings and steel cash registers.

Even more wonderful were the movie magazines. Movies, the flicks we called them, we'd been brought up on them. From the time we were five years old we'd been watching Ruby or Hock or Sadie hand threepences to the glamorous goddesses who sold tickets in little glass booths outside the Metro, the Majestic, the Mayfair, and the Plaza. And then inside, in chairs of plush or leatherette, we'd gaze up at the thousand loops of satin or taffeta and the footlights would play all their colours — azure, crimson, sea green, gold. By the time we turned seven our entire conception of beauty amounted to the interior decoration of cinemas and the faces of the 'stars' projected onto the screen. Jean Harlow and Carole Lombard, Greta Garbo and Marlene Dietrich, they were our vision of womanhood. They were a sort of mirror we looked into and dreamt that one day, perhaps, we might see ourselves.

Then, once we found we could read the movie magazines as well as sit in the movie theatres, the impressions became almost overwhelming.

Lives of the Stars, Hollywood Gossip, Stellar Nights, we leafed through their crackling, importunate pages, gazing and gasping and going bananas.

In our bedroom at Kent Street the big girls had already started to turn the walls into a montage of Hollywood faces and now Ginnie and I attacked *Lives of the Stars, Hollywood Gossip, Stellar Nights* with scissors, hacking out photographs of our heroines and pasting them all around us, so as we woke up in the morning or went to bed at night the teeth of a thousand smiles flashed down on us.

'What I like best are *suave* women,' I said to Ginnie one day.

We were sitting on the floor busy with the scissors.

'Suave women who don't change out of their dressing gowns till it's time for them to put on their diamonds for dinner.'

Dressing gowns were a particular obsession. Dressing gowns meant luxury, leisure. The idea that we might one day actually be able to wear a dressing gown of our own seemed too fantastic to think about for more than one — or at the most two — delicious moments, but we could always try pretending. So we'd creep into our brothers' room and pull an old coat or two off a nail on the wall. Then we'd borrow a tube of lipstick from the paraphernalia of beauty Ruby and Sadie littered all over the window ledge in our room. We'd slip down to the bottom of the back yard and search about in the weeds till we found some dock. Then we'd roll dock leaves and newspapers into cigarettes, we'd slash lipstick across our mouths and we'd slip into our brothers' old coats, and all of a sudden we became Harlow or Lombard or Garbo and the back yard became a poolside terrace on a hillside in Beverly Hills or Cashmere. And Ginnie and I, hunching our shoulders and pouting, would slink about as we thought suave women did.

Love magazines too. We became feverish about love magazines.

Right from our earliest childhood there were always stories about beautiful princesses, peasant girls, orphans. They were always miserable and poor and unloved, and of course our hearts bled for them because — well, they were us. Then the handsome prince . . . And then, well it was only a matter of time, there would be distractions and complications but in the end the prince would kiss her, and up onto the white horse she'd go, and away they'd gallop up and over the hill.

And Ginnie and I would let our jaws drop and our eyes glaze over.

Goose maidens, yes that was us, Sleeping Beauties, yes that was us too, but most of all we were Cinderellas, poor, sad, sweet Cinderellas, bullied and beaten by cruel unnatural relatives, thrust amidst ashes and slop buckets (didn't we have to clean slop buckets?).

'Cinderella, though fair, was poor and unhappy.'

'Ginnie and Fag, though fair, were poor and unhappy.'

Then as we grew older and our big sisters got older still, the contours of the heroines in the stories started to change. The goose maidens and princesses grew bosoms and false eyelashes, they shaved their legs with safety razors and slid them into 'art' silk stockings, they carried powder compacts, and turned up in the pages of *Living Love, Young Romance, Miracles and Oracles,* which were magazines our sisters would buy for a few pennies at news stands and dairies outside the factory when at the end of a working day they stepped onto the pavement and checked to see if they had change for the tram.

Miracles and oracles. A literature of dreamland.

And the dreams came true.

Love, love which conquers all, love which takes goose maidens and factory girls and school kids and Cinderellas and carries them off to . . .

Happiness, of course. Marriage and that.

But if the destination was a bit shadowy it was clear enough that love was how you got there. The journey would be long but the traveller, once she'd finally arrived, could sort of slump into the arms of the prince and slide, drift, slip into bliss. First the unhappiness and the waiting. Then the love and the happiness.

Well, waiting was something Ginnie and I were good at, waiting was something that was second nature.

'Just wait till I git my hands on youse two,' Mum had shouted at us a hundred times or more.

'Just wait your patience,' she'd said a hundred times more.

So we knew about waiting, Ginnie and I. And in the meantime, waiting, we read. And dreamed.

'Wasting yer time with trashy romances,' she said. 'If you think words will pay the rent you've got another think coming.'

'Aw, Mum,' we'd say.

'Only words worth reading are printed on a one quid note,' said Mum.

Fag

Religion started to fit into the picture too, now that we knew how to read. Religion, it turned out, could offer promises and visions of its own.

Mum had always sneered, of course, she'd never in her life been known to kneel to 'that god they're always yabbering on about'. The idea of 'christening' us kids had never occurred to her, and when the time came to celebrate what the parsons in their fancier flights called the birth of 'the Lamb of God', we identified it with the piece of roasted grey flesh which, soused in mint sauce, steamed in the middle of the kitchen table. And when Mum, having made the supreme effort to scrape together a few stray sixpences and present us not only with the roast lamb but also dates, oranges, and even, if the boat was in, a toy, she'd say,

'And you needn't think it was anything to do with any Father Christmas. It was Mother Feron. Now git out from under me feet.'

But when we found ourselves trapped in the airless classrooms at Sydenham School we discovered that not everybody agreed with the Feron line on religion. In fact although state primary schools were supposed to be secular, the teaching staff at Sydenham were all very pious, all very keen on the thing they called 'God', and they took advantage of their authority in the classroom to do a bit of illegal proselytising. So there were sonorous mooings about 'little baby Jesus' and chirpy chantings of 'Jesus loves the little children'. And once a week a parson with scurfy shoulders would talk to us in a strange filleted accent, which we guessed was the way people talked in Fendalton. He'd lisp stories about the Christ child, and camels through the eyes of needles and so on, and hand out what he called:

'Christian literature'.

On hearing the word 'literature', Ginnie and I were on the alert. Now that we could read, we were eager to read everything.

Mind you, the little limp books the parson passed round the room didn't seem up to the standards of *Miracles and Oracles* at first. The pictures of Christ sort of simpering under long blond waves of what looked like peroxided hair seemed familiar — they reminded us of Harlow and Lombard and Garbo and Dietrich — but after opening the covers and dipping into the text we nearly gave up on religion for good.

'Not one of us, yea verily, not even the artless child who seems all innocence as she bends her dimpled knees before the altar of the holy mysteries, not even this small mote in the miracle of creation, shall be saved unless it be by FAITH. For what is faith? Why, faith is unto us as breezes and the sunshine are unto the bird, it is . . .'

But there were juicy bits too if you looked for them, and we did. Like it turned out there was this Mary Magdalene, who was a flapper. We could just imagine what Mum would have said to Mary Magdalene.

'Yer a lazy tart, you just want to git into yer room and git some warpaint on yer face and git into town.'

Then we discovered Christ.

'Imagine, if you can, the sensations of our Saviour as the blade pierced his side, adding new sufferings to the already overwhelming delirium of pain in which he hung, white, naked, crucified and alone on the bare rough boards of the cross, impaled on the cruel nails for our sins, *for your sins*, child, that you might be saved. Christ the Saviour, Christ Jesus the Redeemer, suffering indescribable agonies of pain and, yes, fear, the red blood of his wounds coursing down the white skin of his body, that you might be saved . . .'

Ginnie and I were riveted by this. It was really quite something to discover that this hero, this actual god, had let himself be nailed on a cross to save Ginnie and I.

'Thank you, Jesus,' we said in our private little sessions of worship, reading the religious 'literature' in the back yard and smoking dock leaf cigarettes.

'Thank you for saving us.'

It added new dimensions to the movies and the love magazines and the plate glass windows of the department stores. In the past we'd often pretended that our father was 'away to do work on the Peninsula' or 'up north for a while', or even that Eddie was our father. But now we actually had a god for our father, and his name was 'God the Father'. This was an unexpected bonus because though God the Father seemed a rather distant and high handed sort of individual, still, fathers were like that, kids were always turning up at school with cuts and bruises and saying:

'Me old man did it.'

It turned out that there was also a 'Mother Mary', though we weren't too keen on her. We were inclined to think that one mother was enough.

But it was clear that we were related to a sort of heavenly royal family. There was Mary our 'Mother', who we thought of as a sort of queen, a sort of misty, nodding replica of Queen Mary. And there was God the Father, who we imagined as a bit like King George and bit like old Moneygall of Simeon Street. And that was exciting, it gave us a sort of aristocratic genealogy. It seemed to support our idea of ourselves as princesses, Snow Whites, Rapunzels trapped in towers of corrugated iron.

'Rapunzel, Rapunzel, let down your hair.'

More interesting still was the idea of being 'saved'.

Sin was a stumbling block. We weren't too sure what sin was actually supposed to be. But being saved was something we did go for in a big way, it fitted in just right with all the fairy stories and the movies and the love magazines. They disagreed with one another on points of detail, it was true, but they all made it clear that the thing that did the trick, the thing that took Cinderella or the sinner or the princess from poverty, sadness, loneliness, unhappiness to bliss was love. 'God is love,' the little religious pamphlets told us. 'Only true love can bring true happiness,' sighed the heroines of the silver screen.

So we felt we'd made a great discovery, Ginnie and I, and by the time we were eight years old we knew that it was only a matter of waiting, that in time we'd be saved by Jesus or Clark Gable, who would lift us up in their strong capable arms and search our eyes with their penetrating yet gentle gaze, and would whisper:

'I love you Janet and Daphne. Come with me and be happy.'

Owen Marshall

A Day With Yesterman

Chatterton woke to the birds. The absence of pain may have been the reason. He moved his legs, sucked in his stomach, but nothing caught; just the squeak of the plastic sheet beneath the cotton one. Chatterton was accustomed to the need to occupy himself much of the night; to sidle and belay from ledge to ledge of darkness, but not all that often did he hear the birds begin. He marvelled at the intensity — a sweet hubbub as a base, and superimposed the longer, individual exclamations of thrush or blackbird. He had the pleasing thought that the birds gathered at his house to inaugurate a special day. Chatterton folded the sheet under his chin, so that the blanket no longer tickled, and he made himself a little wider and longer to pop a few joints and check that he was in good shape.

A mild suffusion of light from behind the curtains strengthened as Chatterton sang 'Danny Boy' and 'The White Cliffs of Dover'. He stopped with a feeling something of value was slipping away, and then it came to him, a recollection of the night's dream in which he had made love to an ample woman beneath an elm tree in Hagley Park. It was to some degree an explanation of his mood. Chatterton was sensible enough to enjoy authentic emotion however it reached the mind. Before the experience quite faded he closed his eyes to breathe again the fragrance of the elm and observe a wisp of auburn hair quiver with the pulse of her neck. He lay listening to his birds as morning came. How young at last I feel, he assured himself.

By the time Chatterton was in the kitchen, he could get by with natural light. He poached himself an egg without boiling off the white, and he watched his yellow feet like flounders on the floor. He would never recognise his feet in a crowd, for they were just any old, yellow feet. Truck rigs passed with a roar on the nearby motorway as they tried to get a clear start to the day. Chatterton rubbed his knee to loosen the joint. The skin seemed to have no attachment to the bones, and slid all ways. Only the young body savours its union.

As the birds wound down, Chatterton finished his third cup of tea, and went back to his bedroom to choose his clothes. 'I'll make a bargain with you.' He addressed a small, familiar god. 'Best clothes for best day.' The trousers were a quality check, but big at his waist and so the band tucked somewhat under his belt. A grey jacket, with a chrome zip, that his daughter had given him for Christmas. Tropic Sands aftershave, which the label exhorted Chatterton to splash on liberally, but which he did not. 'Chatterton,' said Chatterton to his own reflection, 'you are an old dog.' He looked at all the bottles on his drawers, and decided to take no medication at all. Before he left the house Chatterton buffed the toes of his shoes with the socks he was putting out to wash. He should have known better, for the bending sent him dizzy, and he over-balanced and fell on to the smooth lino by the bench. He had a laugh at himself, and felt the cool lino on his cheek as he lay and waited for his head to clear. In the corner was a false cut in the lino: Chatterton could remember clearly the wet day seventeen years before when he had laid the lino and made just that false cut. How difficult it is to fault life's continuity. The rain had caught the window at an angle, and drained like rubber tree striations across its surface.

As Chatterton walked to Associated Motors he calculated a route which would keep him on the sunny side of the streets, and he watched other people on their way to work, disappointed that he couldn't recognise them as friends. He nodded and smiled nevertheless.

Chatterton helped part-time with the accounts at Associated Motors; so very part-time over the last months that Susan was surprised to see him. 'And you're looking so smart today,' she said. Chatterton knew he was. He began to use the computer to calculate GST payments. Chatterton enjoyed the computer, and was impatient with people who claimed they couldn't adapt to them.

'Life is adaptation,' he said.

'Right, Mr Chatterton.'

'How I could run when I was young.'

'Could you?' said Susan.

'I was a small-town champion,' said Chatterton, 'and could have been a large-town one with training.' He was wistful rather than proud.

'I like netball,' said Susan.

'Ah, your knees are wonderfully smooth,' said Chatterton: his fingers nimble on the keys.

The Sales Manager broke up their flirtation. 'How are you feeling?' he asked.

'I am in complete remission today,' said Chatterton. 'I can sense my prime again. I'm growing young again very rapidly.' The Sales Manager laughed, for he thought Chatterton intended a joke.

'How about taking a Cressida down to Dunedin then for me. It's needed there today,' he asked Chatterton.

The mechanics watched in envy as Chatterton took a set of provisional plates and two of his own cassettes. They hoped for such perks themselves. 'Hey, Chatters, you lucky old bastard,' and Chatterton winked and executed a no-fuss manoeuvre before them in the yard.

'I thought the old bastard was dying or something.'

'Dying to get away in that car, all right.'

In fifth gear the Cressida was only loping on the Canterbury Plains. Chatterton fed in his Delius cassette and the quiet interior was sprung with sound. Chatterton wondered why he dreamed so often in old age of hang-gliding. Something he'd never done, yet increasingly his night views were from above, the cold air whistling in a rigging he didn't understand. Progress was relentless, and from landscape and people half-recognised he was borne away. He supposed it might be a side effect of the medication. When he was younger he would have tackled hang-gliding. He had been an athlete hadn't he, and a soldier?

At Karitane Chatterton turned off to take the old road. He could avoid the increasing traffic. He liked that swamp flat: rushes, brown and yellow mosses, mallards, and pukekos with their bookish, striding way. Later there was a stranded man — enquiring face and car bonnet raised. Chatterton stopped, and the man came with grateful haste to meet him. His name was Norman Caan. He began to thank Chatterton, who smiled, but was distracted by the peace as he stood there — the quiet road, the crimped blue light over the sea, the headland beyond with an apron of gorse on the steeper ground. The wind from the sea was wine, and it scented the beachside grass and bore spaciousness inland.

'I do appreciate you stopping. I've got something of a problem as you see, and I've a city appointment at one.' Caan was close to Chatterton; his voice a trifle plaintive. He put out his hand and Chatterton shook it.

'Sorry,' said Chatterton, 'but what a day it is. Isn't it? How things continue to fit newly together, year after year.'

'I suppose it is.' Caan looked at the sky, blown almost clear, and the hills and the inlet and the horizon seaward, as though he had just entered a large building and had its architecture commended to him. The coast curved, and a far cutting bore a drape of pink ice-plant, and the sun shone back from it as if from glass.

As they examined the engine of Caan's Volvo, Chatterton noticed a balding spot at Caan's crown, as if a tidy bird had been scratching a nest there. Chatterton passed a hand over his own stiff, grey hair. A dunny brush he'd heard it called. He had to admit Caan's clothes better than his own however; an integration of style and texture which Chatterton could recognise, yet not explain.

'There's nothing we can do,' said Chatterton. 'Lock up and come with me. We can have someone out in no time.' But back at his own car, instead of getting inside, Chatterton was drawn to the bank again. 'Will you look at that though,' he said. 'No pain there at all. Will you look at the ripples on the bars as the tide comes in, and the bubbles over the crab holes in the mud.' The single cloud against powder blue made a cameo brooch of the sky; birch leaves tossed as a mane on the back of a macrocarpa hedge. 'You don't mind just for a moment?' asked Chatterton. 'It's just such a day.'

'No, no,' said Caan.

'It's just such a day,' said Chatterton. Caan had no option, but his face had initially a shrug of the shoulders expression as he watched Chatterton move to the edge of the bank above the coast. He was only a few feet above the sea, yet Chatterton sucked several breaths as a diver would on a high cliff. 'I shall become part of it. I see it all as if I'm twenty,' he said.

Despite concern for his situation, Caan was affected by Chatterton's wonder, and something more — something naive in his cheerful age and the trousers belted too large, and his hair bristling. 'It is rather splendid,' said Caan; diffident in praise of his own country.

'You know,' said Chatterton, 'today I keep thinking of when I was young.'

Somewhere between Lake Grasmere and Seddon the black AJS left the road at speed and took an angle into grass standing high as a field of wheat. There was no way of stopping quickly. The bike's metal scything through. He heard only one sound, that of the rushing grass, and he was aware in the clarity of fear how bright the sun shone on that roadside grass like wheat. Yet there was nothing hidden; no snare, no ditch, and fear gave place to exultation as the grass slowed him and he KNEW that nothing there had harm in it: an instant almost too brief to allow him the dangerous conviction that he couldn't die. The black, heavy AJS off the road; the hissing, even fluster of the wheat-grass in the vivid sun. All in a few seconds, he supposed. All happening in a few seconds and in heightened perception. And the bike had stopped and he found himself quite alone in that landscape, stalled high from the road with grass packed around him, the cicadas coming back to chorus, and fine pollens settling on the black tank of the AJS.

'Like riding through a wheat field,' said Chatterton.

'Sorry?'

'I was thinking back,' said Chatterton. 'Other days.'

As they passed over the hills into the city, Chatterton and Caan, together completely by chance they would suppose, talked freely. Chatterton found it easier to be honest as he grew older, and the knowledge that relationships had no necessary continuation ceased to disconcert him. Besides, Caan was prepared to listen as well as talk. Chatterton liked a positive listener; he could be one himself. They covered the decline of state medicine, the loss of flavour in Bluff oysters, the self-serving of the political powerful, and the suicide of Tony Hancock. There is a good deal of satisfaction to be had from free-ranging criticism. 'But then I'm a deal older than you,' said Chatterton.

'Not so much surely; I'm retired.'

'There are two possibilities as you get old,' said Chatterton. 'You become archaic, or you leave the world behind in your progress. Either way increasing isolation is the result.'

'Well, isolated numerically perhaps.'

'And in confidence. It's hard to be confident and old. The opposite of what most people expect I suppose.'

'But you are,' said Caan.

'An act of faith. Besides, superstition and disease have me now, so I indulge myself. There's days sometimes that favour you, you know.'

'Propitious,' said Caan.

'Pardon.'

'Propitious.'

'Yes,' said Chatterton. 'That's it.'

'Anyway today you're welcome to travel back with me, and have lunch with me too. I'm allowed a guest at the Rotary Lunch I'm addressing. I'll have my car delivered, and afterwards we'll pick up my sister who's coming back with me to recuperate for a while.' Caan was pleased to be able to establish the immediate future, and to provide for Chatterton's repayment within it.

The President of Rotary was a splendid host, just one size larger and more glossy than his fellows as befitted his office. 'So much of what service groups do now is taken for granted,' he said. 'Assistance is an expectation now; almost a right.' Chatterton noticed the barman's black reefer jacket, and it produced before Chatterton his grandmother's sewing basket. The fine wicker-work and the embroidered top — black, black, with a country spire perpetually slate blue. The colours were ribbed, and the tranquillity of even execution rather than the subject had made an ache which allowed of no expression. So he had built childlike barricades of pins around the black field's spire in attempts at the protection which his memory was later able to assume.

'We get told who we should be supporting, and how much,' said the President. 'We get told we're not doing enough rather than thanked. Not coughing up sufficiently.' Chatterton enjoyed a free whisky, and watched the last members picking up their badges. The President led the way into the dining room, and they took their places before three slices of ham on each plate. Chatterton rather enjoyed the Rotarian mood; an aura of confidence and good intent that arises from reasonable success in the world and a wisely unexamined life. Chatterton looked with favour on his ham, and waited for the vegetables. Caan talked to the President.

'I ran my own business for twenty-seven years, then it grew too complex and I sold out. That's one of the things I want to mention in my address: the need to understand there's a point at which a business becomes too much for the managerial skills of its founder alone. A lot of concerns go wrong at that stage.'

Chatterton admired the Rotarians across from him, particularly an assured man in his thirties, eating carefully and smiling carefully as he listened to his neighbour. A man well carapaced in a three-piece suit, and trusting the ground beneath his feet. Chatterton wondered if he himself at any age had looked that way; and knew the answer. The man had a sheen almost; the beauty of a live lobster, an exoskeleton creature, any vulnerability safe within. He was all jointed precision of appearance. Chatterton caught his eye.

'Good on you,' said Chatterton, and they lifted their forks in mutual salutation.

'Few business men can make the transition from personal to corporate management,' said Caan. 'And why should it be expected, or easy.' Caan stopped, and looked first at the President and then at Chatterton as if some explanation was expected from them. His face was pale, and he swallowed several times. 'I feel rotten,' he said. 'I think I might be sick.' His head gave a shiver, and he sighed as if lonely.

'Perhaps the cold meat,' said the President. Caan and he left the table and went through the conversations to find a place for Caan to lie down. Caan walked as if he were carrying a tray of marbles and the loss of any of them would be his death.

Chatterton was offered more vegetables, and accepted all but the peas. Sprouts he had, and potato balls and corn heaped like nuggets of gold. And no pain was swallowed with them; no pain whatsoever. The President returned alone. 'He's lying down,' he said. 'He says he feels a little better.' The President looked searchingly at Chatterton. Chatterton lacked an executive mien, and there was grey hair tufted in his ears. He alone in the dining room had a jacket with a zip. There was a sense of ease though, and good-will and self-will. The President was not a fool. 'Caan suggested you might speak instead,' he said. Chatterton was happy to be of service; he liked to talk to people. And he had his best trousers on, even if they were gathered at the waist somewhat. He had visions to draw upon, his life among them.

When the President's routine business was over and the Serjeant-at-Arms had imposed fines with sufficient humorous innuendo, Chatterton was introduced as a colleague of Norman Caan. As he waited to speak, as the polite applause eddied about the tables, Chatterton was reminded of his last Battalion reunion, and by another step of recollection Birdy Fowler, who died of heatstroke before they came out of the desert. Chatterton hadn't been invited to speak at the reunion, and he thought there was a need for Birdy's name to be heard again. So Chatterton began his talk with several of the stories Birdy used to tell when drinking: the Rotarians laughed at the ribaldry of natural man, and Chatterton laughed in tribute to a friend. Then Chatterton talked about his illness; the prostate and spleen which had been taken, the disaffection of other organs; about how to make it through the nights, the spiritual and practical ingenuities by which it's possible to inch closer to the day. About his wife who had been very beautiful when she was young and he was a coarse, stupid boy. About his dream of steam trains ascending steep tracks through the bush, so that the engine fumed and panted, the white steam like egret's feathers flared against the leaves, wild cattle crashed away, and deep, faded varnish of the inner woodwork still showed a living grain.

The green, sashed curtains quivered at the windows of the hotel. The long tables of Rotary luncheon had flower vases, and pollen beneath some of them was spread like pepper on the white cloth. A waitress with her hair up in gel was at the kitchen swing doors, ready to clear away. She picked her lip, and wondered if she would be through by four. We make the mistake of assuming that our present experience is the world's. The tussock would be blowing on all the crests of Dansey's Pass, glue sniffers sitting with statues of the city fathers, a fine rain flaking on to the pungas of the Ureweras, a sheer excalibur of sunlight from the high window of a panel shop in Papanui transfixing young Marty working there.

The Rotarians were normally uncomfortable with personal revelations, which could easily obscure sound business practices, but as Chatterton was unknown to them they felt none of the embarrassment that acquaintanceship would have brought. They were quite struck by his eccentricity, his passion, and the evident movement of the bones in his thin cheeks as he talked. Chatterton had an innocent pride as he left with the President to find Caan. He was resting on an alcove chair in the foyer. His coat and tie were off, and his head relaxed backwards. 'I think I'm all right now,' he said.

'Well, Mr Chatterton was a considerable success,' said the President.

'That's the second time he's saved the day,' said Caan.

'I just sang for my supper,' said Chatterton. The President's laugh was high-pitched; almost a giggle, and odd from such an imposing man.

Caan's car was delivered as he and Chatterton sat peacefully in the foyer. Caan washed his face with cold water, and then decided that he was recovered. 'You'll understand that Joan's had a hard time of it,' he said when he returned. 'She left her husband to make a mid-life career for herself in physiotherapy and then found she had cancer. The treatment's knocked her pretty badly.' Chatterton knew the treatment, but he didn't think about it as they drove to the nursing home. Instead he enjoyed the dappled shadows on the road through the green belt, the shimmer caused by the breeze on the tops of trees, and imagined himself joining in with the afternoon joggers — putting his weight well forward on the slope and judging a pace to keep both legs and lungs comfortable. The bellows of the chest in full use; cooling tree air on the damp singlet; hair heavy with sweat patting on the back of his head as he ran.

On the front lawn of the nursing home a badminton court had been marked out. Young people played vigorously there, their bare feet silent on the grass, their voices loud and sudden. Joan was waiting in the lounge with her two cases beside her. 'She'll need a good deal of rest of course, but we're all optimistic,' Caan said as he and Chatterton walked past the lawn. Chatterton watched a brown girl leap forever so that her arms and breast were outlined against the sea. He wondered why God still chose to punish old men. As Caan came closer to the lounge he smiled and raised his hand, but his sister was behind the glass, and nothing could be said. She wore a light dress of floral pattern that would be considered cheerful perhaps — when purchased for someone else. She wore lipstick but her eyebrows were very pale, and to hide her baldness she was topped with a tam-o-shanter, green and red. She had the eyes of the travellers of illness.

'I'm sorry we're a bit late,' said Caan. 'It's been an odd sort of day.' As he told her of it, and Chatterton's part as an explanation of his presence, Joan and Chatterton regarded one another. When Caan finished, Chatterton touched the woollen cap in a friendly way.

'I had a hat, but not as colourful as yours,' he said. He took one of her cases, Caan the other, and they waited at the door while Joan farewelled a nurse. 'Chemotherapy as well as the ray can be pretty much a sapping combination,' said Chatterton when she was back. 'Is you hair all out?'

'All out,' she said.

'So was mine,' said Chatterton, 'but it grows in again. Mine grew back very wiry.'

'Very wiry,' said Joan. Well, frankness could work both ways.

'And you get a good deal of strength back.' To demonstrate, Chatterton stopped by the car and threw the case up, and caught it again in both arms. 'See,' he said eagerly.

'You get used to him,' said Caan.

'Are you so very different?' she asked Chatterton.

'I'm in search of natural man now,' he said.

'Too late, too old,' she said, but Chatterton threw up the case again and capered with it. The badminton players cheered; a nurse stood watching from the office and telling others over her shoulder what was happening.

Caan asked Chatterton to drive. After his illness at lunch Caan wanted a restful trip. Chatterton was obliging once more. As he drove he calculated aloud the unexpected profit he was making on the day — the price of the bus fare to Christchurch, and of a midday meal. Enough for a week's groceries, or for semi-gloss to paint his small porch. 'Do you enjoy painting?' he asked Joan. The triviality of it stimulated Joan; she was tired of weighing up life and death. She began to talk of the renovations she had done years before on her house at Port Chalmers. Although her voice was well back in her throat, and somewhat husky, it increased in tempo and her tam-o-shanter nodded green and red. 'Oh, no, no,' interrupted Chatterton decidedly. 'You should always strip back before repapering for a first rate job.'

'It's not always needed.'

'Shoddy, shoddy,' cried Chatterton.

'What would a man know about making a home,' said Joan. 'What does a man remember.'

Chatterton was in the presence of things which gave an answer. The water in the pink heart of flax, and a monkey puzzle tree to hold up the sky. Sheep coughing out the night, and in a winter drizzle the horses smoking in the dray. His mother standing at the laundry, pushing back her hair with her wrist, smiling at him, and the smell of hot woollens and yellow soap again. Old coats without shoulders on nails there like dried fish, and gulls following his father's plough.

At Timaru they had cream freezes, and turned off from the main road at the Showground Hill to rest and eat. Chatterton leant his arms on the top wire of the fence, and watched the downs and the mountains beyond. He led a game to distinguish as many shades of green as possible. 'Nine different colours. To stand and see nine different colours of green,' said Joan. 'All growing from the same soil; all compatible and with the promise of some use or crop.'

When he looked south, Chatterton sensed a change in the weather, and he told the others to expect a southerly. A fisherman gets to read the elements of his locality. Chatterton encouraged Joan to talk as they went on north. He refused to be deferential just because of her trial. 'You have to be careful illness doesn't make you selfish, you know,' he said. 'And you could do a lot more with your appearance — a young woman like you.' He could say such things because of his own illness, his lack of malice, but mostly because of a special innocence which arises from experience and is the mark of rare and successful old age.

'I was never at all religious before,' said Joan. 'Now I'm an atheist by faith rather than logic. And I've got tired of most of my friends: they almost bored me to death when they came. What you expect rarely happens. You, Norman, you're one of the worst.'

'But I'm a brother. All brothers are boring. They lack sufficient biological variation to be otherwise.'

Eventually release was almost overpowering for Joan. 'It's stuffy,' she said. 'I feel dizzy.'

'It's the closeness before the change,' said Caan, 'and you're not used to travelling yet.' Joan took off her woollen hat, and leant back on the seat. Her naked, bird's head had a little downy hair, and the skull plates joined in apparently clumsy workmanship.

'The treatment can have a long term effect on your food preferences,' said Chatterton. 'Peas and beans for instance. I can't eat them at all now; the smell disgusts me, while fruit is a positive craving. Nectarines and satsumas: ah, there now.'

The southerly came through late in the afternoon, catching them before Ashburton. The churned cloud, wind that flogged the trees and bore a scattered rain too pressed to set in. The temperature dropped as if a door had been opened. 'Oh, that's much better,' said Joan.

'Let's sing "Danny Boy". You know "Danny Boy"?' said Chatterton.

'Oh Danny Boy, the pipes — — —.' Three of them together. Chatterton likes to sing, although he has a poor voice. He watched the broad, shingle river bed, the islands of gorse and lupin in the scattered rain. He thought of his nineteen pound salmon near the mouth of the Waitaki; the gravel unsure beneath his waders as he turned, and the cry going up from his fellow fishermen as they gave way for him. The salmon don't feed: they strike in anger or homecoming exultation perhaps. The river aids its fish against the line, and swans form a necklace above the struggle as they pass to Lake Wainoni.

'We're all a bit high,' said Joan. 'I like the song, but we've all light voices and we need someone deeper. A bass baritone, say.' The southerly was blowing itself out, but the coolness remained. Near Dunsandel they saw a hitchhiker with a giant pack and the legs to make light of it. Chatterton pulled up ahead of him.

'Can you sing "Danny Boy"?' he asked. The hitchhiker was willing, although for a time he was embarrassed by Joan's head.

'Where do you come from?' she said.

'Dubbo, Australia.'

'We've all of us got problems,' said Caan.

There were enough voices for a barbershop quartet. 'Oh Danny Boy, the pipes — —.' The Australian sang well. He was out of the weather and travelling in the right direction. Over the sinews of his brown arms were raised a few graceful arteries, and the whites of his eyes glinted in a tanned face. 'The green, green grass of home — —' they sang as Caan conducted. Joan and the hitchhiker, who couldn't remember each other's names and would never meet again, combined their voices, and smiled at each other because of Chatterton's caterwauling.

They dropped the Australian baritone at the city overbridge. Chatterton took his pack from the boot, and Joan gave him a bag of seedless grapes she had from the nursing home. 'Goodbye Danny Boy,' she said. What could he make of them: what could they make of themselves. A hitchhiker's experience is only life accelerated. 'Oh my God,' said Joan as they went on. 'I've had my hat off all that time. What a sight.' She laughed at her own humiliation, and wiped her eyes. She put the tam-o-shanter on once more, for the formality of parting with Chatterton.

The wooden house was like the others that surrounded it; insufficiently individual it seemed to be his. Chatterton stood in the drive as Caan came round to take the driver's seat. The evening was calm, but the evidence of the southerly was there. Leaves stripped by the wind and gathered on the concrete in the lee of the house. Leaves of peach and maple. Leaves of birch with aphids still clustered on the underside. The wind's violence had in its eddy a delicacy of graduated winnowing, and the litter diminished to a whip tail of fragments which included two ladybirds, a length of tooth floss, tuft of cat fur, and ended in a line of most fragile, perfect dust.

'But we'll keep in touch,' Caan was saying. 'You cheer Joan up because you know what she's been through, and she won't have many people to visit her while she's here.'

'If you can be bothered some time,' said Joan. The sheen of her hospital skin wrinkled in a grin.

'You know, right from the start I had a feeling this was going to be a good day,' said Chatterton. 'It's a sort of Indian summer perhaps.'

'Life is sad though, isn't it?' said Joan. She looked up at him with a terrible openness.

'Oh yes, sad, but not dreary, not lacking purpose. But sad sure enough,' said Chatterton firmly. He went to the protected corner of his small garden and came back with a red rose for Joan; an old English rose, dark and red. 'Old style roses have the true scent,' he said. 'Aren't I right.' She had it to her face. 'Eh?' he said.

'Yes.'

Two white butterflies tumbled in the air above the letter box, and Chatterton smiled, not withdrawing his attention from the car as Caan backed out. 'He's a hard case that one,' said Caan. 'He gave a speech off the cuff at the Rotary meeting you know. Hardly a moment for thought.'

'He's certainly got no singing voice, but he sees through things all right.'

Chatterton waited to see them drive away; not the last minute shame-faced turning of some people's farewells, as if they feared what might be being said of them. Only his trousers suggested age; crimped at his slender waist and bagging somewhat at the seat the way trousers of old men do. When they were gone Chatterton arched back cautiously, and pressed with the flat of his hand on his stomach. He decided to stay in his garden while he felt so well. Did he tell them he was an athlete once, he wondered. Unthinkingly he kept his arched stance as he tried to remember. All the things he could do then, all the things he could feel. Chatterton could see his dark roses on the fence, and the two ladybirds upside down and closer in the whip tail dust upon the concrete.

The scent of the rose seemed to linger, maybe only in his heart, for he was no longer sure of such distinctions. What would he think of next, he wondered. He would fetch a beer and have it in his garden, because of the extra money and the friends he had made that day. As he turned to go, he had in recollection the sight of the Marlborough hills, and a hawk the colour of a moth against the sea of the sky.

Rob Jackaman

Palimpsest: I

Fly away you red-wing bird

She'll dream about you when you're gone,
She'll dream about you all her life.

> — B.E. Wheeler, 'Red-Winged Blackbird'
> [a song set in a superannuated mining
> settlement in North America].

The local stone is soft, marks easily,
and buildings turn into   palimpsests
where history aggregates and telescopes:
so on the dado of the Northern
Mrs Bateman and Mrs Hopley
oblivious of chronology
                              entwine
their names — something they surely wouldn't do
(in public) in Victorian Oamaru
surrounded by scratched love-hearts, old initials,
sexual advice.   More recent edifices
have their store of graffiti too — so that
'Bobby Sands lives' by the rail-yard wall
and the North Otago Farmers block plays host
to 'Bob Marley and the Wailers' (without
an 'h')   unlikely as that may seem.
What's written   never quite
                                        disappears
though it may
                    be absorbed or get hidden
under a newer overlay, to emerge
from memory years later as the patina
wears back in time.   So on Wansbeck corner
the New Zealand Mercantile stencil
comes through Dalgety's hoarding in a ghost
script
          smudged charcoal on pitted pages.

So too images
                    linger behind the eye —
Jenny's hair   in gold late
                              afternoon
when we walked on the breakwater and seeing
the cracks I wrote 'Stress Fractures';
                                        her hair
fresh suddenly as a wash of spring
                              air over
weathered stone;
                    boats still drifting round
in the harbour to face the tide — a trick
we all have to learn as absence
                              floods.
Reflections make runes which surface like
mysteries   then break up in shivers
of colour and sink to regroup.
                              Scribed
on a concrete pile beside the water
Anna loves . . .
                    but the name
                              covered over
by moss; a rogue marigold clings
to the scoria used as fill at Friendly Bay,
misnomer for a handkerchief of greyish
sand, seventeen concrete lamp-posts
(an eighteenth uprooted and half-submerged),

sculpture / Sutton Hoo

(palimpsest)
rock-drawings / sign

a fishing smack called 'Redwing' (no smack
in North Otago, baby) — fly away
you redwing bird; there's nothing else
                                        to do.

But the derelict and empty have
their kind of beauty too
                                — the town
full   of poems
                            printed through it.
By here I wrote 'Franklin' and on Wanbrow
with the gulls   'Crowhurst' and most
of 'Love-Rite',   the place
                                    indelibly
stamped on me, mixed with more recent
                                            scribbling —
at the end of the jetty DV loves NB
(though the final letter's   indistinct
making it mean something else), on a rotting
harbour rail   fuck FUCK in lurid
red dribbles, luminous
                                    detail
half a century on from Pound.

steward Poems
      ↑
(palimpsest)
      ↘
      Victorian
          Corinthian
      Colonial

Rob Jackaman

White-Robed Lady

'. . . a Struggle for Life, as a consequence to Natural Selection,
entailing . . . the extinction of less-improved forms.'
— Charles Darwin, *The Origin of Species*
(1859), Ch.14.

'It cannot but happen . . . that those will survive whose functions
happen to be most nearly in equilibrium with the modified
aggregate of external forces, . . . survival of the fittest. . . .'
— Herbert Spencer, *Principles of Biology*
(1865), pt.iii,Ch.12

She walks by the breakwater (having read
The French Lieutenant's Woman, and holidayed
in Akaroa, just in case); the quay
cracks under fists white with menace
and between the blocks where there should be
no gaps you can hear   sea all the way
from Chile   sluice
                         scoria   out.
By a defunct harbour marker where
you can make out the Kakanuis' teeth
behind the town
                    one time we watched some boys
fish up three hammerheads   threshing
                                      glass
gnashing on the empty wharf
                         mindless
relics of prehistoric   ugliness
efficient as cold steel.
                    An old iron
points lever inscribed John Anderson
                         Maker
(date and place obscured) controls a branch
redundant as human gills:
                    railway lines
rust-pocked like the surface of Titan
skew off under the tide
                    into nothing.

Further south even well below Dunedin
(if such a place could be)   fossil

                              forests
are caught in unending stillness by the wind,
ferns forever spread fingers in petition,
trees patiently circle themselves until
waves break the stone
                        and the beaches
will be freed.

                She feels like a character
in a Greek play that has gone on somewhere
else   without her. Her part remains
thinly etched in spider-lines across
the tablet of her mind
                    indistinct   except
sometimes late   when sudden light
                           strikes
at an angle   livid
                actinic so
the past comes up in black and white:
stone pillars against night sky.
Beyond the horizon   remote yet visible
Japanese fishing boats businesslike as
haiku
        with arclamp haloes twenty moons
bright   load up squid by the oceanful
ready   to sail
              into the rising sun.

Rob Jackaman

Leviathan

Some legends say it's a god's canoe, used
to fish up the northern island with a hook,
this whale of a land with an alpine spine
and ribcage full of electric snow,
stranded half-way between equator and pole
on the (ocean) shelf
                  below the latitudes
that count.
             Round the coast it's moored in seaweed
shallows like Maui's skin, mackerel-mottled
(to borrow an ancient formula) with the teeth
of a tattooing chisel.
             At Moeraki
where they once ran trips from Oamaru
in the 1890s a Maori chief
lay on display for sixpence, his *moko*
visible through the coffin lid until
police intervened and another source
of revenue   cut off. On special
picnic days the Garrison Band, famous
in its time, and Bill King (champion
rifle shot and trombone player)
would set up nearby, at Hillgrove
goods shed.

Moko is the face tattoo, applied by chisel to the highest Maori chiefs. Maui, as a god, would have shared the same mark of privilege.

Put your ear   to the shell
and under the static   hiss
                        you may hear
the whale's   lamentation echo through
the chambers of the sea.
                        Inside the shell
is   wind
                in a whorl of pallid air
over green waves of hills   rising
                                falling.
Inside the shell
                is a white city   still
as dead streets at 3 a.m. and the lights
phosphorescent empty.

                When Allen Curnow
composed 'Canst Thou Draw Out . . .', with its waves
of print and pools of shadowed ink,
when he hauled up his book from the typewriter's
tattoo, he'd long gone   north
                        where the big fish
go. His father, Tremayne (who wrote about
frogs
        and playing bowls and Yeats's
crop of beans on Innisfree), was vicar
down here in Malvern parish   big
                                with
mountain   river and sky — too much
                                to believe
brimming horizon   overfull almost
a different dimension like another
time empty   of all but someone else's
history, sun
                down on slopes burning
in the heart of matagouri scrub. Imagine
the pastor wobbling through Otira Gorge
on the top of a Cobb & Co coach, praying
for a tunnel — which he lived to see opened
in 1923, when things were still
flourishing.

The picks flash,
                              the gutting knife
in the poem glints scales the water will
never play again, flensing blades
skitter down light   vindictively
                                        luminous

cutting in . . .

> 1840. Friday, 17th July. *Early in the morning*
> *Mr Miller heard of a whale being in the next Bay*
> *He sent two Boats out to take the chance of the day*
> *. . . . Shortly after cutting the Bone out it came on*
> *to blow from the N.W. . . . . At 5 p.m. Boat returned*
> *with the Bone, and the other two with a raft of*
> *Blubber . . .*

                    (shall they   part him among
the merchants?).
                              When Captain Clayton made the first
paper money, in Queen Charlotte Sound,
did he know what he was starting,
                                        selling
the south   down
                              to the bone, fossil fish
locked in rictus while the lance
goes in under the long white cloud?
You builders of empires, makers
and breakers
                              of grades on a graph,
peddlers of superannuated souls,
                                        spare
a thought for those lost
                              in the long wallow
of south Pacific   swell.

Janet Frame

Willowglen

from *The Envoy from Mirror City*

Arriving in Oamaru, I went at once to the motor camp where I had rented a unit for the night. I bought supplies from the dairy and I stared curiously at the dairy owner, Mr Grant, who had been named next-of-kin when my father collapsed outside the shop. I looked searchingly at the goods I bought as if they and Mr Grant and my father were now in possession of a death I had come too late to share.

When I walked back to my cabin I saw a young man hiding in the bushes and peering out at me. He came towards me. He was a reporter, he said, from the local newspaper and he hoped I would give him first chance to talk to me as the provincial paper was also looking for me. He too had been fed the diet of 'overseas reputation' causing him to form an unreal image of me. He'd been sent to find the New Zealand author who was now jewelled with *overseas*, to gaze on her and share the jewels; and I, in my paste glitter, felt embarrassed. Although the reporter soon discovered that I did not carry the riches he expected, he was pleased to be first with his story, *Oamaru Author Returns*. We walked in the Gardens where he photographed me sitting in the Japanese garden, and I was remembering how as children wearing our Aunt-Polly-made puffed-sleeve summer-breeze dresses, we had been photographed or 'snapped' near the same bridge.

That day also, I collected the Willowglen key from the lawyer who asked what my plans were for Willowglen. My brother was getting married and needed a home, he said. The place was worth little, he was sure no-one would buy it, and so there was little prospect of a division of money from any sale. He advised me to sell my share and not give it away as I had suggested. My father had wanted me to have it, he said. I had already made up my mind to give my brother my share for I knew he had little money and I also knew that throughout his life he had not been as lucky as I.

First, however, I must visit Willowglen in its springtime. Oamaru, as much as ever the kingdom by the sea, had now been declared a city as its population was up to ten thousand, but it was the sea that still clamoured to be heard, making the city like a shell singing in everyone's ears. My return alone to the deserted Willowglen was softened by the green of the leafy trees, and the sight of the once slender pine trees 'down on the flat', startling at first, as they were now a dark forest almost as formidable as the 'second planny' on the hill of Eden Street, and by the sound of the distant roar of the surf pounding at the breakwater on the shore. The driveway of Willowglen was overgrown with cocksfoot and littered with rusting parts of old cars, old stoves, and remnants of a dray. The shed where the pictures and the heavier furniture had been stored after the move from Eden Street was collapsed upon itself, open to the sky, with picture frames and table-legs still angled among the ruins. The cowbyre, the fowlhouse, the old pigsty overgrown with hemlock, the apple shed were all gradually falling apart, boards hanging, swinging to and fro as if the months and years had passed with such violence as to rip them apart like useless limbs. A wild black cat, perhaps one of Siggie's families, lurked in the hawthorn hedge. Siggie had recently died, aged eighteen.

I walked up the path under the old 'ghost' tree, that huge pine with the drooping dark branches. I walked in the porch, the lean-to against the hill, treading on last year's squashed pears and seeing even among the pear blossom a few, shrivelled and shrunken, still clinging to the tree with no-one to gather them any more. The old iron boot-last was still there, just outside the back door; Dad's fishing bag, as I remembered it in Kensington, fishy-stink and scabbed inside with old dried fish scales; and there were his thigh gumboots for wading in the shingle beds of the Waitaki, Rakaia, Rangitata. I opened the back door and walked in. I had not expected it would be as I found it, yet how else could it have been? My father's pyjamas hung over a chair. His long cream-coloured Mosgiel underpants with a faint brown stain at the crotch lay on the floor; even his last cup of tea sat in its saucer, a swill of tea in the bottom of the cup, making an old brown ridge against the china. The latest — two-and-a-half-months'-old — newspaper folded to present the crossword half filled in with the stub of the ink pencil beside it, lay by the cup of tea. There were ashes in the kitchen range with the ashpan half drawn out ready for emptying, while above, on the brass rack, neatly folded pyjamas lay ready for the night.

The old sofa where Tittups the cat had peed and we tried to absorb the smell with our Christmas carnation scent, where the headmistress of Waitaki sat the day she came to give her sympathy over my sister Isabel's drowning, still took the length of the wall facing the shadowing hill beyond the lean-to where the bank was thick with cocksfoot, periwinkle, and small broadleaf plants sheltering in their own clay bed beneath the parent tree.

In the kitchen, the curtains were new, a bright pattern of teapots and cups and saucers, the kind of pattern mother would never have chosen. I drew aside the curtains by 'Dad's seat' and looked out along the path to the cypress tree and the old dunny with its dunny roses spilling in a mass of white buds over the corrugated tin-hat roof.

I walked into the middle bedroom where I hoped to sleep. Books, linen were scattered everywhere. The two front rooms were also strewn with books, newspapers, old clothes, with the room that used to belong to our parents appearing tidier. There, the bed had some bedclothes and the pink eiderdown bought years ago on account from Calder Mackay, and there was a strange-looking electric heater like a copper pipe in front of the disused fireplace. I opened the front door and looked out at the grassy slope to the old orchard, the creek, and part of the 'flat' where my brother had transported an old house and where, I'd been told, Uncle Charlie, Dad's youngest brother, lived from time to time. I stood at the front door. The grass was growing on the doorstep. I remembered the time the cow had come to the front door and looked in. An owl in the tall macrocarpa tree by the old wash-house, startled by a human presence, fluttered from its sleeping perch to the paddock beyond.

My homecoming was as sad and desolate as I knew it would be, yet I relished its importance to the Envoy from Mirror City, that watching self, who was already waiting to guide me to my fictional home. Many times in my life I have received and cherished these gifts of fiction. From my home now in Mirror City I can only keep trying to parcel these gifts in language that satisfies the ear and the heart and the demands of truth. (It is the events of living that are not easily recognized as legends and part of myths that are the test of the value of lifelong tenancy in Mirror City; and it is the discovery of the new legends and myths that keeps building, renewing the city.)

As I explored the house I realized that I had forgotten or never knew about practical matters like turning on electricity, water, arranging a telephone, and I was reduced at once from the glory of my 'overseas reputation' when I received a bill for having the water switched on, and I was questioned by the power board about my ability to pay. I had forgotten in the midst of apparent kindness shown to me on my return home, that the world is still a cruel place, and Oamaru was no exception, and in all the abundance of Oamaru's giving and taking through water — the reservoir, the sea, the baths, the loved creeks and ponds, even the water-race known to us as the 'rolldown sea' by the post office, everything and everyone must be paid for.

I built a fire down on the flat to burn the rubbish collected in the house — old newspapers, receipts going back many years. I read everything before I burned or saved it. I burned family letters. I saved documents that I thought might be wanted by my sister and brother or myself, some that might be looked on as keepsakes — Isabel's athletic and academic certificates, her funeral receipt, other receipts that still bore the anguish of receiving the account so vividly that I said to myself, I remember when that bill came and Mum cried wondering how we could possibly pay it, but now it's paid and gone; how could a sheet of paper headed 'Dr To' (we had always thought of it as *Doctor*) cause so much anguish? I found the Star-Bowkett Building Society book with its detailed payments on the loan that bought Willowglen, and I heard again the anxiety in Mum's or Dad's voice — 'Where's the Star-Bowkett book? Have we paid the Star-Bowkett this month? When we pay the *Star-Bowkett* . . .' There were the Calder Mackay receipts, too, everything paid. And the local receipts — MacDiarmids, Bulleids, the Polytechnic,

Hodges, Kerrs, Jeffrey and Smith, Adams . . . all the tradespeople that inhabited without knowing it our house, our daily conversation, and determined the mood of the family.

I found a pile of letters in a handwriting I did not recognize, and I began to read. The letters were from Dad's woman friend living in another town. I had only recently heard about her from my sister who had said they planned to marry. The new curtains and pillowcases had been bought by her. She and Dad had been good company for each other, for apparently she had stayed often at Willowglen and attended to various household chores, and they had enjoyed themselves over a few drinks, as the numerous empty bottles disclosed. Her letters expressed concern over the house and its furnishings. She also wrote of the presents my father had given her, some of which she asked for in her letters.

As I read, I found myself slowly assuming the role of my mother, feeling the shock of knowing that 'Curly' who never 'touched a drop of drink' had left *empty liquor bottles* in the house, that the love that so steadfastly bound him over the years had been cast aside for this 'cheap' relationship with someone obviously in search of a 'sugar daddy'. I then became the outraged daughter — how dare our father abandon us for this woman? How dare she try to replace our mother! And why had Dad never told me? Not a word in all his letters with their detailed times, dates, costs, journeys, and the state of the government. I suddenly felt lonely, an outsider in my family.

Then as the last of the letters flared and died in the ashes I saw my father as he had been — widowed, living alone, troubled by bouts of undiagnosed sickness, still dosing himself with his 'chalk' to ease the pains in his stomach, coping with the physical effort of cycling each day along that bleak sea-exposed road out past the Boys' High to attend the boiler at the Presbyterian Home, returning wearily to an unlit cold house that escaped from the shadow of the hill only twice during the day, in the early morning when the sun trod briefly on the front doorstep and glanced in the window of the side bedroom, and later when it lay a hand along the front windowsill, then withdrew it, disappearing behind the trees. The frost in that all-day shade was as cruel as ever; and even the glorious seafoam wave of pear blossom at the back door could not atone for the awful chill lying all winter outside and inside the draughty, flimsy wooden house.

I prepared the middle bedroom for myself. I lifted the mattress from the floor and found a gaping hole in the cover and, snuggled within the kapok, a nest of bald pink baby rats. I don't recall how I disposed of them.

I washed the available bed linen and hung it to dry on the wire clothesline that stretched from the top of the hill to the apple shed on the flat. I hoisted the line further in the air with the old manuka-stick prop and heard the familiar squeak-squeak as the stretched line pulled at the tree support, the old oak by the apple shed near where mother used to rest before she 'tackled' the steep sloping path to the house. I saw again in my mind my father's hunched figure, the sugar sack of railway coal on his back, his knees bent to ease the strain as he too struggled up the slope that became steeper year by year.

And that night with the house cleaned and the bedclothes dried, I slept in the middle room. I was wakened by the wind in the many trees, by the silence, by the searchlight glare of the midnight express train as it turned the corner past the Gardens towards the railway crossing. The trees heaved and rocked in the rising wind; moreporks and the little 'German' owls called from the macrocarpa. And in the morning I was wakened by the gurgling, gargling magpies.

I decided I would not stay at Willowglen. I would walk into town that morning to book my return passage to Auckland, and when I had chosen those possessions I thought of as 'keepsakes' for members of the family, I would leave Oamaru.

Although the retraced path is factual and fictional cliché, I'm not beyond indulging my memory. It was a delight to walk down Chelmer Street to the town while remembering other, not happier, times. Chelmer Street, too, with the hilly side of the street facing north, lived in perpetual shade on the north side, with occasional rays of afternoon sun touching the 'Gardens' side of the street. The street was so clearly divided in its share of sun and shade that it was like a street that had suffered a stroke and was left paralysed on one side, with the shade and the frost as the paralysing agents.

At the end of the street I passed the Town Baths and felt again, held within the dull red colour of the rows of seats and their spindly uncomfortable slats, the sense of the old glory of 'being at the Baths', and then I remembered after my sister Myrtle's drowning, the deliberate disentangling, the excision of the baths from my life and the way I then looked on the site as a strange hateful place as if it had been a friendly neighbour who was now an enemy sitting there unpunished for its crime. Now, remembering the succession of feelings towards the Baths, I felt only the sadness of the dull red colour of the seats, that iron-roof, railway-hut, railway-wagon, railway-station red that was painted through my life as part of my childhood rainbow.

I walked through Takaro Park where the circus used to pitch its tent and the sixpenny zoo was held in a row of cages under separate canvas; and there was the old building we used to call the Middle School, used for teaching technical subjects, and always apparently empty during the day. I remembered how I used to walk past it and feel a shiver of curiosity and strangeness at its emptiness and brownness and the tall windows with their cords hanging untouched during the daytime; it was a neutral kind of school, it had fairness, it was middle ground, between the fierce rivalries of the North and the South Schools. I walked by the Oamaru Creek and what I still thought of as the 'Morgue', that small stone hut; and by the green water-race that reminded me of a *weir*, of Maggie Tulliver and *The Mill on the Floss*.

And as I stood in the queue at the post office people spoke to me, welcoming me home to Oamaru; some I knew, others were strangers who had seen my photo in the paper. One woman said she'd been at Waitaki when I was there. I stared at her. 'Oh yes,' and the former rigid classifications came to mind — good at maths; stodgy; not much good at phys. ed. Lives in the country, on a sheep station with a fancy name. Teachers talk with deference of the sheep station. We all turn our heads, envious.

We talked a while. She gave me news of others in the school class. 'Oh? That's interesting, I didn't know. Yes. Oh.'

I walked by the small telegraphic office next to the post office and there was the Social Security Department, and now I remembered my horror and shame as I used to sneak in to present my medical certificate with its telltale writing, *Schizophrenia*, and cash my sickness benefit during my brief stays in Oamaru. I remembered how I used to emerge from the office feeling as if all delight had gone from the day, knowing that I was a 'funny' peculiar person, and wanting to hide forever. I felt dirty, my clothes felt like the clothes of a mental patient, and my shoes looked clumsy.

I allowed myself the luxury of remembering these feelings and knowing that in the magic language of the world of racing — *this time* — everything was different. I need not go to the Social Security Department where the man behind the grille peered at me to see if my schizophrenia were showing.

I returned to Willowglen walking through the Town Gardens with its *Oamaru Beautifying Society* plaques. I passed the fern house and saw the ferns with their hair leaning against the milky windows, and I thought of how as children we used to go to the fern house just to feel the experience of wetness and greenness and the smell of being in the earth with the world above and around. I walked from the Gardens, past Lovers' Lane, the hideaway walk with its tree-enclosed paths, past the children's playground with its seesaws and boat swings and merry-go-round that used to make me so sick I could never play on them. And there was the paddling pool and the murky pond where the ducks and the swans lived, the big white swan with the orange beak and the fierce hooded eyes, and I remembered how I used to think of the Seven Brothers who were changed into swans but there was not enough magic for the youngest who had only one wing and could not fly. And I'd always thought that magic was magic, without limit.

Later that day I searched for keepsakes. I sat among the strewn books that were family books, history books bought by my brother who was always interested in history, 'rogue' books from nowhere, prizes from Waitaki. I chose my sister Isabel's school prizes, Christmas books, London, my Training College *David Copperfield* and school prizes; Isabel's collection of native plants. For June and her family, Dad's book of fishing flies, the polished rod and case won in a fishing competition and never used because he preferred to make his own; various books; dishes, table covers, and the old kitchen clock with the dragons around the glass face. For myself, a pair of old blankets, the eiderdown, Dad's paintings, leaving some for my brother, Aunty Polly and Aunty Isy's paintings, the bagpipe chanter, the bedcover sewn by Dad from the collection of blazer material from throughout New Zealand, used by Aunty Isy at the Ross and Glendining Mills. There was little more that I could take in my luggage. I had no place of my own to live in. My brother could make good use of the rest of the family 'treasures'.

Sitting there choosing and rejecting from the pathetic remnants of a family's life, I could still feel the value of them, my need for them, the need of others to have them as keepsakes. Each object was alive with its yesterdays. I wanted to embrace them, even the books; and when I finally packed them, I looked regretfully at those I had been forced to leave behind: the long kauri form where we used to sit for meals and where my father and his brothers and sisters had also sat, and, like us, had used the upturned form as a canoe. The dining table had been used only on special occasions at Eden Street, but at Willowglen it would fit only into the small kitchen: it had been the Christmas and New Year table, the Sunday Bible-reading table, the table-when-visitors-came; Dad's leather workbag which he always sewed while we watched fascinated as he trimmed the raw leather, cut the bag to shape, stained it, and finally sewed it, first drawing the thread through a lump of beeswax. I pocketed a few of his salmon spoons and sinkers only because we had shared, too, in their making, watching (seen and not heard) while Dad leaned over the stove with the sinkers in their small pan, and the dreaded 'spirits of salts'.

Having a last look over the house I opened the sewing machine drawer where the bullets used to be kept and there they were, two or three, shining with a point at the end like bronzed rockets. 'Don't you touch the bullets,' our parents would say. Curious, we often touched them, and played school with them, marshalling them along the mottled brown varnished machine-stand.

And so with my bundle of treasures from Willowglen I took the train and ferry north to Auckland.

Fiona Farrell

A Story about Skinny Louie
from *The Skinny Louie Book*

THE SETTING

Imagine a small town.

Along its edges, chaos.

To the east, clinking shelves of shingle and a tearing sea, surging in from South America across thousands of gull-studded white-capped heaving miles.

To the south, the worn hump of a volcano crewcut with pines dark and silent, but dimpled still on the crest where melted rock and fire have spilled to the sea to hiss and set as solid bubbles, black threaded with red.

To the west, a border of hilly terraces, built up from layer upon layer of shells which rose once, dripping, from the sea and could as easily shudder like the fish it is in legend, and dive.

To the north, flat paddocks, pockmarked with stone and the river which made them shifting restlessly from channel to channel in its broad braided bed.

Nothing is sure.

The town pretends of course, settled rump-down on the coastal plain with its back to the sea, which creeps up yearly a nibble here a bite there, until a whole football field has gone at the boys' high school and the cliff walkway crumbles and the sea demands propitiation, truckloads of rubble and concrete blocks. And the town inches away in neat rectangular steps up the flanks of the volcano which the council named after an early mayor, a lardy mutton-chop of a man, hoping to tame it as the Greeks thought they'd fool the Furies by calling them the Kindly Ones; inches away across shingle bar and flax swamp to the shell terraces and over where order frays at last into unpaved roads, creeks flowing like black oil beneath willows tangled in convolvulus, and old villa houses, gaptoothed, teetering on saggy piles, with an infestation of hens in the yard and a yellow-toothed dog chained to the water tank.

At the centre, things seem under control. The post office is a white wedding cake, scalloped and frilled, and across the road are the banks putting on a responsible Greek front (though ramshackle corrugated iron behind). At each end of the main street the town mourns its glorious dead with a grieving soldier in puttees to the north and a defiant lion to the south, and in between a cohort of memorial elms was drawn up respectfully until 1952 when it was discovered that down in the dark the trees had broken ranks and were rootling around under the road tearing crevices in the tarmac, and the council was forced to be stern: tore out the lot and replaced them with plots of more compliant African marigolds. There are shops and petrol stations and churches and flowering cherries for beautification and a little harbour with a tea kiosk in the lee of the volcano. It's as sweet as a nut, as neat as a pie, as a pin.

Imagine it.

Imagine it at night, a print composed of shapes and shadows. Early morning, 24 January 1954. The frilly hands on the post office clock show 3.30 so it's 3.25 a.m., as everyone knows. (Time is no more thoroughly dependable here than the earth beneath one's feet.) It's unseasonably cold. A breeze noses in over the breakwater in the harbour and in amongst the pottles and wrappers by the tea kiosk, tickling the horses on the merry-go-round in the playground so they tittup tittup and squeak, fingering the bristles on the Cape pines and sighing down their branches into a dark pit of silence. Flower boxes have been hung along the main street and as the wind passes they swing and spill petals, fuchsias and carnations. There are coloured lights and bunting which, if it were only daylight, could be seen to be red white and blue because tomorrow, the Queen is coming. At 3.05 p.m. the Royal Express, a Ja class locomotive (No. 1276) drawing half a dozen refurbished carriages, will arrive at the railway crossing on the main street. Here, Her Majesty Queen Elizabeth II and His Royal Highness Prince Philip will step into a limousine which will carry them up the main street past the post office, the banks and the shops which have all had their fronts painted for the occasion (their backs remain as ever, patchy and rusted). By the grieving soldier the royal couple will turn left towards the park where they will be formally welcomed at 3.20 p.m. by the mayor and mayoress and shake hands with forty-five prominent citizens. They will be presented with some token of the town's affection. At 3.25 p.m. they will commence their walk to the train and at 3.40 p.m. they will depart for the south. The moves are all set out in the Royal Tour Handbook, the stage is set, the lines rehearsed, and the citizens, prominent and otherwise, are tucked under blanket and eiderdown, secure in the knowledge that everything has been properly organised. If they stir a little it is because the wind tugs at curtains, or because through the fog of dreaming they hear some foreign noise outside the windows where their cats and dogs have sloughed off their daytime selves and stalk, predatory, the jungles of rhubarb and blackcurrant. The sea breathes, Whooshaaah. Whooshaaah.

BRIAN BATTERSBY WITNESSES A CURIOUS PHENOMENON

Midway up Keats Street on the flanks of the volcano there is one citizen who is not asleep. Brian Battersby is sitting on his garage roof. His legs are wrapped in a tartan rug, his thermos is full of vege soup, and with stiff fingers he is trying to adjust the focus on his new four-inch Cook refractor. Thousands of miles above his head a civilisation more advanced than any on earth is constructing a canal and by muffled red torchlight Brian is tracing the line of it: from the Nodus Gordii SE in the direction of the Mare Sirenum, at mind-boggling speed: a hundred miles a day? Two hundred perhaps? What machines they must have, what power!

Above the Cape a meteor flares, green and white, and Brian pauses, waiting for the shower that will follow, but the meteor grows in brightness. Brighter than Mars. Bigger! For a moment the whole town is caught in brilliant silhouette and Brian sits motionless on the garage roof, vaguely aware of music, an odd percussive ticktocking. He cannot identify it, but the fact is that every hen in the town is singing. Necks stretched, tiny eyes like amber beads shining in the warm darkness of their fowl-runs, they chorus: Wa-a-a-chet auf, ruft uns di-e Stim-mm-e. Awake! Awake! Out on the Awarua Road a Hereford cow more sensitive than her sisters is levitating above a hedge and cats and dogs have forgotten the jungle, and kneel paws tucked to soft belly. The meteor explodes at last into a sequined fall of shining particles and the town recovers: hens tuck heads beneath wings, the cow descends with a soft thud and cats and dogs stretch and look uneasily about them into the night, ears flattened.

Up on the garage roof Brian is shaking. He knows suddenly and with absolute clarity that those canals are not the work of superior beings who might offer solutions to fallible humanity but are mere ripples of dust blown this way and that by howling wind, and he knows that he, Brian, is a small, rather pompous accounts clerk who will spend the next thirty years in the offices of the borough council, and that his wife wishes now that she had not married him and that she lived somewhere more exotic than Keats Street. The Rive Gauche, for example. She is bored by Brian, bored by this town, bored by this country and feels her life might be lived if only she were able to live it elsewhere. It's too much truth to handle all at once. Best not confronted.

Brian reaches for his notebook. '24 January 1954. 0357 UT,' he writes with trembling hand. 'Mag.—?? fireball in clear sky. Green and white.' What amazing luck! What a coup! He peers up into the darkness, eyes still dazzled and sparkling, and attempts accurate estimation. 'Travelled 30°–35° start 25° altitude 140° azimuth. Approx 1 min. 58 sec. duration.' What a note it will make for *Meteor News*! 'Accompanying sonic phenomena,' he adds and reaches for his thermos and a shot of hot soup.

Two miles from his garage roof in the Begonia House at the Public Gardens, Louie Symonds, Skinny Louie, aged fifteen, is giving birth.

SKINNY LOUIE HAS A BABY

The Begonia House is warm, steamy, sticky with primeval trickling and the sweet-sour smell of rampant growth. Louie has managed to drag some coconut matting into a corner and squats there, full-bellied and bursting, hands clamped to a water pipe while her body tears in pieces. No one can hear her groan. The Gardens are empty. Only beds of pansies and petunias wheeling away from the glasshouse along the edges of gravel paths, circling the Peter-Pan statue and the Centenary fountain and the specimen trees with their identity labels tacked to their trunks. Louie is on her own.

Far away to the south is the dark little warren where she lives with her mum Lill. Lill isn't in tonight either, as it happens. She's been off for three weeks or so on one of the boats and she won't be back till it leaves for the north with its cargo of snapper and squid, and the girls are put ashore. Lill has a special thing for the Chinks: she likes them small and smooth and she likes the way they pay her no trouble and she likes the presents: whisky, stockings, a nice jacket. It's better than hanging round the Robbie Burns anyway, taking your chances with any poxy john who fancies a bit between jugs. Louie came with her once or twice down the boats, but she gave them all the pip, got on people's nerves being so quiet, hanging around like a fart at a funeral, so Louie stayed home after that while Lill with her Joan Crawford lips and her hair curled went into Port. At this moment she's bobbing about two miles off Kaikoura wondering if she's got enough to go eight no trumps and Louie is in pain. She has walked for days to this place, travelling by night, and by day when the sun slammed down like a pot lid, she has curled round her belly and slept under a bush or a bridge.

She has often done this: got the jumpies, set off walking till she's quiet again, then turned for home. This time she's had them bad. She has walked and slept for days, sucking a stone for spit, following the road up from the city to the hills, past the white rock where she lay once months before to warm herself in the sun. She'd been sprawled, dozing, light tangled in her lashes in tiny scarlet stars, when a shadow fell upon her like a stone. Louie looked up and there was a hawk hovering. She lay very still. The hawk flew closer, settled. She took the weight of him gasping as his talons drove tiny holes in her breast. He dipped his tail feathers in her open mouth. She smelled the dry bird scent of him. Then he rose wings beating into the sun and she lost him in the glare.

She passed the rock two nights ago. Yesterday morning she stopped near a country store where she got a whole Vienna slipping it quick as winking under her coat while the man was lifting trays from a truck. She'd sat under a hedge in early morning half-light and picked out a hole, chewing slowly, and a plump grey mare had come to her from the mist and stood while she squeezed its titties and took the milk, licking it from her fingers, glutinous, sticky, Highlander Condensed.

When the sun was up, she slept. It was wise to hide by day. She didn't trust cars. When she was little, cars came to their house, crawling like grey beetles round the road from Port and when they saw them they'd run away, her and Alamein and Yvonne, because the cars meant questions and picking at their hair for cooties and ice cream sticks forcing their tongues back and where? And why? And how often? And Lill in a paddy, though she was nice as pie to the lady clearing a space and saying would she care for a cup of tea?

But as soon as the car had gone it was bloody cow and why the hell couldn't Louie learn to smile instead of standing there like some mental case because if she didn't they'd have her out to Bella Vista, she looked that daft. Lill slammed around them savage, so they learned to scatter when cars came, hiding like the cats in the smooth places beneath the hedge or the washhouse. But once Ally and Yvonne weren't quick enough and the lady got them, took them away somewhere and they were never seen again. So Louie hid from cars. You couldn't trust them.

Tonight, Louie has crossed some paddocks sniffing for the sea and found herself on a hill above a railway line which curved down into a crisscross pattern of light. Her body was heavy and her back ached. She'd been picking at the bread rolling doughballs when she went to the lav suddenly, no warning, right there in her pants, so she peeled them off and stuffed them steaming into a bush. Cough said a sheep. Louie began to walk along the railway towards the town. The pain her back was growing and another tiny nut of it pressed at the base of her skull.

Clump clump clump sleeper by sleeper careful not to fall between and have bad luck. Around her everything was coming alive: trees tapped her shoulder, fence posts skittered by on the blind side and the grass lined up and waved. The weight in her belly heaved and she had to stop at the bottom of the hill for everything to settle. The railway line crossed a street. Louie stepped from the sleepers onto tarmac and ahead was an arch of flowers, framing black shadow.

Then the pain came up from behind and grabbed her so that she had to cry out as she used to at school when Wayne Norris Chinese-burned her arms or stuck her with a pen nib saying cowardy custard cry baby cry only this was worse and she tried to run away through the archway into the dark. The pain lost her there for a bit so Louie took her chance, stumbling across a lawn to the shelter of trees and a cage where a bird asked her who was a pretty cocky, along paths frilled with grey rows of flowers to a glasshouse gleaming when the moon came from behind cloud where Louie hid, sneaking into a corner. But this pain was too smart. It had slipped in beside her already and was squeezing sly, cowardy cowardy custard, driving her into a black hole where there was nothing but a voice groaning over and over and her body ripping and suddenly silence. A slither. And silence.

On the coconut matting between her legs lay a sticky black thing, wriggling in the sweet stench of blood. Louie crouched waiting for the pain to jump her again but it had gone, sidled off shutting the door silently. Louie wiped some jelly from the black thing and it mewed under her hand. They lay quiet together. Slowly the glass about them turned to grey squares then white and Louie felt her legs twitch.

The warm air here settled round her head like a thick blanket and she needed out. She took her cardy and wrapped it round the thing then stood carefully, wobbling a little, and went outside where the grass was shiny and her feet left dark prints as she walked on water past the bird and the flowers to the archway and the street.

She moved slowly past houses with their curtains drawn still and the cats coming home to sleep, down a long street to the shore. The sea was stretching and waking too and the clouds as she walked up the beach were golden bars with the sun slipping between. She stopped from time to time to wash blood from her legs. She ate the last of the bread. In a cleft in the low clay cliff were a wheel-less Ford, some mattresses stained and spitting fluff, broken boxes, a pile of rotting plums. Louie was tired. She dragged a mattress into the car, and curled to sleep. On the gear shift a nursery spider had spun its web. Baby spiders jittered under the membrane, hundreds of them. Louie prodded gently at their opaque shell and they scattered at her touch but she was careful not to tear a hole because then the cold could come in and kill them all.

That's the story of how Louie Symonds, daughter of Lilleas Symonds popularly known as Shanghai Lill, gave birth. The paternity of the child is in some doubt. It is possible that the father is Wayne Norris, an acned youth who, since primary school, has paid Louie in bags of lollies for a quick poke in the rough ground behind the golf course on the way home. She's particularly fond of gobstoppers. She likes lying back in the long grass listening to the magpies gargling in the fir trees while Wayne wiggles his dicky about prodding hopefully, and when she's had enough of that she can say get off, roll over, and see how the lolly has changed from red to yellow to blue.

Wayne is a definite possibility.

It is equally probable that the father is a hawk.

THE QUEEN COMES BY TRAIN

The Queen was coming. Maura stood with her mother and father down by the railway crossing at the very end of the route. She would have preferred to be in the Park suffering torments of jealousy while some other little girl with perfect curls and a perfect dress handed the Queen a posy while performing a perfect curtsey, but they'd been late and this was the closest they could get.

Dad hadn't wanted to come at all. 'Load of poppycock,' he'd said. 'Mrs Windsor and that chinless cretin she married riding along waving at the peasants and mad Sid and the rest of them bringing up the rear kowtowing for all they're worth. Lot of nonsense.'

'I think she's pretty,' said Maura who had a gold Visit medal pinned to her best frock and a scrapbook of pictures cut from *Sunny Stories* in her bedroom: The Little Princesses at Play with the Royal Corgies on the Lawn at Balmoral, The Little Princesses in their Playhouse which had a proper upstairs and wasn't just a made-over pig pen with ripped sheets for curtains. 'Miss Croad says the Queen has a peaches and cream complexion.'

'Peaches and bloody cream!' said Dad, thumping the table so his tea spilled. 'There weren't too many peaches around back in 1848 when her lot were gorging themselves in London while our lot ate grass, and don't you forget it.' Dad hated the Queen, Oliver Cromwell and Winston Churchill because of the Troubles and the Famine and because they-came-across-and-tried-to-teach-us-their-ways.

'That's years ago,' said Mum. 'Now turn around, Maura, so I can brush out the other side.' Maura turned, glad to be relieved of the tight ringlet sausages which had dug into her scalp all night. 'And what about during the war?' said her mother, who was pink-cheeked today in her best crêpe de chine and ready for a fight. 'They stayed in London didn't they? They stayed with the people in the East End right through the Blitz and the Queen Mother even said she was glad the palace got bombed because then she could feel they were sharing the suffering.'

'Suffering?' said Dad. 'What did she know about suffering, one of the richest families in the world and you know how they got there don't you? Murder and betrayal and half of them illegitimate into the bargain, born the wrong side of the. . .'

'Shh,' said Mum, her mouth tight-lipped round a blue satin ribbon. 'Not in front of . . . Hold still, Maura, for pity's sake.'

Dad drank his tea morosely. 'Eating grass,' he said. 'Eating dirt, so some English bugger could go in velvet.'

A final tug at the ribbon and Maura was released. 'Well, are you coming or not?' said Mum, driving a hat pin into her pink church hat, and Dad said he supposed he would, if she was that set on it, but he was damned if he was going to get dressed up. The Queen would have to take him in his gardening clothes or not at all, and Mum said, 'Nonsense, you're not leaving the house in that jersey, so go and get changed, there's still time,' but of course there wasn't and they could hear the crowd roar like a wave breaking before they were halfway down the hill and they had to run and push even to find the place to stand by the Gardens gate.

The Pipe Band was wheezing and wailing a few yards away and Maura would have liked to go and stand up close to watch the men's cheeks puff and the rhythmic flap of their white duck feet and to feel her ears buzz with drum roll and drone. But they were inaccessible through a dense forest of legs and bottoms: fat, skinny, trousered, floralled and striped, milling about so that she felt as frightened and inconsequential as she had when she'd opened the gate at Grandad Forbes's and the cows had pressed through before she'd been able to jump to one side, buffeting her in their eagerness to get to the paddock. She'd have liked an elephant ride on her father's shoulders; other children swayed above the crowd clutching their flags and safe from harm, but their fathers didn't have bad legs from the war, and she was getting too heavy for Mum to hold.

'Don't fuss, poppet,' said Mum. 'Just hang on tight. I'll make sure you see her when the time comes.'

Maura needed no instruction. Around her the huge bodies pressed and she took sticky hold of her mother's skirt. The crowd noise was like static which tuned in snatches into God Save and cheering. (The Mayor's wife was presenting the Queen with a white gloxinia called Majesty in a silver casket, Miss Croad told them next morning, and the Mayor, Mr Cudby, was giving the Prince a photo of the Begonia House to hang on the wall at Buckingham Palace.) Then the roar built like rain drumming and Mum stood tiptoe saying, 'There she is, there she is! Maura, you must see properly, this is a Once-in-a-Lifetime Opportunity!' And before Maura could protest she had scooped her up, and was tapping a man's shoulder and asking, 'Could my daughter get down to the front please?' Handing her over like a parcel, passed from person to person till she stood at the very edge of the crowd where there was no coach and no horses and no limousine even but an ordinary man and woman walking along the road past the baths, talking sometimes to the crowd or waving, and the woman's face was a bit like the Queen's but not peaches and cream, and topped with an ordinary hat, not a crown. People were calling hurrah hurrah and the pipe band shrilled so Maura waved her flag uncertainly as the man and woman passed by and in a very ordinary way, exactly as anyone might, climbed up the stairs onto the train, turned and waved, and the train chugged (whooshaaah whooshaaah) away down the track.

Then the crowd broke. Maura stood with her paper flag but no hand came down out of the press of bodies and no voice said, 'Ah, there you are, Maura,' lifting her up to safety. She was pushed and prodded, spun and stepped about until she found herself up against a floral arch and beyond it lay a smooth and empty lawn, so she went there, and once she was there she remembered the parrot and then Peter Pan and then the Begonia House where you could pick up fuchsias from the floor and wear them for earrings, and that was how she found the baby.

It was like finding the kittens mewing blind and wriggling in the long grass by the sand pit, except that the baby's eyes were open and it waved its hands sticky and streaked with cream but perfect just the same with proper nails. Maura took her hanky and spat on it as her mother did for a lick and a promise and wiped at the baby's dirty cheek. The baby turned instantly to her finger, opened its pink toothless mouth and sucked. Maura was entranced. She gathered the baby up as she had gathered the kittens, tucked firmly inside the dirty cardigan, and carried her discovery out into the sun.

PEG AND MARTIN WAIT BY THE GATE

They stood by the gate, frantic, pale. 'Bloody irresponsible,' Martin was saying. 'Sending a child her age off on her own in a crowd like this.' He hadn't realised till this minute how much Peg's impulsive optimism, which he loved, also infuriated him and how much he longed to attack and destroy it.

Predictably she was refusing to recognise how appalling this situation was. He knew. He'd seen the worst happen. He'd seen a man step on a patch of desert dust and his legs sever, the trunk falling after in a torn and heavy arc. He went occasionally to mass, but knew it was useless, that this was simply habit, and that you could pray as Donovan prayed on the truck coming out at Sidi Rezegh and die mouthing Hail Mary in bubbles of blood. He voted Labour, argued with Jensen in the tearoom at the Works who said that the unions were full of bloody commies and they'd been dead right to send in the troops in '51, but knew that this faith too was illusion, that there was no common cause, that the reality was each man alone, bleating, as the blow fell.

And here was Peg with a daft bright desperate smile saying the swings, she'd have gone to play on the swings. And Peg was avoiding Martin's eye but knew him there beside her, the heavy dark weight of him and his despair which she can't touch, ever, or relieve. She can make him laugh, she can love him, but when they lie together a bleak and faceless nothing sprawls between them grasping at her throat so she wakes, heart beating night after night. She fights against it in Martin, suppressing panic as she does now, refusing to share his vision (Maura face down on the duckpond, dragged into the water lilies by the swans, hand in hand with some enticing nameless terror . . .). But at this moment she knows suddenly that she won't be able to struggle for ever, that her optimism is a frail thing and that in time she will have to choose: fight or give up, let the blackness take her. Love and survival are in opposition. It's appalling. Too big a truth to face all at once. Better encountered bit by bit.

But look, there is Maura now, safe and sound after all ('You see?'), her blue nylon dress stained and carrying a grubby bundle. And, 'Mum,' Maura is saying. 'I've found us a baby.'

They took the baby along the street to Dr Campbell's surgery and as they passed people drew back on either side like waves parting and quiet for a second with curiosity. But when the family with its grubby bundle had passed, an extraordinary thing happened. People turned to one another and in a sudden rush, earnest and eager, they confessed those things that most oppressed them. They told one another truths, pleasant and unpleasant. McLean, most prominent of the prominent citizens, told Davis the Town Clerk that he bought land on the northern river flats six months before development on a tip-off from a cousin on the Council. Jameson, junior partner in Lowe, Stout and Jameson sought out Lowe and told him he invested £5,000 of clients' money in a salmon hatchery which appeared certain now to fail. Partner revealed that he had swindled partner, parent has coerced child, friend has failed friend. So the day of the Queen's visit ended for some in scuffling and recrimination, for others in forgiveness and pity as people made what they could of the truth.

WHAT HAPPENED TO LOUIE

When it grew dark once more Louie walked along the shingle to the river's mouth. Her legs still ran with blood and her breasts tingled so that she had to lie face down on the cold river sand to soothe their swelling. She followed the bank inland through dank grass willow and blackberry, feeling her body lighten, her feet finding their accustomed rhythm and visible again across the sack of her vacated belly. That night she ate a pie she found in a safe hanging from a tree. Yellow pastry, gravy, meat. On the third night she ate only a handful of leaves so that her mouth ran with a green cud. The nor'-wester blew down the valley, burning the grass to brown crackle and a butter-moon laid across the sky. The river was loud with the sound of stones being dragged to sea. She came to a hall, brightly lit within its ring of cars, and climbed the smooth shoulder of the hill behind. Scraps of music, thump of dancing, laughter, the rattle of sheep running off into tussock and matagouri. Louie stood alone on the crest looking out over the valley. The power lines looped from hill to hill and Louie reached out to swing down and away with them. Like in the movies. Like Tarzan.

She dazzled in a moment and rose splendid into the night sky.

THE YOUNG FARMERS' CLUB EXPERIENCES A BLACKOUT

In the valley the Young Farmers' Club summer dance is interrupted by a blackout halfway through the Military Two. Couples stand arm in arm in the dark while Mort Coker tries the switches and the fuse box in the kitchen. Someone has a look outside and shouts that the whole place is black, it must be bird strike or a line down up the valley. In the darkness body blunders against body, giggling. Then Ethne Moran finds a torch and the beam of it squiggles over faces caught wide-eyed like rabbits on a road. Someone brings in a Tilley lamp. The band attempts a few bars, deee dum dee dum who'syerladyfren, but stops because no one seems to be interested. They stand about instead talking, and a few couples are edging away to the dimly lit corners.

Then Ethne, who has organised the supper, claps her hands and jumps up onto the stage. 'Come on,' she says, lit by the Tilley lamp and holding in her outstretched hands a strawberry cream sponge. 'No point in letting good food go to waste! Give us a hand, Margie.'

Margie Pringle brings out the sausage rolls and finds her a bread knife and Ethne kneels by the lamp to cut the cake into triangles, cream spurting beneath the blade. Side on her white dress is transparent and Ross Meikle watching thinks she's a cracker. Big breasts, curving stomach, long in the leg, and good teeth nice and even, with that little gap at the front.

Ethne looks up. She hands him a piece of cake, then leans towards him and bites his ear lobe very gently leaving her broken imprint in soft flesh. 'You do something to me,' she sings in a buzzing whisper, 'that electrifies me.'

So they go outside into the warm night where it turns out that she isn't that struck on Bevan Waters after all, that she'd fancied Ross all along. On the back seat of the Chev she proves moreover to be astonishingly inventive, so that together they execute with ease a whole series of manoeuvres which Ross had previously discounted as possibly risky, definitely foreign and perilously close to deviance. Ross thinks as a result that it might be worth dropping Margie Pringle who was getting on his nerves anyway with her lisping sweetness and that he'd be better off with Ethne who was bossy, God knows, but had a few clues.

Meanwhile, within the hall, Warren Baty is confessing that it was his ram that had got through the fence and in amongst the Coopers' stud Romney flock last winter, and Jim Cooper, a whole season lost, is saying, never mind, no lasting harm done. And Alasdair McLeod is telling the Paterson brothers that it was him who nicked their chainsaw; he'd come over one afternoon when they were out and borrowed it and he'd meant to give it back but they'd made such a fuss calling in the police and all that he hadn't felt he could face it and he'd be round next day just to get the bloody thing off his conscience. Miria Love is telling Joan Shaw that she doesn't like the way she conducts Women's Division meetings and Pie Fowler is telling anyone who'll listen that she can't stick the valley, they're a bunch of snobs who've never let her forget for one minute that she's a townie and she'll be off back to the city just as soon as she can settle things with Bill.

Around the walls hang the valley teams since 1919, lined up for the photographer, thighs spread, fists clenched, unamused by the extraordinary goings-on in the darkened hall: under the influence of the night, sausage roll in one hand, beer in the other, the young farmers appear to be have been overwhelmed by truth. The room is buzzing with honesty and for some the accompaniment is love and forgiveness, for others bitter recrimination. There seems to have been a sudden rise in the temperature. 'Remember the morning after,' the valley teams counsel, stonily. 'In the morning will come the accounting.'

AND AFTER THE THIRD NIGHT

A Power Board man went up to check the lines next day. They found nothing out of place and the power came back on, of its own accord, at dawn. There was a pair of footprints burned deep in a rock by the pylon; about a size five, they reckoned. That was all.

That's the story of how Skinny Louie, daughter of Lilleas Symonds popularly known as Shanghai Lill, gave birth, and walked up the valley and vanished in splendour.

MEANWHILE

Back by the floral arch at the Botanical Gardens, Peg gripped Louie's baby
with the absolute certainty that this was the answer to prayer. In one neat
move, the grubby bundle solved a problem. Not that Peg would have
expressed it this way: she would have said you had to take the rough with
the smooth, you made your bed and you lay on it, no use crying over split
milk. So if you found yourself lying night after night beside a man under the
bleak pall of his despair, if you had borne one live child to him and now
seemed unlikely ever to conceive another, that was your lot in life. You pulled
up the chenille quilt in the morning, smoothed and straightened, set the
crinoline doll dead centre and got on with your existence.

It was not ideal. It was not good, for example, that Maura was being
raised an only child. Children needed to learn how to share and how to
adapt to others and that was difficult without brothers and sisters, and Peg
could quote in evidence her cousin Joycie, only daughter of her mother's
oldest sister. Tentatively, at the end of each summer, Auntie Alice used to
leave the city to venture along the precipitous zigzag terrors of the coast
road to the farm, her kid gloves stiff with sweat at the wheel of the Oakland,
her heart positively palpitating at the imprudence of the other traffic, the
hairpin bends, the slips and the straying cattle, and all so Joycie could build
up her strength for the winter ahead with farm-fresh eggs and farm-fresh
milk and farm-fresh air for her chest. At their first encounter Peg and Cath
and Jack had decided that their cousin was a sook, a townie and a sook.
They suspected it when she wouldn't take the short cut down the Castle
Perilous to the swimming beach, preferring to walk the long way round,
and when she fell off Trixie when they were jousting on the flat, and when
she refused to stroke Mordred, who was the best by far of Jack's ferrets
with a score of a hundred and twenty but so gentle Jack would carry him
tucked in his coat sleeve to church, and she confirmed it beyond all doubt
when she dropped the gaff when they had the biggest eel they'd ever caught,
four foot long and as thick as your leg, hooked and wriggling and almost
up on the bank, so that it twisted and thrashed and slid like spilt oil back
into the dark recesses beneath the bridge. They had ignored Joycie from
then on, abandoning her as soon as they were out of sight of the house so
that she whimpered and trailed and went back eventually to breathe in the
nice fresh air from the safety of the verandah and wait for her nice fresh
milk with the house cats.

Peg didn't want Maura to grow up like Joycie, fretful and self-absorbed.
And she tried, she really tried, to provide the necessary family. At night in
bed, Martin's leg might brush hers, her arm might fling in sleep across his
shoulder. Once that would have been enough and they would have reached
for one another, certain of the other's pleasure. But now the blackness had
them by the throat. Martin lay cold beneath her tentative hand or worse he

slipped from her in silence and went out to the verandah where he sat, muttering quietly to some invisible adversary and smoking till he thought she would have fallen asleep. Sometimes then he returned and lay far away on the opposite side of the desert that was their bed, but as often he slept instead on the verandah couch where he could lie wrapped in a rough grey army blanket looking out into the deep black pit of the night sky.

Peg tried to understand. (You didn't know what these returned men had gone through. You had to be patient.) But it was hard. She made a novena to Our Lady of Perpetual Succour. She prayed to St Jude. She did the First Nine Fridays. And when none of this worked, she lay in the dark pretending to sleep, breathing in two three out two three and making a private bargain with God. 'A baby. Please. Somehow. And I'll believe in you absolutely, without doubt, forever.' Fearing that this might be presumption. You could not bargain with God. Bargaining in fact invited divine displeasure and God was quite capable of thwarting her in some unexpected way, just to teach her a lesson. She took the risk and bargained nevertheless. A baby. Please.

So when Maura walked towards them down the white gravel path out of the dazzle of heat and excitement and anxiety and brought them a baby, Peg reached out for her recognising a miracle.

JOHN CAMPBELL IGNORES THE RULES

Dr Campbell conducted the usual tests, bending tapping and stretching the baby's arms and legs. 'She seems healthy enough to me,' he said. 'A bonny wee thing.' And he said he'd be in touch with the police and the hospital, see if they could track down the mother; it wasn't possible, not in a town like this, for a girl to come to full term and nobody notice. There had been one case, during the war: that lass at Hargoods department store, pregnant to a GI, who gave birth one night in the manchester section after the rest of the staff had gone home. She'd taken them by surprise, all right. But in his experience that was exceptional. They'd find the girl and in the meantime, he'd take the baby up to the annex.

Peg said, couldn't they take care of it (she didn't dare risk the intimacy of 'her') overnight at least? They felt responsible, you understand? And they'd be short-staffed up at Maternity because of the public holiday and she'd had plenty of experience of neonates after all, and Campbell looked at her hard and said, 'Now don't you go getting attached to her, Peg.'

Campbell believed in rules and methods and the proper channels, not because he was narrowly bureaucratic but because these things were in place to impede impulse; like weirs in a river, they slowed the rush and allowed time for deliberation and a rational assessment of the situation; take away those structures and what were you left with? Anarchy. That was what they had discovered in Russia in 1917, Germany in '32, and Spain in '36. They had not exercised proper caution, they had abandoned steady principle and opened the floodgates to chaos. And here was Peg Conlan, whom he knew to be normally sensible, asking him to behave irregularly.

'It's not usual practice,' he said, but Peg objected: how often did such things happen? How could anyone say what was the 'usual practice'? Martin said nothing, sat on a hard-backed chair turning his hat over and over in his hands with Maura at his knee, watching.

Campbell looked at the baby, who was grubby, with that monkey new-born wrinkled face, and the baby opened her eyes and stared back. It was not possible of course. A baby only a few hours old has a bright unfocused gaze, but this baby looked at him straight and for the first time in years Campbell found himself remembering Janet, who had also looked at him straight one night after ward round and said, 'You have one choice, John. Leave her and marry me. I'll not be any man's sparrow to be tugged in on a thread when he feels the need and let go when he's done.' And he'd made the proper choice, walked into the rain up Lauriston Place and kept true to church vows though he'd dreamed of Janet for years even after he'd cut the affair clean away and placed thousands of miles between them.

'There are times,' he thought suddenly, as the baby flung her arms wide in a perfect Moro reflex, 'for letting go and throwing rules aside.' Peg could take the baby home. She was dependable after all when she was up at Men's Surgical, was not one to flap in theatre or make a silly fuss. She'd cope. Besides, she had it right about the annex: he knew for a fact they were stretched to the limit, ten in since Sunday including the Sidey twins. He handed the baby over. Peg took her, feeling the warm weight settle into the curve of her arm.

No one could discover anything of the child's mother. There were a couple of possibilities: a girl glimpsed hitch-hiking on the north road, another declared missing some weeks later from down Dunedin way, though her mother told the Welfare when they enquired that her daughter often went walkabout and she'd turn up again when she was good and ready.

So the Conlans kept the baby. They called her Mary for Marty's mother and May for Peg's, but Maura had said as they walked home from Dr Campbell's that first night that her name was Celestia, Tia for short. Peg and Martin laughed. Celestia was the name of the talking donkey who lived with Harriet the Hippo and Gerald Giraffe in Mr Whuzzle's Zoo ('Mr Whuzzle sighed. Whatever would the jolly chums do next?')

'You can't name a baby after someone in a comic,' Peg said, but Maura was insistent.

'It's not from a comic. She told me herself. It's her proper name. Celestia.' They let her have her way then because her bottom lip pouted and there'd been enough excitement for one day.

THE VINE

They are written on the branching vine in the Forbes's heavy leather Bible:

Margaret Maud b. 1918 m. CONLAN, Martin Francis b. 1918

And on a leafy twig extending from their conjoined names perch:
Maura Frances b. 1949
Michael Charles b. Sep 1950, d. Nov 1950
and
Mary May b. 1954 (adopted)
They are a family.

Fiona Farrell Poole

Cemetery, Oamaru

April.
Leaves crack and shatter.
Periwinkle binds
a snare for living feet.

————

Angels.
We used to call them fairies.
Chalk white.
Up from the slab
in one night.

————

Under new management
all personal effects
are packaged by the staff.
The corners neat
tucked under for the trip.
Cards lashed to the brim:
'Return to Sender'.

————

It's a family business.
'Those early ones
were laid in pine.
Draped in swansdown.

Embroidered with pansies,'
the undertaker tells me.
'And over there
by the macrocarpa
they fell on stones.
They're still whole.'

But the fruitflies know better
They hang about.

————

Did the trump sound?
And were we too busy in the
garden to hear?
Earth cracks
and in the crevices
hands tear at wrappings.
The party's over.

————

Save the paper.
Keep the string.
The cards in the top drawer.

————

We built huts in the long grass.
We had a fort in the macrocarpa.
This is where Graham fell off his bike.
And this is where we tickled Neil's penis
till it stood up,
pink as a birthday candle.
Hawthorn and brown grass and
pale flowers in glass
centrepiece to the feast.
Then we burst the bubble
and we crawled through the iron gate
onto the slab.

Warm as flies.

Bernadette Hall

Miriama

i. On crossing the border, I always
change my name. A simple precaution
& you to guard my back.
                              Maheno, Monte
Cristo, Waianakarua, Mt Misery & all
the wild flowers.
                              I am heavy with loot
& disappointment, heading south again down
the soft underbelly of the island, shedding
skins like Coke cans on the Kilmog
& already the rain.

ii. You are waiting, with or without
my blessing, in a blue room of pictures
torn from magazines:
                              Mother Teresa, Athena's
sandalled Victory, a sequoia forest, an avocado
pear, gazelles, two babies in a bath with a chimp,
Ayer's Rock by sunset, Hare Krishnas in their
old gold, mud pools, a street kid.
                              You have
a bruise on your cheek.

iii. 'Sit down & I'll tell you a story.

At Moeraki in the old days lived a prophet,
Kiri Mahi Nahina, who taught all the people that
Tiki had made them, not Io.
                         Te Wera, the warrior,
struck him down with his taiaha. Plugged his eyes,
ears, nose, mouth, anus with moss to contain
the heresy. Then he & his warriors ate him.'

iv. Nothing is high, nothing is low, nothing
is hidden.
                    This is the song, Miriama, you sing,
doublestopping on my heartstrings.

Keri Hulme

Slipping Away from the Gaze of the Past

From *Homeplaces: Three Coasts of the South Island of New Zealand*

Moeraki, *is* —
Moeraki means, Place to Sleep (or Dream) by Day.
Moeraki was a complex of kaika and pa, and Moeraki is a fishing port.
Moeraki is beaches and reefs, islands and volcanic dykes.
Moeraki is a motley collection of permanent homes and holiday baches (or cribs, as Southern idiom has it), and Moeraki is an unmanned lighthouse, and manicured rolling-hill farms.
Moeraki is its sealife, and all its ghosts at night (indeed, it is the only place I know of where you can meet ghosts by day).
Above all, Moeraki is people, from the remains in the ancient habitations and urupa and middens, to the lively family cribs.

> *Seaweed floats in a brown tangled rack, a*
> *tack out from the rocks.*
> *It falls and rises, breathing with the water.*
>
> *On the beach, the apricot and gold gravel*
> *turns rusty-orange at wave-edge.*
> *There is a long streak of iron-dark sand*
> *where Matuatiki runs out to sea.*
> *There are shattered black rocks round all*
> *the arc of bay.*
>
> *The cliffs are made of claystone, greenish*
> *and ochre, with odd intrusions of pink*
> *melted rocks. The thornbushes along the tops*
> *slant away from the sea. They are shaved*
> *trimmed and wounded by the wind.*

At each end of the kaik' bay the cliff goes
down in humps to stand blunt-nosed
against the sea. But the rocks creep
further out, become jetty arms, reefs enclosing.
They are full of secret pools —
the unblinking eyes of octopi
at night.

Today, a cloud of midges weaves and
dances through the evening sun.
There are mysterious glassy tracks
on the sea.
Thin waves hush in, pause: slide away.
Moeraki, calm as untroubled sleep

(from *Pa Mai Tou Reo Aroha*)

I have, one way or another, been here all my life. I am not often here, in the physical sense of occupying Moeraki-space and Moeraki-time, but I never leave it. It sometimes seems that I am swept by two tides, one the here & now which is the inexorable, bringing me to death, and the other a wave burgeoning forever out of the past, bearing me aloft and away from any future shore. Fish, water-traveller, that's me, bemused by what-ifs and why-was-that-so? and never sure of anything . . . o, but also the eminently practical, pragmatic Pig, islander and coastdweller, firmly rooted in earth.

An August evening, late winter, and I've come over the hill to here, to pick kareko. The fronds are at their longest now.

For quite a while, my uncle Bill lived at the kaik' beach, and any arrival was welcomed by him. Then, the cribs were warmed and ready for us, and we didn't so much settle in as shrug off one way of life and speed into another, more vivid more real than everyday. Now that Bill has retired back to the family home in Oamaru, there is cold welcome: it is a matter of unlocking doors and windows, and sweeping out dead mice and flies, and setting fires, warming the places to life again. The cribs are right on the shore, and spring tides lap over the fences, or wash up the boat-ramps inside. At first, they are always damp.

I do the unlocking and sweeping and lighting part as quickly as possible, and then go for a wander round the beaches.

Tena koe, e te wahi humarire, e te wahi miharo, tena koe. It's been quite a while eh? I haven't seen you since March, and I've changed a lot since then.

I can always be seduced by a tideline, any beach in the world, but Moeraki tidelines are magical. It's partly because we know them so well, and can recognise and name every kind of shell and seaweed and wrecked bird or crab or piece of debris, but it's also because they are ever full of surprises. We never quite know what will be there, one tide to the next. Over the years, we have found broken adzes, whole pendants, and a snakeskin cowrie (did someone drop that?); a skull; dead seals, and live sealions; two bottles with unreadable messages inside, and a half-full bottle of rum; part of a weather balloon, and fragments of a boat; prints from someone who walked by early in skindiver's flippers, and the marks of two energetic bodies and a neat pile of *seventeen* condoms — now come on, mates, what the hell were you doing? Skiting? Even if you were making balloons of them, you were pretty busy . . .

The tidelines stretch on, beach after beach.

Lying in a bunk in Elderslee, the oldest of the three cribs the family owns at the kaik' beach. The range fire is still going strong, and the room is full of flicker-light. Our bunks are not high, and they give a feeling of comfortable security — your own special womb-room, connected with the living space but apart from it. I imagine that a cupboard bed in an Orkney croft would be similar.

The kettles are singing over the fire: a gull keens out on the northern reef. There's a southerly blow building outside. Before I fall asleep, there is a little wittering of hail on the roof, a here & gone gust. Tomorrow will be a bleak and cold Otago day.

I'm born and bred a southerner.

My father, who died when I was eleven, came of Lancashire stock, people who migrated to Aotearoa in 1912. My mother's side of the family is a different mix entirely. Kai Tahu, and Orkney Islanders, among others, and one branch of the family accustomed to the cold island for over 27 generations.

> '... *Tu-whakarawa*
> *tana ko Te Rare*
> *tana ko Mahola*
> *tana ko Motoitoi*
> *tana ko Maria Stevens ...*'

Maria, partly brought up in a cave out of Purakaunui, partly educated in Dunedin through Pakeha kindness and largesse; married at 17 to an English sailor; widowed at 18 after giving birth to Emma Lillian, my great-grandmother (Maria is better know as Marìa, or Maraea, Mouat, matriarch of a great clan).

When I look over that whakapapa, I know why I can stand waist-deep in a winter sea, and not get chilled to the bone: I know why I can keep on picking this seaweed and not get numb hands. It's not just the fat cover, nei? and it's not only the anticipation of eating the sea herb.

Kareko (also known, in the north, as parengo) is a kind of laver. Called *nori*, in Japan, and *Porphyra columbina* by the botanists, it is a tough, filmy, redbrown plant, growing just below the hightide mark on rocks. When it dries out, as it does most tides, it looks like black varnish. In summer you have to search to find it: in winter, the thallus grows to over a foot in length, and the rocks are suppled, made alive by the beautiful thickness of its fronds. It is common, plentiful — and will remain so, provided people gather it with care. You take the thallus, not the holdfast.

When it has been washed, and dried, preferably by the sun, you can store it for over a year. You may cook it like laver bread (steam it until it is soft, then roll in oatmeal and fry in bacon fat), or add it to chowders, soups, and stews. Some people like to steam it for an hour, add butter and pepper, and eat it like cabbage. In the old days, it was cooked in a hangi. It is especially delicious tao'd with shellfish, and I have pressed it into sheets (after cooking it), and used it to make sushi.

You *can* chew it just as you gather it, straight off the rocks, but it is plasticky in the mouth and tasteless aside from the salt. A prepared jarful promises future feasts, and persons sick with longing for the sea need only sniff it to be restored . . .

There are other seaweeds I collect at Moeraki: *Codium fragile*, which doesn't seem to have a Maori name except for the generic 'rimu', makes a good tea when it's dried and ground. Neptune's necklace (again, just 'rimu') is tangy when you nibble it, and so are the young sweet tips of rimuroa (bladderweed). And then there's rimurapa, bullkelp, *Durvillea antarctica*, a huge, magnificent plant that makes undersea forests round most of the southern coasts. Rimurapa is probably best known, among Maori, for its use in making poha-rimu, the big kelpbags that helped store muttonbirds between seasons.

The two reefs that enclose and shelter the kaik' bay are festooned with rimurapa. As a child I found that seaweed uncanny, sinister. I saw it as a malign plant, full of giant tentacular blades ready to slither round and haul me under if I swam amongst them. Now I find it captivating, cool and smooth against the skin if you swim with it: an enchanting swirl and curve and flow if you watch it. Which I do, for hours.

The rimurapa has caught me, after all.

They say that the hole in the sea off Rerenga-wairua is fringed with kelp.

As children, we made skiddy slippers from the rimurapa fronds, and balls, that bounced, from its stipes. There are six of us today, four female and two male, and I am the oldest. We were more than a handful for my mother to bring up (for she was widowed at 31, when her youngest baby was a year old), but she didn't just cope: she enabled us to flourish, each in our own, very different, ways. Some people are appalling failures as parents, and some never get the experience, and some, like my mother Mary, are extremely good at that most-important job.

I have a theory that far fewer humans are equipped physically (look at the infertility rate), or mentally (look at battered or warped children) to rear offspring than we think. O yeah, it's very easy to start the whole process off, and more than 90 per cent of humanity gets involved with it, but the results are not encouraging. (Do you really think, taken as a whole, we are a marvellous species?)

And yet, for all that most of us would agree with the whakatauki,

> 'E ki ana koe ki a ahau, He aha te mea nui?
> E ki ana ahau ki a koe, He takata, he takata, he takata!'
> [You say to me, What is the most important thing?
> I say to you, People, it is people, people!]

do we organise our societies round the fact? Because the proverb does not say, One kind of people is best, or We, the immediate generation, are the most important. It is all-embracing, all-inclusive, and thinking about *that* can stretch your mind.

For instance, the one homeplace we all share, all people of the past, us now, and maybe all the people of the future, is Earth.

(There is a dimension to the whakatauki I've just quoted that has intrigued me since I learned the words.

You, a human being, are asking me, a human being, what is the most important thing . . . a sandhopper, if stuck with the same question, would presumably twitch antennae/writhe body-armour/emit a stench-response, Te mea nui? He poti, he poti, he poti! Of *course*. How dumb for even asking.)

A beach is promising territory for children to grow up in. There is outside room, a freedom of space, and a sufficiency of change. If you have normal skills, it is a good place to begin to learn life. You learn it from the essential fecundity, and adaptability, of sea interacting with land. You learn it from the omnipresent fact of death — bubu eats seaweed, gull eats bubu, cat gets gull. The crabs and the poti pick the bones. And, if it is a beach like the kaik' beach, you learn life from the past. It can be, in the most real and physical sense, in front of you.

For instance, you early get to know there are layers — strata of names and events that affect one another, interweavings of people from all round the planet. Nobody can give more than the proximate date for the arrival of the first humans here, but you can bet your bottom dollar they were Polynesian. They didn't call themselves 'Maori', but 'the gathering, or company of so-and-so', or 'the family of so-and-so', Te Kahui te mea-te mea, Kati Te mea-te mea. The names of some of the earliest explorers and settlers are lost in that past glowing in front of us, but Kati Mamoe (the descendants of Hotu Mamoe) retain memories that reach over 500 years. And I have inherited from my people, the family of Tahupotiki who battled with Kati Mamoe, certainly, but who also interwed with them, I have inherited knowledge not only of *who* journeyed here, and who lived here, and how they lived and loved and hated, but also what they called the hills and reefs and beaches round.

Layers . . . round at the southern end of Tutakahikura beach (two bays south from the kaik'), is a headland now known as 'Te-upoko-a-Matiaha' (Mathias' Head), Matiaha being the famous Matiaha Tiramorehu, who led his people to Moeraki from Kaiapoi, and who is commemorated in the first stained-glass window depicting a Maori (in the little church Kotahitanga at Moeraki Port). When Maori-English was going strong, the point was called, 'Te *Heti* a Matiahi', but before that it was 'Te-upoko-a-Paitu', Paitu being an earlier chief. And doubtless, Waitaha and Te Kahui a Rapuwai, being earlier settlers still, had other names for it.

All this fuss over one, not large, headland? Well, it *is* at the end of a dramatic beach (of which, much more, later), and behind it *is* an ancient graveyard, Uhimataitai, but the fact is that *every* headland, and rock, and islet, and hill, was named, and sometimes named many times. On the other hand, there were names that stuck, right from the beginning.

Head north, round the beaches: past the rocks of the reef Te Karipi, where I pick most of my kareko; past the island Maukiekie, and the group known as Paeko; past the bluff at Punatoetoe, and on to Onekakara the odiferous beach (and since whales were once tried out there, you can imagine 'odiferous' as a bit of an understatement). Go on, still heading north, round by Millers Bay, which was once called Karere-kautuku and which sometimes has amazing drifts and heaps of live tuatua on it. The first you know that the sea has made a gift of these succulent shellfish is the screaming of gulls. There is never enough food to stop gulls from squabbling over it . . . past Millers Bay, and by now you have left behind the unique gold & ochre gravel, and are travelling over dark rocks and a strange pallid sand that is streaked with something like oil. It is a broad beach you are on, with a correspondingly wide sweep of bay.

The great canoe *Te Araiteuru* had made the voyage from the central Pacific without coming to grief. She had stopped at Turanga, where kumara were planted (and that planting place is to this day called Araiteuru), and journeyed south to Kaikoura, where more kumara were established. Then, still with a substantial cargo aboard — kumara, and gourds, taro and foodbaskets — she came sweeping downwind to the Otakou coast.

What happened then is uncertain: there is an old waiata, song-poem, that says she broached, and was overwhelmed by three gigantic waves — Otewao, Otoko, and Okaka were *their* names — having earlier had the misfortune to lose her bailer. (I have been told by other elders that this waiata applies to a much later, but equally sacred and renowned vessel, the ancestral waka

Takitimu.) Whatever, after that long and useful journey, she wrecked, and is commemorated by the reef called after her.

And she is remembered by something else: here, on the beach with pallid sand, is her cargo.

Mention the name 'Moeraki' to most New Zealanders, and you will be rewarded with a blank stare, or a bright smile and, 'O yes! That's where the boulders are!'

Well, not quite.

But the boulders deserve their reputation. There is nothing quite like them almost anywhere else in the world. The largest is well over six feet in diameter, a septarian concretion with yellow calcite crystals at its core. There are dozens of them (there used to be hundreds, but all of the accessible smaller ones have been souvenired), round and weird, and looming on the bare curving beach.

You think six-feet plus is a bit big for a food basket or a gourd?

Araiteuru was not your average waka: her crew was distinctly strange — many of them turned into hills and rocks in the near vicinity, for example — and so why should her cargo be of an inferior nature? As I grew, I may have begun to doubt the literal truth of the story of *Araiteuru*, but do I remember which canoe brought the kumara, and who came with it?

Forever.

As children, we went mainly to the boulders for mussels, or to play in the sinking sand round their bases. That was a thrill: the pale sand seemed to have no bottom and sucked you in, to your thighs, with surprising ease and swiftness. None of us were ever game to let go and see how deep you could sink. We held grimly onto a crack or a ledge of the boulder (they may take up to four million years to form, but they erode quickly: I have watched two vanish in my forty-odd years) and sort of enjoyed the sensation. A lot of screaming went on.

The mussels, those stubby fat blueblack southern kutae, have eroded away entirely over the years, from the scouring of the sand, and the overpicking by humans.

Things change: things erode: things go.

The shoreward rocks of Tikoraki, the reef that protects the south end of the kaik' bay, are being cracked and hammered apart.

'Shoulda put concrete on them years ago, when we had the chance,' grumbles my uncle Bill Miller. He means, he should have done it when he was younger and had the strength. He knows I won't do it: I'm a believer in the dance of change. The sea gives, and the sea takes away, and if it breaks up Tikoraki and devastates the cribs, even the beloved Black Bach that I look after — and it is most likely to take that crib first, because it is southernmost on the beach — well, so be it.

I know this place as well as I know my own body, and better than I know my own mind. It is where I've done most of my growing up. It is where I'd prefer to be buried, here among ancestral bones. I love it better than any place on Earth. It is my turangawaewae-ngakau, the standing-place of my heart, and I expect, and receive, strength and energy and love from it.

But I never expect it to stay exactly the same. None of my homeplaces do that.

> *That old grey rogue the sealman*
> *has come ashore at last*
> *hollow-flanked and flippers folded*
> *over the curl of his breast*
> *he can still yawn, pink gape and yellowed, warning, teeth —*
> *and rub hinder webs slowly together*
> *as though he really waits upon*
> *the benefice of sun*

There was never a large number of people settled here, although the graveyards —urupa, wahi-tapu — are numerous. As well as Uhimataitai, round on that southern beach, the ones I know best are Tawhiroko, which is on a low, bare rolling hill, hard by the sea, and Kihipuku, just over the back fence of Elderslee. I joke that I grew up with ghosts for neighbours, but it is true in more ways than one. You become — not casual, but at *ease* early on with the idea that humans die, if there is a cemetery next door and the bones turn up on the beaches. (It is the general idea you are at ease with, not specific instances: why is it so hard to imagine your own skull?) And, through that easiness with death-as-established-fact, you accept, from childhood on, the much less evidentially based idea that humans die and ghosts live on. Particularly when you live in an area that is full of — o dear, it sounds woolly-minded and pretentiously mystical to say 'presences', but that is what they are.

I am not a person who sees kehua, and I look first for cracks if there is an uncanny waft of cold air in a closed warm room, and I am more surprised at the noise, than anything else, when one of the Moeraki-based animals sets up an unusual clamour at seeming-nothing — I pragmatically suspect the presence of a small disturbing insect rather than a ghost — but there have been enough odd things happening over the years, and sufficient instances of my being aware of a — presence — for my joke about neighbourly ghosts to have a cloudy and uneasy side to it.

So I didn't do much more than mutter myself, when a friend complained mildly about the person who had sat hunched up by the range fire muttering, most of the night. (I didn't see or hear anyone, the door was closed and only openable from our side, and, no, that friend doesn't drink or smoke at all.) And when the small child of another friend said Those people must be cold eh because they just got sacks on, nobody bridled with disbelief and reprimanded her for lying. True we all went out the half-open door to find nobody there, no sign of, say, the beach variety of street people, no nothing, not even footprints on the tide-washed sand. But she's an unimaginative kind of child, and how could she know that the coarser kinds of kakahu looked very like sacks. And, especially, how could she know it wasn't unusual for the people i nga wa o mua to decorate their faces, as she described, with rectilinear patterns of red dots? And tattoo with *straight* blue lines?

There were two reasons why there was never a large settled population at Moeraki, despite the wealth of food its shores and seas offered.

Penguin chicks, seals, kahawai, red cod blue cod rock cod and ling, and that southern favourite, barracouta (because it can be extremely plentiful, and it dries very well in the sun for winter storage); all of these could be readily taken, and were available season after season. Elsewhere, they would have ensured permanent and growing settlement.

What is essential, and what is lacking, is water.

Matua-tiki, the little stream that carves braids on the kaik' sands, is brackwater. There is one tiny potable creeklet to the north, and the lagoon waters of Waimataitai (which can be translated as 'brackish waters'). There is no good water supply on the Moeraki peninsula. So the kaika sites, and the two main pa, were intermittently occupied over many centuries, and precariously supplied with rainwater kept in gourds, and the like.

Water is still a problem at our beach: you don't wash your hands under a running tap, for instance, and cleaning teeth is an art taught to you before you have too many. My uncle Bill's rainwater catchment system, an amazing slither and splice and tangle of plumbing, is almost the heart of the cribs.

The other reason there was never a large population at Moeraki was, there was never a very large number of Maori in the South Island. Te Waka a Maui, Te Wahi Pounamu . . . the largest landmass the Polynesians ever settled and, comparatively, so few of them to do it.

The estimations of their numbers vary, but it was probably never higher than 6000, and not more than a tenth of that number lived in Otakou at any one time. The earliest settlers were moa-hunters, Te Kahui a Rapuwai and Waitaha (some of their campsites at Waimataitai Lagoon and Shag Point/Matakaea, a little south of Moeraki, have been excavated, and show habitation for the last 12 or so centuries). Small waves of migrants from the north followed, Kati Mamoe, and my own tribe Kai Tahu in the seventeenth century, but the people never bred with the rat-like enthusiasm and efficiency of later generations. And disease kept the populations small — pneumonia and jaw abscesses, arthritis, and stomach cancer (from reliance on that staple bracken-fern root) afflicted a people uniformly described by the earliest European visitors as vigorous and handsome, muscular and tall. (My brother Andrew buried and reburied a small skull he found on Te Karipi's beach so often that eventually it, and bones associated with it, were taken and laid to rest in an inland urupa. The archaeologist who examined the bones said the skull was that of a five to six-year-old child, and the thighbones from an individual who would have stood over six feet nine inches when alive.)

Skeletal evidence also reveals that the old people had hard, short lives, spines and joints and sockets eroded by prolonged digging and paddling, and the average age at death, the late twenties . . .

My mother Mary and uncle Bill have come for the weekend, so I've shifted out of Elderslee and along to the Black Bach. It's the crib I'm kaitiaki for, guardian of & caretaker to: Bill and his mate Tui McNeil built it over 40 years ago, before I was born. They coated the walls with tar then, to prevent rot and protect it against the sea, and it has stayed tar-coated ever since. The walls are not quite the same ones Bill and Tui erected. In 1975, there was a king tide, that dangerous combination of extraordinarily high spring-tide and onshore wind. Waves were breaking over the roof of the black crib before the tide's end, smashing in the doors and filling the living-room and the boatshed with sand. Other cribs fared worse: two were wrecked entirely, and have never been rebuilt. Bill remade the doors, and reskinned the walls, up to four thicknesses of plywood and corrugated iron, after we had spent a merry week digging all three cribs out. I understand there is another king tide due at the end of this year. This time, it will be my turn to lie on my belly on the cliff above the Black Bach and wonder how anything humanly built can survive the power of the sea.

Meantime, I've lit the musterer's stove (a little cast-iron affair a foot by eighteen inches by a foot deep), and got rid of the latest crop of dead things. The tide is coming in, and it's getting dark. On the horizon beyond Tikoraki, a hunter's moon is rising, hugely inflated looking, smokey-orange in colour. I'll get the lamps going soon, and do some reading, then go to bed with the doors wide open and fall asleep listening to the soft swash of quiet waves curling up the boat-ramp and over the doorstep.

It's nearly the end of August, and time to be going home. Slim and Rose Dalton up the hill will keep an eye on this crib until they see I've taken the window shutter down, and have my windfish flying on a bamboo pole outside, to show I'm home here, again.

Rob Allan

from Karitane Postcards

9.

All I know is the world   Karitane
in clear sunlight   the illusion and sensuality
there's drought and refreshment
as the rain begins
apples ripen and the fire leaps in flame.
The poplars in my neighbour's garden
dance through space.
Over at Matanaka   Johnny Jones
prepares for the good city
black passion fruit vines flowering through gum trees
stables open and a smell of hay and wheat
a richness intrudes and passes
maybe the dream of getting here   changing dispossessions
freemen of so many ideas and divided like this.

10.

Part of the song on the edge of singing
where one note stops
that's not silence but part of the song
the waves surrounding Huriawa
all the ways   out to sea and inland
a clear view up the Pigroot
Silver Peaks   and the familiar smells
of sea and land and inlet
the sound the body makes pushing through old pathways
movement and breath want to sing
going further into landscape
till the feelings belong
living the life given   the pleasure of plants growing
the daily service to others
what children bring to family and tribe
more proof of . . . I forget what it was
— part of the song   antithesis of each desire
the centre not final   no time past or coming
and the power here-in resides   in places newly spoken.

Iain Lonie

A Summer at Purakanui

Something in us too is ground
down all the time that can never
be made up again: look at these coarse
grains separate in the hand
that were held together in the kinship
of rock that lasts for ages —

                look at the blackened
sticks of kelp and the bleached
broom twigs and the dirtied
wing of the gull
half covered in grey sand
and fluttered by the wind —

listen to the wind whisper
listen to the sea —
you'll hear a kind of cosmic breathing
in and out
then in and out again.
It too could dry up
and there be nothing: hard
for us to understand
who find this all too easy

the grinding of rock to sand
our walking away and saying nothing.

David Eggleton

Postcard

Opening a refrigerator,
you find Port Chalmers.
Now and then a little light comes on.
Two bottles of milk are white breasts
in the fists of a milkman.
In the dairy
a member of the counter-culture grinds the Turkish blend.
A fly reads the fine print on a fishtail.
Rain is a sad lover,
chucking cheap beads onto the cemetery grass.
Sparrows disco dance in the trees above.
The wind vacuums the flash Wool Board carpet of the sea.
Later, the sunlight tenderly bandages a wounded look.

Graham Billing

[Sunday Krill]
from *The Chambered Nautilus*

Windseer had been about to begin eating his dinner when the boats were in the narrows. He thought he heard a strange, distant sound and then saw Maori men, some with muskets, some wearing only flax belts and aprons, and Maori women wearing blankets or cast-off European shirts and underdrawers, occasionally a ragged petticoat, running past his windows. He saw a few white men walking, not hurrying, some quite unsteadily, down the rocky path and since he could look down on much of the village he could see people from all directions moving towards Wedgewood's Rock. The muskets and war dress alarmed him. He was tired, having already that day preached in English and then in Maori and in the afternoon taken Bible class. The roast pork which his Maori cook Ruihi — Lucy — had at last learned to cook properly in a camp oven over the enormous kitchen fire, was turned out. At the table, a single slice from a giant cedar log, gnarled with a giant and many smaller spirals and polished with the wax of a small native bee that had been green fur and golden brown hair, Eleanor Windseer waited to carve the pork again, at last. She had been unable to carve in the way that a wife should for a gentleman since 21 June, mid-winter's day when her seventh child — the sixth living at the moment of its birth — had been born and on the same day died. Mrs Windseer had been suffering from *tic douloureux* before the birth, an affliction of painful spasms in her facial and other muscles accompanied by bouts of severe melancholy. They had continued after the second child was taken from her. She knew that her hands still shook too much to carve but Windseer's major form of communication with her at Wedgewood Rock was through exhortation, which she supposed he gave her mainly to support himself in his so-far totally thankless mission. Turnips boiled with their greens and roasted potatoes steamed together in their dishes. Her five living children sat around the table, silent, hands in laps, as intent upon their private guessing games on whether there would be gravy this Sunday or not — it depended on Windseer's assessment of the flour being used — as they were attentive for the command to spring up: rise up now and say grace. Heated only by the kitchen fireplace in an alcove half the width of the room, the dining area was naturally cool but Eleanor did not dare attempt the meat.

'I fear there is to be more rioting and disgrace' said Windseer. 'Desecration upon desecration will be performed on this Lord's Day. The air will be all storm and tempest, full of dark vapours and pillars of smoke. The dead will stand before God for this day. O those lamentable suffering people, if I could only make them see, but I am a crumbling rock, I am nothing for them to hold fast to as they must hold fast to see through me the glory of the Risen Lord. You must eat. I must go. I must try to stop it. It is part of my witness, perhaps the sum of it.'

Windseer had a fowling-piece, a double-barrelled, finely-engraved Purdy gun that his brothers in the Wesleyan Mission had pointed out was a complete anachronism for him to own when the Mission provided him with a plain and serviceable flintlock fowler of 'trade' quality for his ruinous parish of the Southern Ocean, the only missionary assigned by God to one whole quarter of the terraqueous globe, all the part of it which lay below 45 degrees south latitude. He was sure the Lord would allow him a gun in his loneliness if it were used solely to shoot birds to save him and God's loved ones entrusted to him from death by starvation or in extremes for his family to use in their own protection, he having vowed to face without arms whatever enemy God might send to try him. Besides, it had been given him by a venerable benefactor of the Mission without whose help he would not have been ordained. He took the gun down from above the fireplace, loaded both barrels with double charges of buckshot, checked the wear on the flints and laid the gun across the table pointing at the front door, the powder flask beside it.

'If you fire one barrel they will leave. It has never been known,' he said, 'that they defied a woman. I must preach twice more today as well.'

As he walked down to the Rock Windseer reflected that the distance must be almost exactly half a permitted Sabbath day's journey of 1,125 yards. He reached the beach in time to see Horako's thirty warriors kneeling on the sand in two spear-straight lines, their naked buttocks to the shore. Each knelt on his left knee, his right raised, his right arm holding his weapon on his right knee and his left forearm on top of his right, eyes downcast. Horako stood in front with his taia, a short spear for stabbing, cutting and clubbing. Grice stood at the end of the columns, silent and enraged but like Windseer unable to intervene. He was furious because while the Maori carried no muskets, each man held a whale-flensing tool robbed from the slipway store when they had overpowered Grice's drunken guard — cutting-spades, bone-spades, head-spades, boarding-knives, gaffs and blubber-pikes, all razor sharp. He was powerless because the priest Matekarite-te-Pua-o-te-Reinga visiting from Heroine had put them through the tira ora which granted them safe passage to, through and from their battle and so made them rigidly tapu, protected by Tu the god of war to whom they were dedicated. To interfere would be to invite Tu's wrath. Windseer prayed. He could see the whales and the boat with no headsman high in the stern. They were almost motionless because it was slack water with the ebb tide barely begun to run. Grotesquely, in a parody of the living whales, a hugely bloated, flensed carcass had drifted back ashore, its scored flesh almost as black and red as tar and paint, to the very edge of the sand with the brimming tide, buoyed up with the gases generated by putrefying krill in its stomach.

'Whiti! . . . Whiti! . . . Eeeee . . .!' Jump up! The world suddenly seemed a stage to Windseer — of the green silk expanse of water, the bloated black nugget of the Rock, the graceful barques imposing though their topgallants and topmasts had been sent down while they worked as floating factories, and the hulk of the whale carcass with its wedding-lace subcutaneous chemise, the sixty-foot, six-foot-beam canoe with its towering stern ornament, the waka taua carved with multiple spirals and the dreadful maraki-hae monster, drawn up stern-first a few feet on to the sand. The place was a whale's Golgotha with skulls, vertebrae ten feet and more across, shoulder blades and shrunken, hand-fingered fins littered about.

'Kia kutia!' ('Close in.')

'Aue! Aue!' ('Ah yes.')

The stamping of the naked feet was like a drum-beat, even on sand. The skulls were about to topple, the flippers to rise up and beseech God. As the fugleman chanted Windseer could hear an enraged 'tsi-tsi-tsi' sound coming from them and when they turned their faces to look down the columns he could see their wild, staring eyes and twitching face muscles and protruding tongues and thought with horror of Eleanor and her suffering and how she could not stop her face and they could and they did it thinking of death while she struggled for life. Now they called upon the whale to sail into their trap, now to 'gaze up at us, gaze up at the face of raging death'.

How could one not be stirred, Windseer told himself, then shivered with revulsion. They were running for the canoe, in it and rowing with Horako seated chanting high over them amidships and the helmsman chanting at the steering oar, not a traditional configuration but oars and steering oar were also innovations, more efficient and learned from the whaleboats. What they could do with blubber spades and boarding knives — long knives used for cutting limbs and between vertebrae, with spade handles — was not clear. The ships' boats had so far kept their distance. Lynch's boat was two hundred yards up the channel, being towed by the whale although he could have caught up with her at about five knots, heading towards what would one day be Port Paradise. In thirty feet of water which would rapidly shoal to twenty, much less than twice the diameter of her drum-like body, she would soon have nowhere to go. But now, standing down on the sand, seeing the ship boats begin to move and their cheering resume along with a concert song:

Take good heed, my hearts of oak,

Lest her flukes, as she lies,

Swiftly hurl you to the skies,

Windseer also heard the voices of the Maori women. They stood about him on both sides. Their leader was next to him, grinning up at him — Hinehaka, widow of Toowaro, her mouth grotesquely swollen with its tattooed moko pattern pulled awry, her gangrenous nose pitted and running, her eyes weeping pus. She was mata ngerongero — she had leprosy, would die from putrefaction and was laughing and happy, holding his pale hand in her fingerless one as she had held the hand of Toowaro, a great chief who had died of the ancient disease before her. She turned away to the side and other women took her place. Windseer ignored them. How he longed for the day when they might begin to remember the Sabbath, when they would bathe in the crystal waters of innocence and shower the degenerate, the ungodly, the white, with the wisdom of their blessed obedience, teach them that through the merits of Christ even their sins would be forgiven. That was his vision — the Maori soul captive in the Lord and by His shining light reflected, leading the debauched, the so-called Christians to the very gates of Salvation. His mission was to the Maori, that was his plan, his stratagem for the Lord. He was about to move. His feet were hampered by a dirty white flannel petticoat.

'A . . . a! E ringa pakia!'

The women around Windseer were dropping their skirts, throwing off their blankets, stepping out of petticoats, out of trousers, tossing them on the sand so they could obey the command to slap their open hands rhythmically on their naked thighs. They had broken the tapu, he thought in panic. Now that he could, he ought to stop them. He must summon God's word. Their dirty faces, their dirty bodies had a wild beauty as they moved.

'A . . . a! E waewae takahia.'

The women began to stamp rhythmically with their right feet. Windseer felt himself being touched, their hands touched his, caressed him, their naked thighs touched his hands as if from habit, with the ordinary and free sensuality of Maori women. They sang the verse of their song, about nobody ever being allowed to conquer them, and the bay seemed taken over by complete confusion.

Windseer's account in his journal is scant because he notes that he was beset by a double set of embarrassments. He says that for some reason all he could think of in 'a raging sea of noise' was the sound of 'Great Tom tolling from Christ Church Cathedral as I used to walk across the Meadows on a summer evening and the water sounds of the Isis under Folly Bridge. I thought of all the civilized glory of Oxford. I thought of home.'

Grice's daybook is little more than a log of whales caught and work done and blames what was to happen on the rebellious, 'nay mutinous laziness' of the boats' crews that did not go to sea with the others and had been ordered to clean up the slipway and its surrounds. Lynch had little time to observe from seaward and the log from an American vessel records that for a moment they thought war had broken out ashore. Fortunately Eleanor Windseer wrote to her sister in Oxford a letter that has been preserved and fills in some detail.

As the women danced a number of boys, black (Tartoux's), brown, coffee-coloured and spuriously white were running in and out of their lines with flatfish spears — about eight feet long and tipped with sharp barbed heads fringed with wandering albatross chick down, the bloated, stranded carcass was an obvious surrogate enemy. At last one boy ran in to hurl his spear into the distended stomach of the whale that swelled more than three times his height above him. It was the immediate explosion of pressurized gas that made Captain Benjamin J. Nute, of the *Nimrod*, suppose an insurrection. It was thump like that of a double-charged-and-shotted 64-lb carronade, he said. It was a sound so deeply impressive that the ship-boat crews forgot their self-imposed restraint and sped into action against the living whale with every kind of whoop and war-cry in their several languages and tattered garments impressed for flags. For Windseer, Heaven seemed to rain putrescent krill until Eternity. It continued to fall, splattering layer after clotted layer over the original red-running bloater-paste that covered him in the blast. A good deal more than half a ton of krill now spilled from the obscene, vulva-like split like an opened dung heap.

Windseer knew that he had to either stay or run and that either course demanded the same firmness of resolve. He could run home, saving the Lord from disgrace with every horrified footstep. He could stand and preach, a stinking offence to the Lord on a beach made tapu for the men, a tapu now broken because the women had danced where they were forbidden — the explosion was the atua's punishment and the beach was now accessible as a pulpit. He could employ another kind of courage and run to the rescue of the boy all but drowned in shrimp meal, laid out by the blast and covered in a mound from which a hand protruded like a torn boat waif in a dung-orange sandcastle. He realized that nobody else would save the boy. He was, in effect, in the latrine, the abode of evil spirits, the very source and spring of necromancy, the fearful makutu, and undoubtedly he was eating the filth and being swallowed up in the kete tuatahi, the basket of knowledge of evil; and if he were eating and becoming an evil priest, tohunga makutu, he could not be touched. He was infectious with death, let alone contagious with a generalized, quite eclectic evil.

Windseer threw off his dripping, low-crowned billy-cock hat that had stayed on because of its stormy-weather chin strap he always kept down as a precaution lest its wide, curving brim caught the wind, and began to run towards the boy with an idea of which he entirely disapproved forming in his mind — to the Missions Committee it would seem almost blasphemous, skylarking, trifling with God by performing theatricals in his name, like setting the Lord a-dance with a bear at a village circus. In his mind clear memories of words he had written in his journal not long ago raced with engraved clarity.

'The Popish Missionaries are now to the north of me at Seldom and are doing all they can to ingratiate themselves with the natives there by presents etc. The French have a schooner the *Santa Maria* and outnumber me five to one. Their mode of worship and wonderful legends (if I were not a strong believer in the power of truth), would lead me to fear that Popery would prevail over Protestantism in the native mind. I am far from happy in New

Zealand, I am often miserable. I wish I could have been spared the pain and shame of being sent to a place where my disgrace will be used as a preventative of my usefulness if I exert myself in opposing Popery. I wish I were on the other side of the world, and if I had not a wife and family dependent upon me I should wish myself out of the world, my body hid in the grave from the strife of tongues, my soul in the *lowest* place in Heaven, that I think must be my place if God in his infinite mercy grant me one. O God pity and save thy unworthiest servant.

'The Popish Bishop has visited and by dint of gaudy ritual, tapers, attitudes, dazzling vestments and superstitious forms and giving presents produced some effect to the disparagement of my plain dress and equally plain mode of service. If I can visit Seldom before a Priest is appointed I may succeed in reclaiming some Maori and preventing others from falling into that corrupt system. These natives are fond of forms and shew. I belong to a church that dispenses with parade and unmeaning gesticulation and am moreover of a temper that shudders at such things and that could not be brought to use them.

'Would you rather have a new coat or an old one, I asked some Maori who claimed the vile popery they had listened to was older than my faith. A new one to be sure, is the reply! Well *if* Popery is an old religion patched and tattered and *if* mine is a new one, it is just thus: he brings you an old coat patched and tattered; I a new one without a rent. The Popish Bishop has taken his leave for some time taking a number of natives with him to be initiated and intends to return with a Priest or two who are to be fixed somewhere on this coast and to baptize those who have been taught the Paternoster, Ave Maria and Creed in a dialect not their own — that of the Northern Island and largely incomprehensible here — the meaning of which they know little — I can now teach in the Murihiku tongue with the help of my dictionary and phrase book nearly adequate — if baptism can be dispensed on such terms I might administer it forthwith to most of the people here about but they ought, I am sure God wills, be taught much more and pass through a considerable lengthy trial. But to be a Papist however ignorant, and I fear however wicked, is a sure passport to Heaven. O when will the moral curse and plague be stayed!'

As he churned the decaying krill which flowed like quicksand about his legs, catching in the button-holes of his stiff leather coggers, strong gaiters, and the liquid flowed over their tops down into his Blucher half boots, round lace and tongue and eyelet holes and slowly soaked his clerical grey moleskin trousers, he remembered what he had written condemning the Papists. He reached the hand, pulled and the body came easily, partly propelled by a new surge from the stomach. This boy was born again, born spotless again from death, Windseer thought. This boy could be baptized while in a state of grace, indeed he had to be baptized and blessed since he might be about to die, a blessing on this beach that would scourge the tapu from its sands and waters, that by association would bless and cleanse the women who would see the boy rise up living from the sea and recognize the miracle of Grace. The boy now dripping in his arms was now trying to push the muck out of his mouth, still not breathing. Windseer tasted it for the first time in his own mouth, spat, even swallowed, the smell was worse when tasted, and tipped the boy up as he walked into the sea, holding him upside down and spanking his back just as he had held most of his own children giving them breath when they first emerged from Eleanor's thighs. This was Jonah, he thought, come not from the mouth of the whale but the womb, a man-fish with a sacred future, a Maori Jonah, the man whom God taught charity, whom God taught that anger, raging against fate, should in our hearts be turned to pity and understanding.

The tamaiti choked out a glutinous gob of krill and began to cough. Windseer had to snatch him up because a large, hairy black-and-pink pig, standing beside him and till then unnoticed immediately grabbed the expectoration, then lunged at the boy's head. There were three or four pigs belly-deep in the water. He looked over his shoulder and began to wade. There were dozens of pigs on the beach, kicking and jumping and tossing their heads about the whale's stomach cavity; there were dozens of dogs of every kind, some already inside the whale tearing out offal; there were black and brown roosters and hens coyly lifting their feet in the tide of filth and pecking up single, whole crustacea; there were cautiously nibbling goats. He looked to the Rock. All the women had retreated in fear. He too must be now tapu, a tohunga makutu. They lined the rim of the Rock and crouched in its crevices. Windseer waded on, the boy too frightened to move. When he was waist deep, the tails of his Brandenburg surtout — it had been specifically inchered for him in Oxford in 1820, a long loose winter coat trimmed with cord and fastened with frogs, his only remaining good coat — floated out around him. He looked up at the women on the Rock. He felt the filth begin to ooze away. The women were absolutely still and silent. He spoke, as best he could, in Maori. They must be expecting a sacrifice, he thought: they think I will drown him.

'Do you know what you have done? Do you know what you have done on this Day of the Lord? You have brought down his wrath upon yourselves. He has punished you here today because your men went whaling. The Lord God tells you to rest on his day. Nobody must work or He will be fearsomely angry. And you women have sung songs and blessed the men going to work. God was angry with you and sent the dead whale. You ignored the Lord's Day and this little boy was nearly killed. But I am the humble servant of the Lord and I have saved this boy. I have saved this boy in the Day of Desolation you have brought upon yourselves; I have saved him from the belly of the Devil's Whore. I have saved him, and look, I have made him breathe again; I have raised him and look: his soul is new found, he is new, he is cleansed and made pure, this boy I have saved on the Lord's Day, and the Devil has had to give him up, my God made the Devil give him back to me from the latrine, the Devil thought he had dragged this boy over the bar of the latrine whale, into Hellfire but the Lord God of Hosts saved him. Do you hear me?'

'Aue! Aue! Aue!'

'Now I am going to baptize this boy. I am going to offer him to God to be his child.' The boy's eyes were closed and he clearly thought he was dead. Windseer shook him. 'Tamaiti, Tamaiti! Whakaara!' The eyes opened. 'Now help me call upon God the Father through Christ our Lord and his mercy to give this child the thing that no other God can give: let him be baptized with water and the Holy Ghost and be received into Christ's Holy Church. God baptized Jesus Christ and he made it sacred to wash sins away with water. Christ loved children and was kind to them. He was very angry when people were unkind to them.' He held up the boy and called, 'Do you renounce the Devil and all his works?'

'Aue! Aue! Aue!'

'O merciful God, grant that the old Adam in this child may be so buried that the new man may be raised up in him.' He lowered the boy into the water, supporting him with his left arm and raising his right. He called, 'Tamaiti, tamaiti. Whakaarua. Mau tou koiwi kei te tiwhaiwhai. Waiko te tiwhaiwhai o-te-Ihu hanga koe ma. Haere mai ahau kei Ihu.' Then he called it in English. 'Child, child, wake up. Bear yourself on the wave. Let it in, let the wave of Jesus make you clean. Welcome. Come with me to Jesus.'

'Aue, aue, aue!'

'Sanctify this water to the mystical washing away of sin and grant that this child now to be baptized herein may receive the fullness of thy Grace.' Windseer pushed the boy under the sea three times, held him up spluttering. 'I baptize thee in the name of the Father and of the Son and of the Holy Ghost Hoani Wetere.' John Wesley, the women knew, was the most famous man in England. They came laughing and running to gather in their new-born child.

Lynch and his boat had meanwhile fled on their 'Nantucket sleigh ride', past the ships with their cheering crews in the main and foremast ratlines, towards the shadow of the snowy ridges. The main channel to Port Paradise still runs as it did then square across the harbour from peninsula to mainland rock wall directly behind the sandspit dam, then down the landward side past a series of short points with sheer cliff sides and shingly beaches in between. At the end of the first point from the sea was a small basin formed by tidal scour and with an extreme depth of 8 fathoms. It was nearly a cable's length athwart the tide and not quite so long fore and aft. Sensing this pool ahead, the whale lunged forward and to the crew's surprise took out half a tub of line. For a moment the following ship boats thought them under water too because they were almost hidden inside the long curling bow wave. Then the whale line went dead. They were over the centre of the pool. They had had no knowledge of its depth. The line hung limp, straight down. The water was more black than green and they could not tell whether occasional great upwellings in it were caused by the whale or the tide. Lynch told Manx Oscar to haul in the line, but carefully until it was just firm, to see where it tended. A frightened right whale could spend up to 20 minutes sounding, perhaps more if it was lying on the bottom using no energy. Pupuha tapped Lynch on the knee. 'Te tohora i ki raro tatou. Waka pakanga. Taua tinihanga te tohora.' The whale is under us, he said. We must deceive him like a war canoe.

'Ship your oars, lads,' said Lynch. He was sweating. His skin felt coated with ice. Twice he had been in a boat when a whale charged from below, hitting them fair on the keel, leaving the boat a collapsed bundle of planks with them in the water and those sad ones hurled to the clouds or hammered on the surface of the sea, the whaleman's dread hard anvil, by her raging flukes. The dead could be unrecognizable but for the carved initials in their trouser suspenders. 'Poop, you slack away that line. Manx, you pay out and keep it slack. Paddles out lads and stern all.' Using the tide, Lynch eased away until they found less than a fathom of tide at the channel's edge. He had little time. The ship boats were nearly up to the deep pool. 'Ship paddles. Out oars. Stern all, ye poxy cods-walloping scum, stern all.' He had to bring the boat upstream of the whale and at the same time by twisting the harpoon force the whale to end its sound. The ship boats could not see what was happening.

When the whale blew it charged downstream lobtailing like a spermaceti, its drum head catching one boat broadside, driving it down until it was run over, its thwacking tail accounting for two more. Lynch's boat sleighed through the wreckage, oars at the salute and none of the other four ship boats bothered to pick up the survivors. The tide would bring them down. Whales were more important than men for the moment and the dead needed no assistance. Lynch knew that the whale would go back to its calf, now under tow to a boat from the Rock. If he could come close enough on the ride, about a mile now, he could run the boat in with the built-up momentum and while the whale's senses were distracted by panic and the calf's change of position, hand over the steering oar to Manx Oscar, spring forward along the thwarts, pick up the long, diamond-headed lance of malleable iron, plunge it into the whale's heart just behind the fin, stand off while she tired herself in agony, lay in again with a fresh lance and churn it in a fresh wound just as one churned butter in a standup barrel-stave churn, getting at the life of her, up and down with the lance, tearing more and more tissue as the blood began to come fresh and bright from her blowholes, getting at the life of her until she spouted heavy dark blood over the sea and all of them, lay on her side with one flipper raised in submission and her life got. Before this happened the Maori war canoe lay in her way, athwart it between her and the calf. It was as long as she was. She did not charge it — she sailed under it, heaved it up with her flukes and brought them down in the middle of it. The canoe snapped like the dry stem of a flax seed-head and fell neatly, one to either side of Lynch's boat. He observed that the warriors were either dead or laughing with complete abandon.

Windseer was unable to watch what happened on the water. The boy sprang from his arms and swam to the Rock to lose himself among other children. The leprous old Hinekaka called 'E ringa pakia' again. Some of the women, now abandoning still more clothing, began to stamp and some rushed into the water to Windseer, and grasping his arms led him onto the sand. They ran their fingers through his soft pale missionary hair, wiped krill from his eyebrows, singing the words of a made-up song about the events they had just seen, stamping now and then, slapping their flesh. Bewildered, he looked about the beach and saw that it was littered 'with childish things' — there were broken dolls carved from flax flower-stalks, soft like balsa wood to take stick arms and legs and albatross feather piupiu skirts and heads to be tied with lichen hair, broken carved whale boats and canoes, broken kites — the seagulls were shrieking now, gorging themselves — pieces of cooping iron filched from the cooperage beside the boatshed, sleeveless tackle blocks, even, miraculously alive, a fantail squeaking in a birdcage made of the supplejack lianas; at least, he thought, it was opening its beak to cry. There were blubbery playing cards blown out between the slats of the boatshed doors, thick cards with crude numbers and mutilated royal faces. The faces around him were those of once beautiful South Seas maidens, ugly and evil-smelling, streaked with grease and soot, with yellowish pupils red-veined from liquor. Some did not drink, he knew, but these, with their broken-fingernailed, tobacco-stained hands were removing his clothes.

And Gargantua's mother with her hanging shytten tripes also confronted him. They were undressing him as they swayed and sang and he was speechless. How could he fling them away? That would destroy all the good he had done. He had made himself the god to be adored, to be touched, touched, touched: for the god must be aroused, the god must have his favours. His Brandenburg was gone — surely they would not dare steal it: no, it was in the sea — they had taken his dreadnought coat — some of their hands were soft and clean — they had unbuttoned his coggers and unlaced his Bluchers, they had unbuttoned his straight-collared shirt of oatmeal flannel, they had loosened the draw-strings — some of their faces were clean — at the back of his trousers and stripped his legs — ere you go forth display your legs to your women — yet leaving his ineffables, his wool stockinette darned all colours, square-cut drawers that were barely touched with whale filth. They were washing his clothes in the sea, some of them, while others held him and stroked him in time with the song and some were in the belly of the whale. The bladdery blue-and-white intestines had also split, spilling out long-beaded tapeworms like comets coloured death white, their eggs in tails and their hooked swollen heads that fell free and lay spread by the blast like gargantuan spermatazoa nudging the gigantic tubes and gonads of Gargantua's mother, their tails lashing. Some of the women made the tapeworms into poi: made them like the balls of bullrush covered with woven flax they used in a more langorous, more sensually rhythmic dance. They were coming towards Windseer with armfuls of tapeworms, wrapping them round themselves, between their breasts, in waist girdles and between girdles walking and swaying — some of them with clear eyes — they were giving the worms to the women who held him who were untying his parson's stock which was tied in an osbaldistan knot instead of a plain one, a flourish in Popery's face he had allowed, and not a plain parson's neckpiece: they had taken it off and his shirt and his drawers.

He was moving in the white surplice of worms that he now wore, the belt that he wore with two heads in a knot at his navel. Moving. The poi tails sometimes clashed together, letting the eggs fly into the women's hair. Some struck his face. He called out, 'Death and Hades get thee hence. O Lord let not the invisible world give up the dead. O Lord let not the powers of heaven also be shaken. Let not the sea give up the dead therein. O Lord let this corruptible put on incorruption. O Lord they have no rest day or night but the smoke of their torment ascendeth for ever and ever. Say to me Lord, blind wretch, thou camest naked from thy mother's womb and more naked into eternity. Say not depart yet cursed into everlasting fire. Lo, Hell is moved from beneath to receive those who are ripe for destruction, O Lord thou hast bought me by thy blood. Let . . . me . . . not . . . perish!'

He had reached the sea, tearing the fishy jewels away from his temptation. He stood waist deep and washed himself again and again, and as the women ran suddenly to the Rock — they had seen the canoe destroyed and could see Lynch coming up with upraised lance — he walked slowly to the deserted beach, dressed in his washed clothes, washed his hat which they had overlooked, and walked slowly home. As he reached the try-works the calf was already on the slipway being cut in, the long blankets of blubber being torn from its body with a crackling sound and dragged across the sand to the tables where they were chopped into foot-square horse pieces ready for the pots. The calf looked like carved hard soap, he thought, and then hoped that Grice might give him a piece of the heart for tomorrow's dinner. It was like fillet beef. Soap, he thought: perhaps they could make soft soap from whale oil and the ash of say, kamahi wood which was very hard, to yield a fine ash lye, to cleanse his clothes. Or rum would be cleansing, though it tended to preserve things. Nelson's blood was the rum he was pickled in, stolen on the way home. It might kill the fleshy detritus of whale spew. Often whales coughed up their stomach contents as they died under the churning lance. This one must have died fast. This one today had died for love, had followed its loved one inside the Gates of Perdition and died for it. It had been human in a way. The dried krill might shake out or be brushed out of his clothes or at least might not smell. Soap would prevent infection. So would sunlight but there was little of that at The Craggs.

The calf was being cut up. The whale was coming up on the windlass. His house was among the last of those in sunlight. He would have to have clean clothes. The pity was that these were so old that they could not be harshly washed. He knew he still stank because he could still catch the taste of it. He would tell his family that he had slipped on the Rock where he was preaching against the desecration of the Sabbath and fallen into the sea near the slipway, where it was dirty. He remembered the leper woman's twisted moko and her long shark tooth ear pendants.

('So you can take your pick among those stories,' I said to Lydia. 'Windseer rescued a child and damned himself— he'd overcome that easily as far as the Maori were concerned — but he damned himself again to himself, the worst sort of thing to have to live with. The whale gave herself over to grief. It wasn't noble. It was foolish. I'm sure a whale would know her calf was dead. For a start there'd be no underwater sonar signal and none of that squeaky talk they make to each other. She must have heard every squeak of her calf dying. She truly was grief-stricken, enough to follow the calf in and die willingly. She didn't after all make a fight of it. She let Lynch leave his lance in and churn and churn until she vomited krill and spouted heavy dark blood and died, raising a flipper there, right under the rock, saluting her child ascending to the cutting-in plant. She couldn't bring it back. She knew she couldn't but she behaved as if she could. Don't cry.')

Cilla McQueen

Map

Here is the map used by Charles Brasch in his hiking days, a Lands and Survey Department map of Otago Peninsula published in 1942. Its folds divide it into 24 tattered squares, held together by a fragile muslin backing. The paper is creamy and brittle.

The city and the coastal area take up the left hand side of the map, the right hand side being mostly sea of a southern blue. A fine purple grid is superimposed on the landscape, which you may reach by slipping through the one-dimensional map as if it were the surface of a mirror.

Charles and Rodney are standing on the spine of the peninsula, facing north. Rodney is puffing and his eyes are bright. In one hand he has a stout stick and in the other the map of Charles Brasch. Charles is tall and thin. He has bushy eyebrows. He is dressed in khaki shorts and shirt. In his rucksack he carries a compass, a pair of binoculars, a water bottle, a green pullover, a battered Auden, two notebooks and several pencils.

Running due south, the centre fold line passes through the graceful font of the word 'Dunedin' at the top of the paper, through Aramoana township and across the narrow harbour heads, through the marae at Otakou, the church and the graveyard and the cockle beds, across the peninsula and the tidal flats at Papanui inlet, through Mount Charles and out over the cliffs of Allan's Beach, towards Antarctica.

Rodney wishes he had a gin. He mops his face with a silk handkerchief. Charles is sitting on a rock, writing in his notebook. His handsome face is stern. From up here they can see the whole panorama. The length of the peninsula lies before them, the harbour on their left and the ocean on their right.

'Purple!' chortles Rodney suddenly, as he unpacks his rucksack.

Charles looks up, frowning.

'What?'

'Purple passage, let's have a purple passage,' carols Rodney. He spreads the groundsheet. 'A purple passage before lunch.'

Forbes Williams

from Dunedin

from *Motel View*

Friendly City of the South

Dunedin, port and capital of New Zealand's largest province, Otago, is the country's fourth city. Dreamed into existence before the site itself had even been considered, Dunedin was the product of the New Edinburgh Scheme, an 1840s plan to establish a Scottish settlement in the South Island. Since then it has earned and jealously guarded a reputation for good sense and friendly hospitality, growing into a robust, prosperous city, successfully keeping pace in the cybernetic age without losing its sense of history or deep respect for all things cultural.

A Proud Tradition

Dunedin is unequivocally Scottish; indeed, Scottish tourists are often heard to loudly proclaim that the city is more Scottish than Scotland itself. 'Dunedin' translates to 'Edin Hill', though the more common version renders it 'Edinburgh of the South' — and everyone knows how the central town plans of these sister cities are identical. Today Robbie Burns sits proudly overlooking the Octagon in the city centre, and the Robbie Burns liquor outlet is the city's biggest grossing retail concern.

Less well known is that 'Edin' apparently in turn translates to 'New Athens', rendering Dunedin 'New Athens Hill' — or, if we follow the usual error, 'South New Athens' — perhaps, for convenience, 'South Athens' — and indeed, Greek tourists are also often heard to loudly proclaim that the city seems as Greek to them as Greece itself. 'Athens', of course, comes from Athena, goddess of wisdom and patron of the arts; it is difficult to imagine a flag-bearer more apt.

Uncrowded and Spacious: Health and Geography

Dunedin's founders chose for their settlement one of the most magnificent harbour settings in the country. Today the city spreads up and over the hills ringing the head of Otago Harbour, offering the majority of home-owners sweeping vistas of hill and sea. In fact, like Rome, Dunedin sits on seven hills, a detail first pointed out to me by a psychiatric patient *from* Cherry Farm — incarcerated precisely because of his fixation on this unhappy coincidence, which had grown to a point where the dire prophecies in Isaiah and St John applied not only to 'Babylon' but to Dunedin as well, catastrophe averted only with the aid of a complex set of bizarre, private rituals that took up all his time and which unfortunately did not appear to anyone else to be normal. The seven hills are arranged in the manner of holes in a plughole: six around the central one, disrupted only by Saddle Hill, squeezed some way out of the encircling six like a sulking child.

As in all hilly cities you tend to make friends with those at similar altitudes, so that visits don't involve any climbing. Going down is often just as bad: on a cold winter's morning Dunedin can be irresistibly downhill. The valleys slowly fill up with people and cars. You might break the odd bone or two, you might even smash up the car — but hey, you'll probably just end up laughing. Hills are like that. You just never can tell.

Dunedin and the Treaty

The Maoris also have a name for Dunedin: Otepoti, but do you think the Post Office are worried? You can try sending mail to Otepoti; more often than not it will simply boomerang, returning some months later covered in question marks, try Otemata, Otaki and Outram (so close!) and of course the final definitive ink-stamp of a straight purple finger accusing the letter back to its sender. Otepoti — Otepotu is also correct — notes the position of the site at the head of the harbour: *where the points of land come together* or *place of the steep points* . . . you see, there they are again, the hills.

A Relaxed Pace

Dunedin has more centenarians per capita than any other city in the Southern Hemisphere. And how many major cities are there left in the world where it is still possible to drive four or five miles from a city office to a suburban home for lunch and return within the hour? To suggest that Dunedin did not have a traffic problem would be unrealistic — the traffic problem is an inescapable fact of postmodern living. But in Dunedin it is by no means as great as in New Zealand's other major cities. Oh and by the way, it's actually illegal to use your indicator within city limits. That one often catches the unsuspecting visitor.

I had a friend who moved out of town to the peninsula, not far out, but enough that no one visited him any more. He was hurt and even angry that a few miles could make such a difference to friends and always made a big thing about how it was only six-and-a-half minutes from the Octagon to his driveway. Of course you had to really speed to get even close to that — though he always loudly maintained he'd carefully kept to the speed limit the whole way when he measured it. Really, though, it wouldn't have mattered if it was twenty seconds. He'd moved out of town. End of argument.

Youth, Sport and Culture

Despite its proud sense of the past, Dunedin is above all a city for young people. New Zealand's oldest and the world's southernmost university attracts large numbers of students from out of town and many are enticed to stay on after completing their degrees or dropping out, ensuring the city's gene pool remains vital. A thriving underground arts, literary and music scene helps keep Dunedin's vast numbers of young black-clad unemployed away from serious crime and it is remarkable how many rock-stars you can meet in ten minutes of walking down the main street. Attractive, aromatic and medicinal flora and fungi abound, experienced most fully on the many scenic walks around the city where in autumn in particular the youth are so often to be encountered. Sometimes their mysterious fungal forces seem to fill the very atmosphere: a simple afternoon stroll can assume the grandest proportions.

Tomorrow's Forecast

Dunedin's cold, squally, unpredictable weather is maligned by visitor and resident alike; not so well known is that the city has less rain than any town in the North Island, fewer rain-days annually than Auckland, average temperatures only one degree cooler than Christchurch, and a higher percentage of bright sunshine in winter than Wellington. The news always has the day's maximum too low. Try not to judge Dunedin by your first visit — for all first visitors it is cold and wet. Dunedin is like someone you meet for the first time who acts like a real arsehole but later somehow becomes a close friend.

The future looks bright. With continued global warming it is anticipated the climate will improve to Mediterranean standards at least. As the sea-level rises the squalid low-lying South Dunedin suburbs should flood, so that the peninsula becomes an island in the manner of Salamis, the harbour a channel overpopulated with yachts, and my City Rise cottage — where currently the coats at the door are to be put on when you come in — an envied waterfront apartment, prime Pacific real estate sought eagerly by rich and famous the world over.

. . . *acknowledgement is made of scenes and samples from* DUNEDIN Friendly City of the South *by Alan R.T. Brady; published by the Dunedin Rotary Club, October 1966.*

Graham Lindsay

Maiorum Institutis Utendo

1
Gulls flying
motes of ash in the updraught, up in the sunlight
the sun declining on the western faces
of hills, houses
people readying themselves to go home from work
to the pub from work:

see them in the Oriental
faces afloat in a dark tank
the old gropers grinning boyishly
holding freshlit filtertips aloft in their fingers
spilling first glassfuls from full jugs on pedestals
easing their arses on the awkward hotel furniture
settling in for the night;
others walking
head down along the golden streets.

Two wood pigeons on the powerlines
great fluffy feathered white breasts, forest green necks
red eyes red collars red crowns transcolouring
three purple claws visible on each leg
symbol of transcendence of the carved ancestors.

Signal Hill in the binoculars, that place that presence
the War Memorial statue on the peninsula, away over there
the stone hillsides.

Bracken View by the Northern Cemetery
where the lovers in cars cradle each other blind
behind the windscreens to the view
which nevertheless settles down through their hoods and all around
where the hoons heave their empties vaingloriously
in beautiful glinting parabolas of bad taste
leave their piss in half filled bottles on the parapets
beam headlamps like searchlights in a swathe across the city as they
drop clutch and depart
in slithering mud-spinning vollies.

In the Northern Cemetery east of the main gates Bracken lies
under a view he would not have cared too much for:
wharves, cranes, gasworks, bits of railway track
silos, oil depots, chimneys, sweepage of houses and industry
probably the earth has caved in his bones —
he was dug in there in 1898
and fastened with a monumental plug.

On the Lookout pedestal we're accorded
this civic charm of his:
Go, trav'ler, unto others boast
  Of Venice and of Rome;
Of Saintly Mark's majestic pile,
  And Peter's lofty dome;
Of Naples and her trellised bowers;
  Of Rhineland far away:—
These may be grand, but give to me
  Dunedin from the Bay.
He didn't get it, we don't either
more than a glimmering.

A bronze compass disk points out the places of 'interest':
Cargill's castle, First Church
Otago Boys', the Technical College
and other architectural and engineering amazements
of the city fathers, the councillors those mothers
monuments in masonry to their everlasting memory
their foresightedness;

Queens Gardens, the Early Settlers' museum
a bust of James Macandrew beside plaster colonnades and acanthus leaves
D.M. Stuart D.D. daydreaming through a hole in the past, out on the
       reclaimed beach front
Queen Victoria with down-turned orifices
the mournful cheeks of the chaste maids Justice and Wisdom
tears of rain rolling down their heads
Wisdom suffering impressment, her eyes direct
merely watch what you say they ask —
hard pips of the nineteenth century
in the brown core of the present;

the Cenotaph like a Mandarin arms folded
until you see the crosses on its breast
to THE GLORIOUS DEAD 1914–18
an emaciated marble lion guarding the plinth
griefleaves of shadow cascading up the spotlit spine

(the Sixty-Fifth moves out onto Anzac Avenue
elderly men running shikkered to catch up with
the Holsum Bakery Kaikorai Band
it's too much)

Norwich Union breaking wind with MFL
monstrous mausoleums transfixing the night-time gaze
of out-of-city children
AIRPORT HOUSE about to take off
the Gresham Home Supply not going anywhere
men spitting vomit alongside the Café de Curb.

The directions — get it right — that way north, trans-border
stand with your arms flung like a weathercock
planes coming in from the upland
crossing the Sorbonne of the low night sky
over Swampy and Flagstaff (Johnny Jones' highway)
the geophysical barriers reducing to silhouettes
way over them the world flies out

that way the aurora
over the cold flat plexus of the southern ocean
all the way to Antarctica our kindred land-form from Gondwanaland days
an odd angle it seems, with us on Te Waka a Maui aslant like this.

2
Bell Hill in the harbour
grief envy, what keeps us back
'The estimated cost, £355,000, would be covered, it was believed,
by the return from the sale or leasing of the land created' —
between thirteen and fifteen metres were cut off
and First Church erected in its stead;

the pommel on Saddle Hill sheared for basalt
the great girth of the hill underneath sliding toward Mosgiel;

the reserve on Signal Hill, contrary to statute, leased to a farmer
who bulldozed the bush regenerating on its summit, presumably
because it was eating up space and nutrients
his dozen or so sheep could increase on
because that's the model for the New Zealand male, if he means business;

two quarries on its spurs
the lower a great amphitheatre for the prevailing winds
and detonations jumping in the bowels of Black Jack's Point
the upper a silent auditorium for the post-mortemed rock.

The peninsula heavily frosted from 'shoreline to skyline'
once-upon-a-time
when Tuckett came through looking for the New Edinburgh
where Kahukura stood, one foot on Hautai the other in Tainui,
watching over the ambergris of the cells of man
as it floated landward.

George O'Brien painting the lines of his times:
sunset over the harbour from Waverley
the 'kidney' clearly visible at the Heads, where they plan,
the councillors those motherfuckers, to raise an aluminium golgotha
so they and their cohorts can continue buying in
their bright new Japanese cars, and dispense with the bumper stickers saying
        'We love Otago' and
'Otago Needs Jobs'

they're going under
the Skeggs' eggs Bolgers Birchs Coopers Couchs, minions of late Western
        capitalism, are going under
and they're taking with them their
charismatic catastrophe;

painting also Kaituna, from Te Pahure o Te Rangipohika, or Signal Hill
where he was, 1860s, deforestation already commenced
the passive imperturbable upper harbour ringed now
by the orange lights of Portsmouth Drive on the Southern
Endowment (sic).
Reclamation

protestation . . .
Pelichet Bay, Mud Terrace:
the former taken 'chiefly for the convenience of land-owners in the vicinity'
the latter through the surveyors drawing Princess Street through blue water;

Andersons Bay, the Southern 'Endowment':
the decreased volume of water in the harbour reducing 'tidal scour
            necessary to prevent shoaling';

proposed widening of road facilities beyond Careys Bay
proposed reclamation of twenty-nine hectares at Te Ngaru
pretty soon plans will be revived
for an international tarmac on the upper harbour.

A dead octopus suspended in the tide
where the water empties through the causeway laid by Taranaki prisoners
many of them dying of bronchial and tubercular diseases
the nineteenth century equivalent of germ warfare

stretch-marks on the water's surface
black spools of current unravelling
into seemingly insoluble bird-nests
riding over rapids and dissolving
in the coves the water like moiré
reflecting hanks of copper light from the lamp-posts
on Burns Point shimmering wind-rippled.

Across the Bay those spaceships the highrise are readying for lift off
from the cavernous dark roar of the water-front
the gloom of night pours heavily into the hill above Ravensbourne
cars battle round the bays and headlands
an ambulance flashes deathly scarlet beside a prone cyclist
the industrial isthmus looking like a ghoulish school playground
the curvature of the world evident
in the meniscus of the Bay.

3
Fancy finding 'New Zealand' on an AA Otago roadsign
the 'New Zealand Centennial Memorial' beside the simple seal of a country
       road
simple grass verge-hedge-paddock, and
ten-acre farmlets on a hilltop!
Eucalyptus trees full-grown, kennels, nurseries, stone out-houses
a hamlet 'over the rainbow'
a stone's throw behind the city shoulder.

Alone at the wheels of their big cars
the poets who lost their lives, maybe lost their wives and children,
have been up here
gazing into the crystal ball of Separation
they descend now through black gates, back to the shadowed trenches
of Caversham, Maclaggan, Leith and North East Valley
the cattle-stops rattle behind.

We must grow into the immensity, the phantasmagoria of
Dunedin, New Zealand, the World: that large!
That way north, over there, over those hills
stand with your arms flung like a weathercock
over Maniototo, that plain of the fruition of vision
where the world flies out, outwards and upwards
that way the aurora
east-west the transmeridional
demarcation of our spirit.

'At the beginning of the dominion's second century this monument is
       dedicated to the memory of the pioneers who braved the first'
History and The Thread of Life commanding the vistas
the patriarch heavy-browed, in boots
with a hollow book and a solid pencil, gazing west — padme gate padme
       gate
the hooded woman in sandals with a bale of twine or
fishing line, gazing into the birth. And

Edinburgh, here!
'This rock hewn from the rock on which Edinburgh Castle stands was given
      as a centennial
memorial token by the people of Edinburgh to signify the bond which forever
      binds the cities of Edinburgh and Dunedin'
cloaked in indigenous lichens
and here too is Robbie Burns inscribed: Auld Lang Syne.

From the Seal of the Province of Otago — Maiorum Institutis Utendo*—
looking down on our home town
a freighter casting chevrons and demi-spheres in the harbour dawn's mercury
     bowl
the bridge of the Memorial soaring out over the city
old brain of the chieftains Pukemamaku, Whanaupaki, Kapukataumahaka,
     Te Pahure o Te Rangipohika
demurely regarding the slip of gold at their feet.

* 'By following in the steps of our forefathers' (translation from K. C. McDonald,
City of Dunedin)

Hone Tuwhare

Snowfall

It didn't make a grand entrance and I nearly
missed it — tip-toeing up on me as it did
when I was half asleep and suddenly, they're there
before my eyes — white pointillist flakes
on a Hotere canvas — swirling about on untethered

gusts of air and spreading thin uneven
thicknesses of white snow-cover on drooping
ti-kouka leaves, rata, a lonely kauri, pear
and beech tree. Came without hesitation
right inside my opened window licking my neck

my arms my nose as I leaned far out to embrace
a phantom sky above the house-tops
and over the sea: *'Hey, where's the horizon?*
I shall require a boat you know — two strong arms?'
. . . and snow, kissing and lipping my face

gently, mushily, like a pet whale,
or (if you prefer) a shark with red bite — sleet
sting hot as ice. Well,
it's stopped now. Stunning sight. Unnerved,
the birds have stopped singing,

tucking their beaks under warm armpits: temporarily.
And for miles upon whitened miles around,
there is no immediate or discernible movement,
except from me, transfixed, and moved by an interior
agitation — an armless man applauding.

'Bravo,' I whisper. 'Bravissimo.' Standing ovation.
Why not . . . Oh, come in, Spring.

Cilla McQueen

Recipe for One

Take a Dunedin winter's afternoon,
a woman blown along the road,
a leaf, a russet umbrella
Take heed of the weather:

Take the washing off the line
and listen under the tree
to the storm coming seawards
over the mountain, cold taffeta

Take into consideration
the blackbird and the worm,
the world beyond the surface:
a jump through the meniscus

A glance, a chance, a step, a risk
a fancy, care, the liberty;
a moment held for time enough
to let the tones untangle.

Take all of this to heart.

Now,
take the rain.

Cilla McQueen

from Berlin Diary

In the attic bedroom
there is a writing table
under the window

At this hour, Dunedin is asleep
The cat is asleep in the valley of bedclothes
The chrysalis on the kowhai tree
is silvery with frost
The car is frosted outside in the street
The tree is whispering
as it whispers in all weather

Distance is of the body alone

A place, an island
a pool of light

New Zealand
Dunedin
Grange Street garden
Berlin
St Kilda

House, protection

Skin, the function of skin

Dreams within dreams,
chiselled ivory balls
and the space within.

Michael Harlow

Stop-time: Galata Kebabci/ Dunedin

Not wanting to serve anything
but the 'real' thing he served
nothing, or so his hands spoke,
and down we sat at a table. Islands of plates and bowls, the
cones of paper serviettes
carefully arranged, small sculpted
hills ragged at the edges. And
we ate off empty plates so deep
I wanted to touch them with my
fingers and go travelling. Tilting glasses of air, we toasted
our families' names, mothers'
mothers, fathers long gone beyond way back; we talked through
mirrors of ourselves, the landscapes of bodies. His hands
weaving a language I understood
imperfectly, but still can
taste the resonance of, fine
print of inner speech. Touching his heart with the flat
of his hand, he asked if I had
heard the watch of nightingales
in Arnuvutköy, 'making love'
to the young girls who live,
as we all do, *effendi*, inside
the songlines of our story.
Have you? Seen them, I mean
strolling along the Bosphorus,
arm in arm, up and down the sea
road, listening under the lace-
work parasols of trees for that
heart-stopping swarm of notes

to call down the green hills.
And they listen: touching each
other at the wrist, their bodies
light-filled with the invisible;
in their embroidered scarves
knotting keepsake loops for
love, promissory notes they
will dream through in the
watery dark above the Golden
Horn. When we finished, the
table cleared, not a scrap of
emptiness left, I called for
the 'count', waiting for the
numbers to appear in the open
palm of his hand. And here
at the end-words of a feast,
I begin to listen to a world
outside this carpeted room,
beyond the palette of prayer
rugs, bowls of artificial
flowers, and I hear: flying
down Princes Street in a
funnel of wind, the deep trill
of birdsong from the steeped
hills of Arnuvutköy; carrying with it stop-time: a song
so rich with desire it can
cross frontiers with astonishing ease, and settle as
it does now into this brief
conversation, this deep space
of an Antipodean spring.

Marion E. Jones

Shadow

Another damn Monday morning. I stumble to the phone. Hello. Hello.

Happy Birthday. It's my father. I have told them not to telephone New Zealand. Them is my father and stepmother. I cannot bear to speak her name. My father has never phoned before.

Thanks, I reply. I shiver in the dawn. Air shifting penetrates to my skin. My thin frock catches on something. Someone works quickly to secure a rope about my waist. A parachute opens. The fall becomes more gradual. The ropes beside us sway in the silence. Space surrounds the rocking. Soon the mist will turn to ice. Far below people move in and out through an open door. I am to go into that light among people I do not know.

Is it happy? he asks.

Not especially, I reply. I appreciate your contact. That, I think, is wrong. An invasion of my breathing space even now. After twenty-four years. Across eight thousand miles. Have you chosen, I find something to say, any photos yet? To send, as you suggested, from among your old negatives?

It's hard to tell with negatives. Everything is reversed, my father replies. I've been preoccupied.

I understand you've been under stress. Of course, with her illness. It does me no good to keep on understanding. I need the photos you took, as I've written, of my mother. All of them.

Do you have the professional photograph? he asks. The one that stood on the corner of your dresser?

It's vague, I hesitate. I think so. High up. Between the closet and the drawers. Something was always in front of her face. My mother's loose hair passes as a shadow from that time toward me through light beginning to soften the rooms. We moved from that house, I add, when I was seven.

And the studio photo of yourself when you were twelve? he asks.

With plaits, I reply, and white bows. Yes. I look like a skinned animal.

She had faced away from the sun where she stood in the shadows cast by a leafy hedge. The hair was drawn back each side of the face. The Easter dress was sheer cotton, dotted swiss, small white dots on yellow. Grosgrain ribbon tied about the waist of a short gathered skirt. The puff sleeves had too much puff. The crisp material smelled of stiffening. Her stepmother had commanded her to stand still so the hem could be pinned in. That year was the only year for the next half century her birthday was to fall on Easter Sunday. They would have an Easter party, her stepmother had said. For her fifth birthday that Saturday afternoon. At nine o'clock on Saturday morning, she had put on the new dress, new yellow socks and white shoes. Then undress again. The photo this time, her father had promised, would not take long.

On the sinkbench, she had looked up at the smooth shells. Each time the spoon lifted a boiled egg up out of the water, the shell was darker purple, orange, pink. Darker green, darker blue, darker red. She had not been allowed to watch for long. While she had her nap, the eggs would be hidden in the grass for the Easter Egg Hunt. Before her nap her stepmother had said she must take a bath.

Take off your clothes, Hurry up. Get into the tub. There is nothing to be afraid of. That day her stepmother had not forced the palm of her hand over the plug hole. The big fingers had not bent the little fingers over the drain. When the water sucked down on the Saturday noon of her birthday party, she had not screamed. She sat far back at the shallow end of the tub. Down the pipe the darkness was still there. Down there she would have to breathe water instead of air. Down there she could not get away from the darkness, the silence, the falling that had no end. She had begged to be allowed to stay awake on her birthday. No, after her bath and after her nap, the party would begin.

She had not known each child who came to the party would bring a gift. Or why each gift was put high up on top of a glassed-in bookcase. She could open only one gift, her stepmother had said, at the table. The other gifts must wait until after the children had gone.

At the table by each place, a paper cup held gumdrops. The drops were all colours sprinkled with grains of white sugar. She had never sat at the head of the table before. She did not eat her piece of cake. The almond icing had tasted strange, strong and terrible. Special icing for her birthday cake, her stepmother had said, was to have been a surprise.

There would be a prize for the one who found the greatest number of Easter Eggs. The others ran off to look. She had stood in the middle of the lawn. You can't find even one egg, her stepmother had said, at your own party. Around and around she walked looking. Eggs in the grass, she had thought, must be pretty hard to see. Over there, her father had whispered, along by the hedge. Then the Easter Egg Hunt was over. She was the only one who had found only one egg at her birthday party.

Happy Birthday. My father is about to hang up at his end of the line. What does one say on someone's birthday? I do not ask why he thinks my birthday might be happy. Or whether he is happy today. Or whether, before I hang the receiver back on the hook, he remembers my mother died on my birthday.

Between the parking lot and the solicitor's office, I pass the Returned

Servicemen's Association Centre. TO ALL THOSE WHO HAVE FALLEN IN THE SERVICE OF . . . The words never change. My birthday must have been a deathday for my father. Perhaps he telephoned instead of sorting the negatives.

From the street I walk up two flights. Unlock doors. Switch on lights golden against the dark blue dawn at the windows. Patches of snow lie cruelly along the tops of the hills that circle the city. At noon the walls of the buildings will tower sheerly over icy shadows in the streets below. Because of the phone call, I am an hour early. Suppose today spelling errors slip through . . . occasion, occasionally, regret, regrettable, reconcile, reconciled. Suppose by mistake I erase a tape before I type it. And if they lose confidence in me? Fear rises as I put out stapler, copy stamp, telephone books. In the chill I turn on typewriter, cassette player, adjust the earphones and listen.

LETTER TO . . . REFERENCE . . . NEW PARAGRAPH. We believe this country is hell bent . . . Anything that previously appeared as a subsidy is now unacceptable. Nevertheless mortgage funds are available subject of course to . . . We look forward to dropping down to see you when your ground temperature rises above zero.

REFERENCE: PROFILE ENTERPRISES LTD. You were always aware there would be insufficient funds in total to repay the mortgage advance. But you have gone a long way toward that. Kind regards.

The receptionist arrives at nine o'clock heavy eyed as in a daydream.

LETTER TO: Ms Jane Smith. REFERENCE: DEBT RESTRUCTURING. We enclose a note of our costs and disbursements and a full Statement of Account.

Absolutely miserable weather. Sylvia, Mr Rathbone's assistant, unwraps her scarf. Sylvia with the dark eyes, long skirts and graceful manner. I'm frozen, she says.

NEW PARAGRAPH. We had considerable difficulty obtaining insurance. Guardian Royal decided they did not want to know us anymore. Perhaps you would be kind enough to assist us to get a conclusion on this matter.

Mrs McClaggan! Mr Rathbone strides from his office to the reception area. Lovely to meet you. Come this way, please. The door at the end.

Mr Rathbone's voice drones through the earphones. May we remind you that four o'clock on a Friday can be a trap for the unwary. There is a condition the Contract is subject to you arranging satisfactory finance by four p.m. on Friday the 24th of July next.

At five minutes to five o'clock, Mr Rathbone speaks into the telephone in Sylvia's office. You cannot imagine what I am looking down on from the second floor. Silence dangles from the other end of his line. Whether he hitches his trousers above the hip bones because they fit his previously larger waist, whether he hitches up his trousers because they fit the size waist he thinks he ought to have, is difficult to determine. I am looking down on a dead pig, he says, in the middle of Princes Street.

Horrible! Sylvia frowns, shudders and turns from the window.

I might add, Mr Rathbone continues into the phone. The pig is lying in the centre of a trailer. Hitched behind a ute. Stopped at the lights. The ute, when I move to the window to look down, pulls into the intersection. Then slows for oncoming cars. The pause wobbles the pig flesh. Which wobbles again as the right turn is negotiated.

That, I say, is absolutely disgusting. Blood had smeared the neck of the pig in a great red cloak about its shoulders. Mr Rathbone, I imagine, sends his shirts to the laundry. A clean shirt every day. As well, the latest styles. They must have bled the pig, I say to Sylvia.

On her eighth birthday, her father had told her he would build a swing. Very high. Out of four by four redwood timber. Redwood does not rot in the ground, he had said, for a hundred years. He had sunk the legs of two triangles into holes he had dug. A horizontal beam joined the triangles across the top. Higher than the arbour he had built down the centre of the quarter acre city section. Simpler than the enclosures he had built for rabbits, chickens, cow and pig. Neighbours never complained. People did strange things during the war. Despite rationing, her stepmother had said, they would have plenty of food. Before and after work, her father did the milking morning and evening.

Then her stepmother's father had shifted into the house to help with feeding, breeding and oversight of the young. One afternoon it had been impossible to imagine why that man had his hand under the cow's tail. The cow, her stepmother had explained, had not had a calf before. It was time to get that cow used to the idea of being pregnant. They did not want to hire the bull a second time.

She had never told anyone how the grandfather would stare across the dinner table at her body. By staring back into his eyes, she could stop him staring at her breasts. That man had a jowly face. He chewed with his mouth open.

Early in the morning the squealing had begun. They had cut the vein in the pig's neck. Her stepmother had said, Stay in the house. She had gone out anyway. Blood flowed down the pig's neck and body. Around and around the enclosure the pig ran in the path of its own blood. The squealing had pulled at her stomach, her lungs, her brain. A noose drew tighter against the gasping. The shadow followed behind, catastrophe clutching, falling through space, the cutting off, the darkness before oblivion.

Ropes were attached to pulleys attached to the frame of the swing. The arbour beams, her father had said, were too low. The men had pulled the body of the dead pig higher as they skinned the carcass, cut the flesh, sawed the bones. The guts spilled out on the grass. Meat on the kitchen benches piled up to be packed in plastic bags tied with string. The bags were stacked in boxes. The boxes were taken to a commercial freezing works to store the meat in rented drawers. For two days the house had smelled putrid with fat boiling to make soap the old-fashioned way.

She could swing again, her father had said, after he readjusted the ropes and put back the seat. He had washed the grass with water from the hose. By sundown the next day under the swing a strange damp smell was gone. She never felt dizzy the arc of the swing was so wide. She sat in the swing and looked up at the sky. The ropes cast shadows across the scaffolding from which the pig had been hung.

At five o'clock in the afternoon in winter in Dunedin, ice gathers in the shadows on the stairways and along the footpaths. Out on the street I look across and up at the words, PERMANENT BUILDING SOCIETY. The framework of sashes stretch in a black grid across the fluorescence of lighted rooms on each of the eight levels. I think of the bones my father cannot bear to look at. The glow of my mother's flesh he dare not remember.

I fasten the collar of my coat as I pass the Centre, TO ALL THOSE WHO HAVE FALLEN . . . To all those, I think, who must pay to keep from falling . . . pigs, mothers, daughters. To all those who must obtain insurance to secure assets against falling. To all those who must restructure an inherited liability. To all those who must mortgage the present to the past to keep from falling.

Christine Johnston

[Prayer Dove]

from *Blessed Art Thou Among Women*

On 9 September 1959, Carmel Maria Connelly knelt before Our Lady of Perpetual Succour in the Cathedral of Saint Joseph in Dunedin, New Zealand. It was the custom when Mass was over for members of the faithful to approach Our Lady with a special intention, and so it was that Carmel knelt down on the red velvet cushion at the altar rail for the second time that morning — she had received Communion during Mass —and prayed that her father would lift her mother off her feet and whirl her around the kitchen.

The prayer was not framed in words, but was rather a sweet and treasured memory that the nine-year-old child laid at the altar. It could be said that her prayer was the result of Carmel having approached Our Lady because she enjoyed the theatrical (and nothing was more theatrical than to leave one's pew and approach the altar where the smell of extinguished candles hung visibly in the air, and to kneel before the icon, an object of such lavish and exotic beauty in a church of plaster statues, while the restless congregation choked the portals of the cathedral in their eagerness to get home to breakfast). She arrived at the place for special intentions absentmindedly recalling the occasion when her father had swept her mother off her feet in the kitchen, whereupon Carmel's sigh of pleasure and nostalgia together with her longing for a repetition spawned a prayer of such heartfelt emotion and such unselfish purity that it was seen by one Joseph Saba to emanate from her head in the form of a white dove and wing soundlessly to the highest point in this scaled-down colonial-Gothic cathedral and apparently pass through the stonework.

Nine-year-old Carmel's prayer-in-the-shape-of-a-dove was seen to emerge from the grey slate roof by Father O'Neill, who was at his window in the building known as the Bishop's Palace on the rise opposite the cathedral, and wing heavenward, causing Father O'Neill no surprise — he was not an ornithologist — but making him recall, inexplicably, his second cousin, Pauline Corchoran, for whom he had once had feelings that were neither priestly nor cousinly.

Old Joe Saba, however, although likewise no ornithologist, was arrested by the vision of Carmel's prayer to the extent that he dropped the rosary beads that he was holding in his right hand. Reaching to retrieve them — they had never been out of his hand in the presence of the Blessed Sacrament for the previous 30 years — he was struck a blow on the forehead, striking him (doubly) as appropriate punishment for having inadvertently broken a vow, and was obliged to sit back on the seat to regain his equilibrium. He had seen a white dove rising from the head of a child praying before Our Lady. A marvellous thing, a miracle of course. Its meaning was clear to him. He had known many marvels since his birth in Lebanon in the previous century.

By this time Carmel had vacated the praying place for the extensive Kennedy family who prayed collectively that their eldest boy, Francis Xavier, would answer the call and accept his vocation to the priesthood, a prayer which had no paranormal manifestation for Joseph or for anyone else. The prayer was in vain in any case, as Francis's girlfriend, Marilyn, a non-Catholic, was shortly thereafter to fall pregnant and they would be married in the sacristy, among the brushes and brooms it was said, to the very great shame of the Kennedy clan. But that was another story, a common enough one in Saint Joseph's in the 1950s, a story that surprised and moved no one including Joe Saba.

Lebanese (or Assyrian, as he and his countrymen were known), Joe lived in a tiny room at the back of his niece's house in Carroll Street. He was always fingering his rosary beads, which had become almost translucent with use, indeed the rosary seemed to pass through his fingers of its own volition, the fingers being so gnarled and arthritic as to be incapable of manipulating the tiny beads. His lips moved continuously, whether in English or Latin or his own language it wasn't known, and the beads moved through the crippled fingers day and night, his prayers seeming to God like the murmur of the waves or the chirping of the sparrows. To the Fenesseys and the Toomeys, the Flynns and the Currans, in short to all the parishioners of Saint Joseph's, the prayers of old Joseph Saba were, in spite of his name being the same as their patron saint's and in spite of his brown tweed suit, an extravagance which gave rise to doubts as to whether his devotions had anything in common with their own. Obliged by pressure of numbers to pray alongside old Joseph, they were distracted by the working hands, the working lips and the smell of foreign food.

It has often been observed that God works in mysterious ways, and indeed Mr Saba was granted a vision that morning in September 1959 which was denied all others, save Father O'Neill (on whom it was lost), of a prayer dove rising out of the bowed head of Carmel Connelly, aged nine, in front of an icon — Our Lady of Perpetual Succour, brought home from Rome by the first bishop, who had fallen in love with the foreignness of the almost-black face of the Virgin Mother, that very same foreignness which had so confused and distracted members of his flock. The current bishop's devotion to Our Lady of Perpetual Succour was outstanding but was witnessed by very few. However, Carmel Connelly's mother, whose name was not a saint's name but significantly the name of a flower, spent an hour every Friday night keeping the Blessed Sacrament company — and she had seen the face of the young bishop uplifted to the beautiful black face of the Mother of God. This sight had exemplified for Camellia the beauty and harmony that were sadly absent from her immediate domestic situation and she had felt inspired by the demonstration of the young bishop's devotion. Camellia too was devoted to Our Lady of Perpetual Succour. She dared to believe that the Virgin had addressed her one evening in 1943, turning her life around with a promise as yet unfulfilled. For this reason she came faithfully to her hour of adoration and was occasionally rewarded.

So it was not by chance that Carmel brought to Our Lady of Perpetual Succour a fond memory and wished earnestly for its repetition. Chance has no part to play in this story.

Joseph Saba was to keep all these things in his heart for many years and just as he had once vowed never to let his rosary beads fall from his hands and to make his every breath a prayer, he now resolved to discover the identity of the prayer-dove girl whose face he had not seen. He would search for her among the many white-skinned, mousy-haired daughters of the parish while the beads slipped through his fingers and his lips mouthed mysterious prayers. From that day on Mr Saba gave great attention to the hair and necks of mousy-haired girls of a certain age. It was a habit which did not endear him to parishioners.

By this time the prayer bird had reached its destination. Its snow-white purity was matched in beauty only by the sad black face of the Queen of Heaven. The Divine Attention was arrested and drawn to the hitherto unremarkable Carmel Maria Connelly, who was even now stumbling down the cathedral steps in the mistaken belief that her mother had gone home without her. (Camellia was obscured behind a pillar of the porch, purchasing a copy of the *Tablet* and endeavouring to avoid a number of large, bossy women whose company she did not relish.) Mousy hair and pale cheeks notwithstanding, Carmel was at that moment as pristine, unselfish and unworldly as she would ever be, aspiring only to have her father take her mother in his arms, and God was sorely tempted to take her to Himself.

At the time when the prayer dove manifested itself, a certain Danny Neary, formerly of that parish but now lapsed and fallen from grace, living in substandard accommodation in Elm Row, was calling upon God, albeit blasphemously, to relieve his constipation. He had already been sitting in his outhouse which was held together with ivy for a good ten minutes, and he feared he might not be the first at the shop when it opened, to collect his *Star Sports*. Danny decided there and then as he resumed his trousers that he would buy prunes along with his *Star Sports* that Sunday morning. He would also take his car to the shop so as to maintain his habit of being the first and to avoid the crowd of churchgoers who were always ready for some indulgences after Mass (indulgences of the sweet and sticky kind). He was keen to avoid the grace-filled, God-sanctioned congregation because the sight of them on Sunday morning aroused in him feelings of rage and murder which surprised even himself. At all costs an encounter with the parishioners, some of whom would know and recognise him, was to be avoided.

The Ford Prefect started first time and Danny took off at speed. He was appalled to see the cathedral steps already thronged with people who spilled out onto the footpath. It was unlikely that any would have reached the shop yet, but Danny took the corner in front of Saint Joseph's sharply in a last-ditch effort to be outside the shop when it opened.

Carmel Connelly was anticipating her mother's annoyance at her slowness and so she paid little attention to the traffic, which was normally only parishioners driving home. She stepped out onto the road.

The impression must not be given that Carmel Connelly was saintly or in any way more pleasing to God than any other nine-year-old. No more was her prayer at the shrine at all typical of the general run of her special intentions. Why, only the previous Sunday she had offered the promise of a lifelong abstinence from licorice in return for the transformation of her brunette walkie-talkie doll into a blonde one exactly like Brigid O'Shea's. She had at various times prayed for pink wallpaper, an inside toilet, stiff petticoats and even for Catherine-Mary Blackie to lose the power of speech. She bit her nails, fibbed, invented sins and had strenuously denied breaking a treasured teacup and burying the pieces.

Even so, her fresh young soul was shining with grace that morning when at one minute to ten she stepped off the kerb and it should by rights have been dispatched in mint condition to its Creator, while Carmel's earthly remains twitched hideously in the gutter. Not so. Was God's hand stayed by the black-eyed beauty? Was this an example of Divine Indecision? Or did Carmel herself stake a claim to life by exhibiting then a trait which would, as it turned out, dog her throughout her days? At any rate she stepped back onto the footpath and Danny Neary's Ford Prefect passed harmlessly by, with the driver berating the Roman Catholic Church for filling its children's heads so full of nonsense that they came out of church ready to step under the wheels of passing cars and startled level-headed citizens on their way to pick up the *Star Sports*. He had already forgotten about the prunes.

Carmel Connelly was groping in the gutter when her mother's voice startled her.

'Carmel, what in the name of God are you doing, grovelling in the gutter in front of everyone?' Her gesture encompassed the steep steps leading up to the cathedral, an amphitheatre of non-spectators to Carmel's non-death. 'I thought I saw a thruppence,' said Carmel.

Her mother scanned the gutter. A thruppence was a thruppence after all. She sighed.

'I don't see a thruppence, and look at your glove, all messy. Can't you look after your clothes? God knows, money doesn't grow on trees. I get you nice white gloves to wear to church and you end up with your hands in the gutter. Let's get home for heaven's sake or your father will be wondering if we've been run over.'

A thruppence was a wonderful thing in 1959, a tiny, light sliver of silver with the most beautiful diminutive design — two crossed Maori clubs, objects at once indigenous and alien to Carmel and her mother. And it was legal tender. So mother and daughter both turned and scrutinised the gutter again before walking away. In silence they laboured up Brown Street, which provided them with no relief, only a retaining wall on either side, coarse grey concrete full of holes like sponge cake and sporting virtually the only piece of graffiti seen in Dunedin in the 1950s — a V-for-victory-sign. (There was a representation of male genitalia on the wall of the old horse sale-yards in the notorious McLaggan Street, but male genitalia meant nothing to Carmel in 1959.)

How different it might have been if Carmel had not fancied she saw a thruppence in the gutter! All this had been in the eye of God — fellow parishioners running up Brown Street to fetch Charlie Connelly and impart the dreadful news; Camellia, nauseated and distracted by the sight of her only child ground into the gutter, asking only that her husband should come so that she could lean upon him and need him; the couple eventually brought together, weeping in each other's arms, while priests whispered of God's ways not being our ways and suffer the little children to come unto Me. Camellia and Charlie being led away to the Bishop's Palace for a cup of tea and a brief audience with the young bishop who was in no doubt as to Carmel's readiness to meet God, since she had received Holy Communion and prayed at Our Lady's picture. The funeral, days and sleepless nights later, Charlie and Camellia supporting each other, united in grief, strong in their faith, glorious and beautiful at the graveside, returning home to sort out her things, reading her school exercise books cover to cover. ('We want you to have these, Mrs Connelly. She was a good little worker and a neat writer.' Sister Mary Michael, OP). Treasuring her little prayerbook with its holy pictures, smiling wistfully at her tortured attempt to knit a peggy square, closing the door of her room and walking slowly upstairs to lie weeping in the dark silence night after night. But after some weeks, when each marvelled at the other's inner strength, they confessed a very great love, an intensified love of each other and sought consolation in coition, after which they opened up frankly and warmly, enjoying an intimacy they had never known before and which both valued and nurtured. In the time that followed they became like young lovers, Camellia growing daily more beautiful and Charlie, finding new reason to live, turning his back on the Grand Hotel and the Christian Brothers' Old Boys, hurrying home to be with this fine, strong woman, his wife. The day came when he surprised her in the kitchen and gathering her into his arms he whirled her around the room, while she laughed and squealed — an act to which neither attached any significance. Then Camellia could tell Charlie that from that tearful-joyful coupling would come a child, to be born in the new decade. Her eyes shone. She knew she would not miscarry.

'How do you know?'

'I just know.'

And how excited little Carmel would have been!

How excited little Carmel would have been indeed, to have had a little brother, Michael Joseph Connelly, born in July 1960, while large snowflakes fell and the city glowed in reflected light. But it was not to be.

And as for Danny Neary, whose dingy room in Elm Row overlooked the Connellys' garden of pear trees and convolvulus, how would Carmel's untimely death have altered the path of his life? Danny had lost his faith as a result of the watersiders' strike of '51. His religious zeal had been Jesuitical but it had withered overnight, leaving him with a vacuum so terrifying that strong drink was frequently called upon to hold his life together, in much the same way as his outhouse remained erect with the aid of ivy.

Convicted of dangerous driving causing death, Danny Neary would have suffered a personal upheaval as devastating as the Connellys'. He would never again purchase the *Star Sports* and accepted constipation as the punishment it truly was. The discomfort in his bowels could not be compared to the troubling of his conscience. The Catholic values so recently submerged in his life surfaced to condemn him. He lived in Hell.

Danny would not have been recognised on Friday nights in a dark corner at the back of Saint Joseph's, his eyes fixed on the bowed head of Camellia Connelly. His heart was full, although he hadn't touched the drink, but he dared not approach her or the altar. Father O'Neill saw him but attached no importance to his presence, so carried away was he by the tide of his own great problem and the problem of Pauline Corchoran. Weeks would pass before Danny Neary could approach the altar (though he could never bring himself to approach Camellia) and then his gesture of prostration was so dramatic, if not theatrical, that it interrupted the devotions of the young bishop to Our Lady of Perpetual Succour. He was alone at the front of the cathedral because of Camellia's confinement and it was he who offered the renegade the elixir of the confessional and a cup of tea.

Do not think badly of God, Who entertained the notion of crushing Carmel under the wheels of a Ford Prefect. (This method of dispatch was not personally favoured by Him, but was rather dictated to Him by the times.) Such were the eternal benefits which might have accrued to at least three souls in the parish of Saint Joseph's but for the illusion of a thruppence in the gutter, a thruppence which was never found, which in all probability never existed, but which, given a vein of acquisitiveness in Carmel — inherited from Camellia and compounded by poverty — was enough to tip the balance in favour of Carmel continuing to live.

Joe Saba must not be overlooked. Imagine his reaction on finding the mousy hair matted with blood, knowing as he did that it had been the nest, if you like, of the miraculous prayer bird and that he alone among all the McIlroys and McAlevys and McCarthys had been singled out to witness its ascent to the Gothic heights. Might he not have interpreted these events as indicating a calling to the Communion of Saints, seen himself as a lone disciple of the mousy-haired martyr and whipped up for her a following in the Lebanese community? A sect is born in Carroll Street and High Street, high above the city's commercial centre, a movement of Dunedin's Lebanese Catholics with a saint of its own, a miracle, and a prophet called Joseph Saba, whose rosary now whips through rejuvenated fingers and whose lips now speak loudly in tongues, incomprehensible even to him. The parish is divided and the movement of Lebanese Catholics into the ruling Presbyterian class of Dunedin is arrested forever.

How would the young bishop's devotion to the black Virgin hold up with such a schism in his flock? Would he not one Friday night prostrate himself in imitation of Danny Neary before the altar of God, only to see the shapely ankles of Camellia Connelly at eye level and her hand raising him up? He might well have been won over by Camellia in the dimly lit cathedral and have taken to Rome the cause of Carmel Connelly, the application for beatification and eventual canonisation.

But this is speculation.

The truth of the matter is that Carmel Connelly's identity was unknown to the Lebanese community in September 1959, except to Susie Farr, her classmate, who didn't particularly like her. And anyway a bona fide saint should by definition be dead, and Carmel had clearly sidestepped death and was matching her mother's stride as they arrived at the top of Brown Street, pausing briefly for breath and reconnaissance. Camellia sighed and her gloved hand brushed her daughter's shoulder. How she loved the view — city, harbour, hills and ocean.

Dunedin is a city which in turn encloses and liberates. A vista of azure laced about with hills gives way to the view of a retaining wall and a bank of old man's beard. Turn right to the South Pacific, turn left to a sunless hollow, a tangle of convolvulus and sycamore, smelling of death.

Camellia's eyes sought and found the blue horizon. She could hold fast to that distant line — the promise of heaven beyond the hills.

Camellia Connelly was a handsome woman. She was tall, dark-haired and dark-eyed, with a good figure and beautiful ankles. Her daughter on the other hand was fair. Carmel took after the Connellys.

Camellia's reaction on seeing Carmel at the foot of the cathedral steps with her hand in the gutter was the thought that her daughter had been sent as a cross for her to bear, as a punishment for loving Basil Crighton and not marrying him or for marrying Charlie Connelly and not loving him, not loving him enough, for love him she did, of course. But God knows, he could be difficult. God knows. Or for denying her true vocation, perhaps? That was a sin, worse probably than letting a married man (a non-Catholic) kiss you. Until she had put a stop to it. And she had put a stop to it. Eventually. An occasion of sin? Probably. Definitely. But. The situation had been impossible. Still was.

And Basil had been charming, handsome in his own way, rich, confident and her boss. It was hard to find a good job in wartime and the money was needed. And the kisses. Well. Just romance.

A desperate situation calls for something. The convent like a suitor always hanging about. Twenty-five, twenty-six, twenty-seven. And the babies, her picture-book nephew and niece, sent to tempt her into motherhood.

Enter Charlie. No, re-enter Charlie, seen in a new light, seen in the wrong light. There had been some romance. But.

The convent had at once attracted and repelled. It was possible of course to reach a degree of holiness in marriage. Sainthood was not ruled out by . . . . But. God knows.

Such were Camellia's thoughts as she walked home with her daughter on the thirteenth Sunday after Pentecost. Thoughts? They were more like little spirals of abstraction arising from the present, departing from it in giddy fashion and collapsing. 'Ah well.' Leaving her with the present. 'Ah well.' Basil Crighton. 'Ah well.' Charlie Connelly. 'Ah well.' Cupboard drinking. 'Ah well.' Leaking roof. Hole in bathroom floor. Threadbare carpet in hall. 'Ah well.'

God — now there was something pretty solid. It seemed to Camellia that God probably had something better in store for her, in this world as well as in the next. It seemed unlikely that He would bring her into the world as the daughter of a prosperous businessman and his beautiful musical wife to enjoy a few short years of affluence, before the Depression reduced their circumstances to such an extent that they could not comprehend it or believe it, and then, and then, lead her into the temptation of Basil Crighton which she had withstood, and then present, re-present her with Charlie Connelly, who seemed a pretty safe bet, being a Catholic, although from out South, and being as he said 'in love' with her, and then, and then allow them to slide further into poverty (not to mention debt and cupboard drinking) for ever and a day. That didn't sound like God at all. It seemed more likely that God had a rosy future in store for the Connellys and Camellia had conceived a way by which God could restore her fortunes, remove temptations and set her on the path to sainthood. It was the Art Union.

The Art Union was won regularly by New Zealand families just like the Connellys, setting them up in new 1950s-style homes and providing washing-machines, electric ovens, vacuum cleaners, even cars and bicycles, all of which the Connellys lacked, not to mention Selby shoes, Burberry coats, pigskin gloves and other necessities of life. All Camellia had to do was skimp a bit more, buy the tickets and keep an eye on the results in the *Evening Star.* And pray. There was ample opportunity for that.

There was another scenario. Charlie, finding inspiration in the *Australian Home Beautiful,* would launch into an energetic programme of home restoration, instead of making marquetry pictures of English village scenes, so that Number 19 could match the tidy frontage of Number 21. Both houses had been built in 1901 to the same design, and to the extent that one was well maintained, so was the other (theirs) neglected.

And a start had been made — logically enough — on the foundations or piles as they were called, so that this scenario could be considered less fanciful than the other. But what had happened that Saturday afternoon nine months ago when Charlie, after an hour and half under the house with a bottle jack, had come up, turned on the cricket and sat down to listen to it, smoking his Capstan Corks as if it were the most natural thing in the world? He had subsequently announced that he was going 'down town', which meant the Grand Hotel. That was the end of it. He sometimes mentioned to people that he 'was doing up the piles', but there was no evidence that he ever intended crawling under the house again. Camellia supposed that it was hard work raising a house, Herculean perhaps, and marquetry was more in his line. But. Ah well.

They were almost home, but just as they turned the corner into Duncan Street, Camellia stopped short and announced, 'I've just remembered. I dreamt about the bishop last night.' With surprise (always with surprise), innocence and delight she recalled her dream.

'I was going down the garden with the washing and there he was in his cassock with the purple buttons beside the apple tree. "Camellia," he said, "how charming you look with your basket of apples." Basket of apples? I looked and there in the washing basket instead of the sheets were so many big, red apples. They were the biggest, reddest apples I'd ever seen. And I said, "May I offer you an apple, My Lord?" And he said, "Alas, Mrs Connelly, I cannot accept." Now fancy that. What a strange dream! He would never say anything like that. Far too shy. That just goes to show how stupid dreams are.'

Carmel had watched her mother's face as she related her dream. Camellia had laughed with delight and her daughter saw her mother suddenly become quite animated by mirth and pleasure. Camellia stood with her hand on the gatepost where the old wooden gate had been until it became unhinged and had to be pushed back under the hydrangeas. She wanted to hang on to the dream and Carmel was right there with her, smiling too at this fantastic conversation under the apple tree, taking it a step further, seeing her mother carefully hanging out the apples on the tree, like the Hand of God, while the bishop sang like a thrush.

'He must have been fasting,' added Camellia as they went in.

Charlie was not up but would soon emerge and prepare himself for eleven o'clock Mass. His habit of attending a different Mass from his wife and daughter was puzzling, because it is a fine sight to see a Catholic family kneeling together, receiving Communion together and walking home with the *Tablet* tucked under an arm, thereby fortified against the temptations of the new week. It had not gone unnoticed that Charlie preferred to pray alone. Perhaps he liked a lie-in? Perhaps he disliked his wife's manner of praying, or her taffeta coat, in which she resembled Jennifer Jones with her thick, black hair and fine, dark eyes? Did he dislike escorting his tall, beautiful wife, who seemed to be growing taller and more beautifully statuesque in spite of poverty, while he himself was shrinking visibly? Or, more to the point, did he dislike Camellia? It seems improbable that a man of 32 would 'fall in love' with a woman of 27 and marry her, only to discover after some years and a child that he disliked her. Only Charlie could say for sure whether or not he disliked his wife, but of course the question never arose.

Suffice it to say (with certainty) that Charlie disliked his wife's taffeta coat for the reason that it suited her too well. He disliked a certain 'theatrical streak' in her family, chiefly in her mother. This theatrical streak would in time show itself in Carmel (the beginnings had been exhibited that very morning in front of Our Lady of Perpetual Succour). Along with this failing, Carmel would inherit an acquisitiveness (already noted) for objects such as gloves and shoes, tablecloths and fine china, cut glass and diminutive reproductions of the Madonna and Child painted on silk. These tendencies would in time further alienate Carmel from Charlie. All this was to come, although the seeds were already sown that Sunday morning when Camellia and Carmel entered the dingy hallway of Number 19, united by a dream of huge red apples as much as by the bread of angels.

'You go and change out of those good clothes, Carmel dear, and I'll put the kettle on for a cup of tea and then you come in and watch the toast, but don't leave your prayerbook there on the chair or you'll be looking for it tonight when we go to Benediction.'

Camellia took the electric kettle out to the scullery and filled it in the gloom. She heard her husband descending the stairs.

'Oh, hello, Charlie.'

'What's the time?'

'It's ten past.'

'Who said Mass?'

'Father West.'

'Preached?'

'Yes. On the rosary.'

'Aw.' Charlie didn't think much of the rosary. 'Where's the *Tablet*? I'll have a look at it before I go.'

Of course it would be childish to argue over who read the *Tablet* first, so Camellia plugged in the kettle and went upstairs to hang up her taffeta coat and change her dress. Their bedroom smelt of cigarettes and the chamber pot, and the urine smelt of alcohol, just a little. Open the window, insert a piece of four-by-two, and ah, the view. Fly, little bird, from the heart of Camellia Connelly, née Chambers, across the grey stone city, over the ships at the wharf and down the bay, away, away from this rank little room with its smell, his smell, and its sagging wallpaper with the map-of-Africa watermark. 'You deserve better,' her mother had said. But then. But. Ah well. No point in.

Camellia sees herself in the mirror, a handsome woman in a dark blue taffeta coat standing in front of a dressing table with its cut crystal powder bowl and its cut crystal scent bottle — empty. Camellia lifts her chin and looks herself in the eye. She pats her hair — it is strong, thick hair which bounces back. She eyes herself critically, judges herself by a standard that is her mother's standard. She makes a half turn before the mirror. She is not without vanity. Then her eye strays to the stained wallpaper hanging loosely on the scrim and to the pieces of scuffed underlay which serve as carpet.

There is an irony here. There is an irony in Camellia's good looks, in her stylish coat, her neat little hat, her kid gloves and her elegant shoes. The irony is not lost on Camellia.

In comes Carmel, changed from her Sunday best into her Sunday worst, showing her blue knees and those hands. Too much wrist and naked hands. She is an awkward, graceless child.

'Mum, the kettle's boiled.'

'Did you turn it off?'

'I think so.'

'You think so?'

'Well, I turned it off, but it seemed to keep going, so I switched it the other way and then I couldn't remember . . . What's this for?'

'That's for scent. You do this.' Camellia takes the ornate crystal stopper and dabs her daughter's neck with imaginary scent.

'It's lovely. It's so cool.'

'With scent it's even cooler.'

'Hey, Mum, why don't you get some scent?'

'Huh,' Camellia is full of scorn. 'Where am I going to get the money to buy scent?' She sighed and breathed in the cold, damp air of her bedroom, his bedroom. The irony of scent. Carmel watches her mother's face.

Camellia: Are you reading me?

Carmel: Yes, Mother. Reading you loud and clear.

'You never wear this.' Carmel is fingering a marcasite pendant that her mother keeps in a box with other trinkets and broken strings of pearls.

'Oh no. You don't wear that sort of thing for the day. You wear marcasites at night. For balls and that sort of thing. The Charity Ball, for instance. You could wear marcasites to the Charity Ball.'

'Have you been to balls, Mum?' The Seven Dancing Princesses wore out their dancing shoes every night.

'Well, dear, I was presented of course. Years ago. And I went once with Charlie when we were first married. But.'

'Mrs Mooney goes every year, doesn't she?'

'Well, of course they're on the committee. And she's a chaperone. It's all very well for the Mooneys. He's a solicitor. And Nancy has her own money.'

Listen well, Carmel, and pass it on. You will have daughters one day and daughters are nourished with such talk — of balls and marcasites, of being a chaperone, of marrying a solicitor, of having your own money. Think on it. Consider the empty scent decanter, which teaches a lesson for daughters to learn.

And so it is that Charlie enters his bedroom to get his missal and finds his wife still resplendent in her taffeta coat and his daughter holding the marcasite pendant and learning the lesson of the crystal scent bottle and he feels a rage of bilateral jealousy, that his wife should be here in his bedroom with his daughter, filling her head with tripe, and that his daughter should be here enjoying an intimacy with his wife from which he is excluded. And he senses the shadowy presence of a third party of whom he has every reason to be jealous, who occupies first place in Camellia's heart. So he strikes at his wife with: 'The kettle's boiling away.'

'Heavens!' cried Camellia, tearing off the offending coat, hanging it up roughly, kicking off her high heels and with a murderous look at Carmel she is off down the stairs in haste.

'I thought I'd turned it off,' remarks Carmel lamely, feeling glum. She goes downstairs murmuring: 'Up's off, down's on, up's off, down's on, up's off, down's on.'

Carmel had come close to sainthood that morning but it afforded her little joy at half past eleven with her father gone to Mass and her mother reading the *Tablet*. It seemed to her that neither her mother nor her father liked her much, any more than they liked each other. The prospect of taking in arms and whirling about the kitchen was remote indeed.

The model of the Holy Family was always before them, but somehow they always fell short. Carmel felt as her mother did the lure of sainthood. If only she were given a vision like Saint Bernadette or the three children of Fatima. Then she would be a nun. Not an ordinary sort of nun, like the faceless novices who cleaned the convent floors with old tea-leaves, but a celebrity nun, performing miracles and converting non-Catholics.

If Carmel thought such aspirations were pleasing to God she was wrong. They were in fact repugnant both to God and his Byzantine mother and had old Joe Saba been present, he might have seen a vision of snakes and vipers. Such prayers, if prayers they be, do not even rise but rather ebb away down the cracks in the linoleum and end up with the bottle jack and the bottles in Charlie Connelly's hell of under-the-house.

Poor Carmel. She saw in the sweet love of man and wife a lost cause and set her sights on the martyrdom of spirit. As ye sow, so shall ye reap: a relentless logic which the children of God observe and even admire. But what of the temptation of the crystal scent decanter? And balls? And acquisitiveness?

For everything there is a season, says the Bible. Carmel had sidestepped death, thanks be to God and the dream of a thruppence. Her life lay before her. She could manage a future of balls and Catholic solicitors, she could envisage an abundance of thruppences.

Alistair Campbell

Growing Pains in the War Years
from *Island to Island*

At primary school we Campbells were the only pupils to have Polynesian blood, although a family of Maori children were to arrive a little later. They were also 'homies' and were to achieve academic success, one of them being the first girl from the orphanage to pass Matriculation. At high school I was alone. It's incredible to think that in my four years there I was the only coloured boy. I used to wonder about two Jewish boys, refugees from Nazi Germany, with whom I felt some kinship — but I never got to know them.

In those days racism was more blatant than it is now. I remember coming home one day and running into a contemporary who was walking along with a girl, laughing and talking intimately. He was one of those flashy types, with vapid good looks, whom I normally disdained.

'Good-day,' I greeted him.

He grinned at me vacantly, his mind still on the girl he was trying to impress.

'Oh, good-day, nigger.' He turned back to the girl who looked at me and laughed.

I had become accustomed to being addressed as 'snow', 'darky' and even 'Hori', often by adults who would have been surprised had they known they were giving offence. And at high school Stuart was known as Sam (short for Sambo). But 'nigger' was the ultimate, the unforgivable epithet.

Still enraged I rang the boy that evening.

'Yes?' Wary and a little nervous.

'Listen, you bastard. Call me that again —'

'Look — who are you?'

'Quit it. You know well enough. Call me that again — and I'll bloody well kill you.'

To be honest, there was a deeper reason for my fury which I never admitted, even to myself. I was passing myself off as a white person — as I was to do for many years —and this boy had contemptuously exposed me.

Stuart and Margaret preceded me to high school, Stuart going to Otago Boys' and Margaret to Otago Girls', but neither could settle down to serious study. On completing the third form year, Stuart left to become an apprentice panel-beater and Margaret to work in a cake shop, much to the disappointment of friends and teachers, who deplored what they considered to be a waste of talent. What they forgot was that they'd started school late, as I had, and that

Stuart was 16 in form 3, and Margaret a year younger. Being proud and sensitive, they must have found it intolerable to have classmates so much more childish than themselves. I was also 15 in form 3, but thanks to my birth certificate, which happened to be wrong, I thought I was 14. That one year's difference may well have been decisive in determining my future.

My memories of Otago Boys' High School are closely interwoven with memories of World War 2, for I was at high school during the critical years, 1940–43. The billboards at the Dunedin Exchange, which I read each morning and evening on my way to and from school, kept me posted with the latest news — Dunkirk, the Battle of Britain and the mounting 'cricket' scores of German versus British aircraft losses (67 for 11, 180 for 34, 185 for 26), the Battle of the Coral Sea . . .

Even so, the war was never as real as passing 'Matric', beating King's High in rugby, or plucking up the nerve to speak to that pretty girl who travelled to school each day on the same train as I. (I never did pluck up the nerve.)

It may have been this air of unreality that made it difficult for us to take the Home Guard seriously. All those grown-up men in ill-fitting uniforms, solemnly playing at soldiers in their spare time. What would they do with their wooden rifles when the Japanese came? Beat them over the head? Trip them up? Poke them in the ribs until they died laughing?

Then came the astonishing news that the Rector himself had joined the Home Guard. How could he lower himself? Had he gone soft in the head? Well, we thought, they'll have to make him colonel, or at the very least a major. Picture our surprise when we learned that he was only a private. We began to see him in a different light, as if he might be human.

Small of stature, with a high, bulging forehead and a long, slightly puffy, upper lip that he drew back over his teeth when he was angry, H. P. Kidson was a formidable headmaster of the old school, who had the power to intimidate pupils long after they had left his charge. I remember him in retirement at Wanaka, not long before his death, and the sight of that brooding face and sternly puckered mouth made my heart quail, and I was back again in the lower sixth, enduring the lash of his tongue for failing to answer correctly a simple problem in logic.

'A man is an animal. A donkey is an animal. Therefore a man is a donkey. True or false, Campbell?' I was confused and said nothing. 'We are talking about the fallacy of the undistributed middle.' No reply from me. 'Tell me, Campbell, it is possible I'm addressing a donkey?' Still no reply. His face darkened with anger. 'Oh, sit down, boy — and pay attention in future.'

It had been a rough session for all of us, and in our haste to get out of the room there was some jostling in the doorway. Into the midst of this strode the Rector and dealt a blow at the chief offender and sent him reeling. We were appalled, terrified, exhilarated. What could have caused that Olympian self-control to crack? Looking back, I suspect it had something to do with the humiliation that he'd inflicted on me.

That Kidson loved the arts was evident from his weekly art and literary appreciation classes with the sixth forms, and from the recordings of classical music that the whole school was often obliged to listen to. We used to file into assembly to the sombre strains of *Finlandia* — stirring stuff for those dark days of the war. What was less evident was that he himself was an artist in prose.

Was the author of that article in *Landfall*, 'Annus Mirabilis', a lovingly detailed account of a year at Wanaka, really the same H. P. Kidson? I remember Charles Brasch, poet and editor of that literary journal, smiling at my utter disbelief. 'The very same.'

'But how —?'

'He's a highly cultured man — and before you go any further perhaps you should know what he said about your "Elegy" when it first appeared. He was much taken by the poem, and said you were a master of language . . .'

At Wanaka, on the occasion mentioned earlier, Kidson was to repeat his flattering judgement, almost as if he'd been waiting all these years to say it to me personally.

We were sitting outside his lovely stone cottage among alpine flowers and plants in their natural setting, with a view of the mountains across an arm of the lake, while Mrs Kidson brought us tea and biscuits.

'I knew you were miserable as an orphan boy,' he was saying, 'with no choice but to pursue a lonely course. We discussed your problem more than once at staff meetings . . .'

I was touched by his words, but I wondered at a system that kept producing masters who were unable or reluctant to show pupils their concern. It seemed to me a pity that I came to appreciate H. P. Kidson when it was almost too late.

As I write, my masters of those days pass before my eyes, and I remember them with affection — Grub Garden, Pussy Bridgman, Dreamy Watt, Nigger Martyn, Creeper Bailey, Blobs Anderson . . . Their nicknames are a testimony to the schoolboy's unusual flair for affixing the apt appellation. Take Creeper Bailey, who taught us maths, and who owed his nickname to the way he seemed to glide along a few inches from the ground, or Pussy Bridgman, who taught us English, and whose nose seemed to twitch in a cat-like way above his thin moustache when he was amused. Bridgman was the first poet I knew, and I remember being impressed when the Rector announced one morning in assembly that he'd won some poetry prize.

Blobs Anderson, who taught us chemistry, was one of the characters of the school, with his baggy pants, crew-cut hair, slightly popping eyes and mildly risqué jokes delivered in a plummy accent. There was one preposterous story, long in the telling, about how he once tried to cure a lady's nose bleed by placing his key on the back of her neck — but the dashed thing slipped from his fingers, and the problem was how to retrieve it, by George! 'I had to feel inside her dress — a most delicate operation, you understand — and I felt a perfect oss.'

He had been ordained in England and was known to preach the occasional sermon. His favourite expression, which naturally we adopted, was 'Correct me if I'm wrong', and it was told with relish how he would sometimes surprise his congregation by using it in his sermons.

Then there was the legendary Nigger Martyn, so called, not because of his colour, but because of his sallow features, deep-sunken eyes, craggy brow and heavy, sagging eyebrows. When he spoke, his voice rumbled in his throat like the wind in an unswept chimney. His smile, which was rare but which I sometimes provoked by my mathematical ineptitudes, was bleak and fleeting.

Generations of boys had stood in awe of his mathematical genius, but it was his droll wit that I relished and his precision in the use of terminology. Few things irked him more than to hear us say 'nothing' when we meant 'nought' or 'zero'. 'Nothing,' he would rumble, 'is the complete absence of something.' He must have been well past retiring age, but the war, which had caused a general shortage of teachers, had brought him back into service.

It was at high school that I first tried my hand at verse — ponderous lampoons on masters, to begin with, lush exercises in imitation of the worst excesses of Keats, piteous war poems in imitation of Wilfred Owen (the first modern poet I discovered), and, capping them all, a frothy sonnet sequence, full of 'oh' and 'thees' and 'thines', which I composed at St Kilda beach one afternoon, after I'd skipped military drill. I wrote it to impress a girl and succeeded only too well, because she flatly refused to believe it was mine.

Lists of athletic successes are generally boring, so I'll mention in passing that I was a better than average sprinter and a more than useful back, experienced in every position from half-back to wing. I admit I enjoyed being in the first fifteen, partly for the status it conferred — we were, after all, *la crème de la crème* — and partly for the close fellowship that developed among us over weeks of practising, travelling and playing together in many parts of the South Island.

Of my contemporaries, the first that comes to mind is R. D. Fraser, whose friendship meant much to me at a time when I was trying to establish my identity. I remember his mother's kindness to me the first time I was ever drunk. She took me in, put me to bed and placed a bowl by my head in case I was sick. Genial and popular, Bob Fraser was to be head boy and dux of the school, and later a doctor.

Another contemporary was E. J. Carr, who had an aristocratic approach to sports, which was then new in my experience. A natural athlete — a fine swimmer and a swift runner — he refused to train. In spite of that, he often excelled, but took his achievements lightly. Intriguing, too, was the rumour that he composed avant-garde music and was particularly influenced by Stravinsky. Edwin Carr, who is now a distinguished composer, is one of the few classmates that I still see from time to time.

Throughout my years at the orphanage, I saw much of my Uncle Tom (my father's elder brother), my Aunt Flo and my cousins Allan, Graham and

Tom. Uncle Tom used to fascinate me as a small boy by his trick of putting his thumb to his mouth and blowing his biceps up. A Saturday at Uncle Tom's was never complete without a visit to the Captain Cook Hotel not far away, where Aunt Flo's brother was the licensee, and where I could always be sure of a solid meal in the kitchen, a raspberry drink in the bar and always, before I left, a dozen pennies still in their paper roll.

I was to see a little more of our great-aunts during this period. They were Em, Torie and Bean, who had recently joined them, and they lived in a poky little house at 4 Douglas Street, one of the more depressing streets in St Kilda. They kept the place in darkness, even on the finest days — blinds down, curtains drawn.

Margaret told me that she called to see them once, when she was working in a cake shop just around the corner. She knocked repeatedly, and, although she could hear them moving round inside, no one came to the door. She was so cross she wrote them a note in lipstick and called out, 'I know you're in, and I'm not coming back — so there!'

My experiences were different from hers — perhaps because they preferred boys. They used to fuss over me in their dark little kitchen and bring me wine biscuits, or seedcake, and a cup of tea, and they would hover over me, their dry hands fluttering, until they were sure I had all that I needed. Em and Torie, from what I remember, were frail like Grandma, and Aunt Bean, who'd been so round and jolly, had become a ghost like them.

Grandma died on 2 January 1942, in Onehunga, and her body was sent to Dunedin to be buried in a grave beside her husband in Anderson's Bay Cemetery. It may have been in the semi-darkness of the great-aunts' living room that I saw her coffin. I can't be sure — but I do remember an occasion when Aunt Peg came into a darkened room and saw me and nearly had a fit. 'My God — Jock!' she said. For a moment she'd thought her brother had returned from the dead. I was 17 at the time.

I used to ride a push-bike 3 miles to High School — quite a distance in hilly Dunedin. I gave it up after I'd come a cropper at the bottom of Silverstone Street, where it turns quite sharply into Musselburgh Rise, and could have been killed if a car had been coming towards me.

Sometimes at high school I felt I didn't belong, not only because of my colour, but also because I was poor. I'd take it hard to have to leave my friends after football practice, when they went to the tuckshop for a milkshake. I was never given pocket-money — except sometimes by Margaret and Stuart, who were both working then — and I couldn't join them.

These were restless years for Stuart. After working for a while as a panel-beater he joined the Otago Mounted Rifles — our father's old regiment. But after his accident, he left the Army and drifted north, where he was directed by the Manpower Board to work in a dairy factory at Kopuarahi. From there, he joined the Air Force as AC2 in the Central Camp near Hamilton. He loathed the life, and in 1944 he joined the Maori Battalion, where at last he felt at home. He wrote to me, 'We've got a great crowd here — they're rough as guts, but they can drill.' Later in the year he left for the war.

I still spent my Christmas holidays at Robertson's orchard in the Cromwell Gorge, picking fruit, and it was there that I received a telegram from Margaret in Dunedin, announcing that I'd passed Matric. I remember bounding with joy through the orchard, shouting, 'I've passed Matric! I've passed Matric!' It was a big day in my life.

One year two senior boys from King's High School came to work on the farm, one of whom I remember clearly, because of a fight we once had, using broom handles for quarterstaffs. It was friendly enough to start with, but it soon became serious because of my will to win. Being some years older than me and strongly built, he easily parried my strokes, smiling all the while, which made me madder than ever. In the end, exhausted and humiliated — I wasn't used to being bested — I burst into tears. His reaction, totally unexpected, was to show such concern that I cried more bitterly than before. How dare he beat me and be so decent! His name was Ron Keller and he was to join the Air Force soon afterwards as a navigator, and was killed in the Battle of Britain.

Evening was the best time of the day, when the warm air was scented with thyme and horehound, and I would take my gun and wander over the hills in search of rabbits. I usually went alone, but when a girl accompanied me we would sometimes end up by the river on a patch of sand still warm from the day's heat. I remember one such occasion because the smell of my feet in sandshoes came between us just as we were about kiss. I was embarrassed and found some excuse to go back to the house. I was never to have a second chance because next day she went home to Dunedin.

A swaggie had a regular beat up the Cromwell Gorge and was a familiar sight, with his torn felt hat, tattered long overcoat, and his sack over his shoulder containing all his worldly goods. He never hurried or varied his stride, and was always courteous, touching his hat to Mrs Robertson as he asked her if she had some little job that he might do. She would set him chopping firewood and, when he'd finished, would give him a little money and feed him.

He had a gift of water-divining. We used to watch in wonderment as the forked willow stick he was gripping, a prong in either hand, twisted and dipped towards the ground, as if with a life of its own. 'Dig here,' he'd say, turning to Mr Robertson, 'and you'll find your water. About 15 feet down is my guess.' But Mr Robertson never took his advice. The performance was what he enjoyed, and he wanted to share it with us.

Those were good days, with ice-cold dips in the green swirling Clutha; cricket matches with other orchard crews played on pitches so bumpy and hazardous — the ball would pop up, shoot along the ground, or disappear down a rabbit hole — that victory was determined less by skill than recklessness; Mrs Robertson's cooking for which we could find no adequate superlatives; and, above all, the irresistible combination of fruit in abundance and lightly clad nubile girls smelling of apricots. The horn of plenty indeed!

Graham Lindsay

Green Island

In the quiet weekday suburb of Green Island
someone in a garage hammering away
a photographer with time in hand, passing by
stops short before a silent brick bungalow
dazzled by its eave
the backdrop is a vista of hinterland
against the blare of sun's particles
nebulous distance and a plain of orange sky
stretching back over Central
voices issue through the wind's white noise
a couple straight out of the Fifties are taking leave of each other
the man striding round his car to the suicide door
the skirted woman skipping down her driveway
into the sun-bleached air
three scant children come into the picture
playing on trikes and carts sweeping out into the roadway
theirs are the last children's sounds
on the side of the suburb
(across the valley families pose beside a deepening fissure
the hill a mudstone skid with the chocks kicked out)
the photographer takes a shot ('Vision of the Post-War Madonna')
and climbs above the houses into farmland
walking along plateau-top lanes with dusty hawthorn hedgerows
the sun flaring as though through dark glasses
glancing off the flaxen grass
to a view of the sea
dust and spray commingling above the margin.

Bill Sewell

Sutton

(for Bunty & Eric Herd)

A landscape which lets us let go of time.
Rocks which might be ruins, but are not:
far older, they have twisted their shadows
away from the sun and held back time.
                                    So
everything slows down there (excepting time)
into a routine which has no tedium:
parts of the day for assembling, for gin,
steak, Scrabble; others for ambling away —

To vegetable patch, siesta, the hunt for rabbits
or mushrooms; whatever. Like the rocks these
are constants, however quickly they vanish —

So we can understand, that in the summer,
when it's time for the lamp at last, the light
wants to linger, making the far land glow.

Neville Peat

[Winter Solstice: Strath Taieri]
from *The Falcon and the Lark: A New Zealand High Country Journal*

ONE

Above the crater, where a few clouds have gathered, the sky begins to glow — light ochre at first, an earthy colour, hardening in minutes to orange. Shades of pink flank the orange core. Suddenly the sky is aflame, bursting red.

From my vantage point on the lower slopes of the Rock and Pillar Range, I can just make out the dark, pouting lips of the crater on the Taieri Ridge skyline east of Middlemarch — the opposite side of the valley. Despite appearances, the fireworks in the sky do not signal another eruption, a rerun of the events of 10 million years ago. This landscape is largely made of schist, a kind of non-volcanic sedimentary rock. The lighting is simply explained: the sun is coming up over Taieri Ridge.

Yet this is no ordinary sunrise. It is the one that ends the Longest Night and prefaces the Shortest Day — the Winter Solstice sunrise.

The pause is not perceptible but you know, because it has always been so, that somewhere in the railway yards of our solar system the points are switched, noiselessly, automatically. It happens twice a year, winter and summer, and the planet, leaning as it spins, sets out on its orbit to favour the opposite hemisphere with sunshine, encouraging an all-over tan.

Golden brown is the prevailing colour the year round in the Strath Taieri. This morning it is white-dusted with frost, the product of a still, clear winter's night. As the sun lifts out of the distant crater its rays seek out the valley floor where Middlemarch, population 189, lies in a cold cuddle of fog. I am well above the fog and predict it will disappear as the day warms. It barely covers the big pine trees round the village showgrounds and is already breaking up at the edges, a fleeced effect.

This fog is nothing like the winter fogs of old that used to lie for days on end, conspiring with hoar frost to keep the village deep-frozen around the clock. The story goes that it got cold enough then to freeze the steam engine's whistle. Cold enough, too, to freeze a candle flame solid — to put out the light you snipped the flame with a pair of scissors.

I am aware that the first hour before sunrise is usually the coldest, which is why I have come well-insulated to this lookout point above my base at Gladbrook

Station — woollen hat and gloves, woollen seaman's jumper under a padded cold-weather jacket, woollen socks and thermal socks inside lace-up gumboots, and, yes, long-johns. To farewell the Longest Night I take no chances.

Ten minutes before I feel the first twinkle of solstice sun it is painting the Rock and Pillar tops, a thousand metres above me, a brilliant amber that falls as a curtain across the entire face. The range seems to hum its approval and, on impulse, I haul out my harmonica, its metal casing bitingly cold, and contribute a couple of verses of *Amazing Grace* to the show.

A fortnight ago these mountains sported a dapper waistcoat of snow, but a thaw since has reduced it to tatters. Irregular white squiggles are all that remains — high-country hieroglyphs.

Across the top of the range, outcrops of schist rise in jagged formation above the alpine meadows like the teeth of a much-abused saw. They give the range its name — Rock and Pillar. In fact, they are much older than the range itself, which was uplifted along a fault line just five million years ago. Its schist actually started out as a rock called greywacke, which was formed from sediments laid down on the ocean floor 400 million years ago. Heat and pressure from upwellings of the earth's molten core slowly transformed the greywacke into schist and in the process infused into it quartz lodes bearing gold, scheelite and other ores — a treasure chest.

But rock of hybrid origin does not necessarily develop hybrid strength. The name, schist, is derived from a Greek word meaning to split, and this the rock does spectacularly well in the Strath Taieri.

It splits, crumbles and weathers along lines of weakness. Curiously, many outcrops are sliced clean through across the grain; in others the layers are folded into corrugated patterns, hooks and chevrons. You may stumble on perfectly round holes filled with red algae which geologists, exercising not a little imagination, describe as 'Druids' sacrificial vessels'. Altogether, then, the schist leads a rotten life, shattered by frost, baked by summer sun, and thrashed by wind storms. Ancient gales were responsible for the loess soils surrounding the outcrops — wind-blown silt and dust from western inland regions and possibly even from the continental shelf out east, long since submerged.

The biggest and toughest of the schist outcrops still standing above the loess are called tors. In a few places these tors form ridges and from my sunrise lookout I can see some of the best examples away to my right, on the Sutton Hills, which deflect the Taieri River east towards its gorge and mark the southern boundary of the valley.

From this height and distance and in the frosty primeval dawn light the ridges show up as the spiny backs of dinosaurs poking out of parallel graves.

8.27 am, 21 June. The sun hits the dinosaur I have chosen to sit on. It bursts through a gap between crater and clouds, shockingly bright but devoid of warmth just yet. I whisper a prayer for its ascent into summer. How dull to live on the equator when you can enjoy the extremes of climate at this latitude, those extremes determined by the coming and going of the sun, the seasons, the cycles of life.

Now I check out what is lighting up around me, right to left, eyes swinging, panning, mind snapping the pictures still . . . Click! Sutton's dinosaur ridges and a dinosaur watering hole nearby called Salt Lake, a uniquely saline pond without an outlet, a silver disc at dawn . . . Click! Bulbous Mount Stoker, where the earliest people to see the dawn in these parts left bowls of polished kowhai, dried weka skins and other artefacts . . . Click! Bald Hill, tor-less, guarding an amphitheatre containing the most exquisite leaf fossils, a buried still-life forest . . . Click! Click! The Sisters, twin knobs, strikingly smooth, at the southern end of Taieri Ridge, and below them a tree-topped sibling called Smooth Cone . . . Click! (terribly exposed). The crater, blitzed by the rising sun, a sunken ruin of black boulders described on maps simply as The Crater, the one and only . . . Click! Kakanui Range, a distant glint of snow, with sharp peaks forming a wall at the far end of the valley, another geological story . . .

Such panoramas take the breath away — especially in freezing air. The big view is mesmerising. I am reminded of how our eyes dominate all senses to a point where simple and delicate things escape our notice — the whispers in the silence, aromas in the breeze, things as subtle as the texture of lichens on weathered stone.

Lichens are plants of ancient ancestry and as a matter of fact I am seated on a grey-green species. Every plant in the vicinity can salute this lichen for its work at the frontline of life, and not only the plants but all the grazing animals, the sheep, cattle, and rabbits.

Now I have some warmth on my face. The air is not as rasping on the cheeks. Finches, ever energetic, have begun their daily rummaging — goldfinches, chaffinches, greenfinches. Starlings have also left their overnight communal roosts and swirl in the air. Two vocal magpies are telling a harrier to get out of their air space. The harrier takes the hint, wheeling away with lazy wingbeat. Had the attack continued it would have rolled over in mid-air, talons bared, at each pass of the magpies.

The world is well awake. The sun will continue its passage without any coaxing from me. I wonder if anyone else has seen what I have just seen — the Winter Solstice sun rise up out of a crater.

TWO

The first rays of mid-winter sun stabbing over the top of Taieri Ridge catch the falcon slumbering on her overnight perch high up on the Rock and Pillar Range — a prime site for viewing the valley and the hills right out to the Otago coast.

It is a favourite fair-weather perch of hers, a twisted, rigid branch of an old fire-scarred matagouri tree. Unlike some of her rocky landing spots and lookouts, which she uses in gales, this roost allows her to sit up straight with her long tail tucked in behind the branch and talons firmly gripping it. She is relaxed. Her small head is erect, her feathers tight and smooth against her body — a picture of sleek nobility illuminated. Her eyelids, lightly closed over her dark brown eyes, flicker fractionally. She could be dreaming falcon dreams.

A predator like her, occupying top place in the food chain, can afford to lounge through sunrise. Natural enemies are few. Also, falcons do not mind a sunbathe first thing in the morning. There is no rush to start the day. In winter they are solitary birds with only themselves to feed.

This falcon has seen four winters and four summers go by, not counting her summer as a nestling. The next summer will be her third breeding season — her young have all departed to start adult lives in other hills — and she will expect her mate to come courting in early spring. Through the winter the pair live apart but stay more or less within a known territory.

Come spring, the territory will have unseen barriers erected around it within which no rivals will be tolerated. The ground within a few hundred metres' radius of the nest will acquire the status of an inner fortress to be defended, if necessary, to death. No wilder creature exists than a falcon in its home range at nesting time.

Right now, letting the winter sun caress her, the female appears anything but wild. She rouses (a gentle body shake and fluffing of feathers). It is a sign of wellbeing. It also helps insulate her from temperatures well below zero. One leg is retracted.

Half an hour after sunrise it is time for a stretch — first a leg, which she flexes backwards in the manner of an athlete warming up, then a wing. The wing stretch reveals the whitish bars on her dark brown, almost black, flight feathers. Her head, back and tail are brown-black, her front is dappled — a mixture of lighter colours, from cream to tawny, interspersed with black bars and vertical streaks. Front on she blends superbly with the rock and tussock landscape.

Down each cheek runs a black stripe, a 'moustache', which stands out in sharp relief to her buff chin and throat. Reddish-brown feathers cloak the upper areas of her yellow legs. Her toes are yellow as well, ending in talons as black as her beak and hooked as menacingly — efficient, deadly tools.

From bill-tip to the end of her tail she measures almost half a metre, her full adult size. Her mate, fairly similar in colouring, is smaller.

Upright again on her perch, the stretching exercise completed, she eyes the new day. Far below, flocks of small birds are exploring the morning, sprinting then landing then sprinting again, oblivious of the calculating gaze of a predator. But they need not fear an attack just yet. The falcon caught a rabbit yesterday and has the leftovers cached in a rock crevice near her overnight roost — enough food for the morning at least.

At this moment she is more concerned with bodily care than with feeding.

She tilts her head slightly to focus her gaze on a gully away to her right, one of the wrinkles on the face of the Rock and Pillar Range, where she knows there is water. Even at this distance the ice-lined trickle is audible to her. A drink, a bathe then she will fly to a nearby rock, another roost, where she will expel from her mouth a pellet of undigested feathers, bones and rabbit fur, called a casting; then she will begin a preening session.

To facilitate preening she uses oil from a special gland at the base of her tail. The water from her bathing helps disperse it. She preens each feather individually. It is not just for looks. Her feathers must be in top condition. She lives by hunting prey on the move, from the larger insects right up to hares and shags. She is only as efficient as her flight feathers.

But consider that efficiency. She can muster astounding speed and agility in the air, whether soaring, gliding, stooping (fast, steep attack) or tail-chasing, across open country, around craggy faces, through trees. She stoops to conquer, sovereign of her skies.

And now, braced and leaning forward, her tail approaching horizontal, she pushes off from her matagouri branch and glides towards her bathing place to perform her first task of the day.

Brian Turner

Lawrence Cemetery
(*for Ngaire*)

An artist takes snaps of cemeteries
irresistibly, *click*, with light
angling in from the left, say,
or the right, shadows staining headstones
and neglected plots, rusty iron
fencing off the last small pieces of land
that are definitely not ours.
One walks with care on such impenitent ground.

The sun dazzles and sprags
like a splinter in the corner
of your eye. Late light genuflects
upon the nearby hills: distantly
mountains turn gun-metal blue.
It feels quite neighbourly, you say,
picking a path among the broken vases
and the perky faces of wild flowers.

Brian Turner

In the Nineties

Say this. Say it reminds you
of days long ago
which seemed to go on
forever, and the dreamlight of morning
enhaloed everything
all day, and the twilight
embalmed you, and starlight
was the glitter in your brother's eye
when he holed out
on the 18th at Royal Melbourne
and won.

Say this. Say you remember
everything that did no harm,
the good more than the bad.
Say you're biased, say you're
jaundiced, say
So what? Say you
remember the first time you heard
Bruch's Violin Concerto
and Beethoven's *Emperor,* and the tears
brought on by Tchaikovsky's *Pathétique* ...
say how Lilburn and Sargeson and Mansfield
and Glover and McCahon
showed how culture, how art meant here
not always elsewhere.

Say how the words Dordogne, Milan, San Remo,
Paris, Oxford, rolled off the tongue — not deferentially,
not batedly, not scornfully, but more naturally.
Say you remember how your heart leapt
at the sight of silver cloud
pouring over and down the Pisa Range
and you followed the blue-green Clutha
upstream to its source in the mountains.

Say you felt at home here
and not averse to elsewhere
in times when you still thought
a lifetime a longtime.

Say violins remind you
of moonlight on snowfields in spring,
pianos of high country streams,
and a flute of dun hills
swept by tussock
above which hawks turn, stall
and turn.

Say you felt you grew up
in a place as close to Paradise
as any left on earth,
and it wasn't only your imagination,
that the outer pageantry
fired the inner, and vice versa.

Say what is, now
is what you wanted,
what you deserved.

Say you're bewildered.
Say you're betrayed.
Say you don't care.
Say, enough . . . *enough*.

Philip Temple

Rocking

from *Dark of the Moon*

At first light the rain stopped and Rockeye flapped through the canopy of the mountain beech, shaking branches and showering the others with water drops until they were all awake and grumbling. 'Come on,' he said. 'Come on come on come on. Let's get there before any other rockers; show 'em what sunrise rocking is all about!'

'Go away!' Starkle cackled, hunching up and poking her beak under her wing. 'Go and rock on your own stupid claws.'

Rockeye gave out a low, looping whistle, something few keas could do. It was intended to impress. 'Woken up on the wrong side of the perch, have we? Just another fairweather, eh?' Starkle opened her beak and lunged at him, but Rockeye flapped quickly up one branch and sat above her, joined by Redeye and Tweaker, and they cackled and chortled and bounced the branch up and down so that the treetop began to shake and more water cascaded over her.

Starkle flew into the next tree without a sound and shook herself dry. It really had been a terrible trip over from Blooming. Rockeye had found the pass through Sunrise before the cloud and rain came, but then, for no reason at all it seemed, he had given the flight lead to Redeye, who she was now certain had some kind of wing sickness. She was unfamiliar with all the land of Behind Sunrise, yet had been certain they were flying in the wrong direction; but, with four cocks around her, she had been reluctant to call out. As it was, they had ended up almost flying into the cliffs of the Claws of Ka. If Rockeye had not noticed at the last moment . . . even with Rockeye in the lead again, they had flown around the wrong side of Top of the Echo. By then it was almost dark and it had started raining again. Too late, Rockeye realised they had flown *past* the legs cave they were supposed to be partying at and so missed meeting the right keas in Far Sunrise Country. They had somehow found their way through the first mountains and arrived at the second legs caves; 'much better than the first one anyway,' Redeye had assured. Then it had waterfalled down all night and she had had trouble keeping her head dry.

Kriki cautiously sidled along the branch towards her as the other cocks flew off. 'Coming down to the legs caves?' he asked.

'Not before I've eaten something,' Starkle snapped. 'My stomach feels as if I've lost my beak.'

'Rockeye says there'll be plenty of food down at the caves . . .'

'If his judgement about that is anything like his navigation, then we'll all starve.'

'Yes. It wasn't much of a flight over, was it?' Kriki said tentatively.

Starkle looked at him sharply. 'Well. What are you waiting for?'

'What?'

'If there's so much food down at the legs caves.' Kriki blinked and pecked over his shoulder in distraction as Starkle climbed up the tree and snatched angrily at a beech twig. 'The beech leaves are not much good here either.'

'Then try this, petal,' she heard behind her, and turned to find Rockeye perched with a lump of prized yellow fat at the tip of his beak. 'Want some? Plenty more where this comes from.' He stretched his neck and head towards her so that the tempting morsel was no more than a wing-stretch away. He fluttered his eyelids. Starkle almost reached out to take it, so insistent had the twitching in her stomach become. But she kept her wings together and said, 'If that's the case, you'd better show me where it is.'

Rockeye retracted his head with a sniff and lazily licked at the rich grass, working away with his tongue until every last grease spot had gone from his beak. Starkle turned her back on him and fluffed up her feathers, quietly grinding her beak.

When she finally went down to the legs caves with Rockeye and Kriki, Starkle found that Redeye and Tweaker were tucking into a bowl of food which looked like a mixture of seeds and lichen flakes drowned in glacier water. 'Good stuff!' chumbled Redeye when he saw her hop tentatively over the big flat rocks before the cave. 'Try some.' Starkle, and Kriki behind her, cocked their heads and looked carefully at the longleg, a female judging by its hair and the shape of its legs, which was crouched in the entrance to the cave. It held nothing in its claws, and the shape of its face and the look in its eyes gave Starkle the confidence to go closer to the food. But she remained wary, because if there was one thing she had learned about longlegs, it was that their faces and eyes could alter as quickly as the changing of shadow and light when clouds passed over the sun in a southerly gale.

Starkle found a piece of the yellow grass beneath the overhang of the food bowl. Oh, what nectar! She had eaten it only once before and she still found the taste almost indescribable: it was a little like a mixture of fresh huhu grub and daisy root, but really it had a special, exotic taste all its own. And the richness! As it slid down her throat, she knew that she would be sick if she ate too much. 'Not bad, eh?' chortled Tweaker, bunting her with his wing, and she flew at him, squawking, 'Don't get fresh with me!' Then she took his place at the food bowl, shaking slightly as the new taste sensations flooded over her tongue.

There were thumping noises inside the cave, the rumble of a voice, and a male longleg appeared at the entrance, standing over the female. Starkle looked up from her feeding as the male's voice became suddenly louder. The tone was a warning, and she and all the other keas except Kriki were alert and able to react quickly as the male's featherless wing swung back and an object — which they had only seen before on longlegs' feet — flew through the air towards them. It hit the bowl, splatting the food over the rocks. As the foot-shaped object rebounded, it gave Kriki a thump on the backside as he took off. Redeye's breast feathers were drenched in the food's liquid. They gathered on the ridge of the cave roof, where Rockeye let out a rattling, angry screech as the male longleg waved a stick at them and the female scolded him. 'Like Snowflier and Dew on a bad day,' Tweaker snickered.

'Are you all right?' Starkle asked Kriki.

'I think so,' he said, hunching and carefully twisting his tail.

'Nothing that a bit of roofing won't fix!' squawked Rockeye. 'Let's do it! Up your nostrils!' he screeched at the longlegs as he skated down the corrugated roof and flew over its edge just beyond the reach of the male longleg and its stick. He flapped back to the roof ridge, screaming, 'C'mon! Everybody roof! Everybody roof!' and swooped over the other keas' heads. Starkle ducked and opened her wings involuntarily, and suddenly found herself scratching and sliding down the roof with the others. All except Redeye, who remained at the top and screamed as hard as he could into the chimney. 'Wakey, wakey!' Redeye screeched.

'Go for it, Redeye!' Rockeye exhorted.

'Deal it to 'em!' shrieked Tweaker.

'Wakey, wakey!' Redeye screamed again down the chimney.

'Let's get them all out!' Kriki cried.

'Kreeks!' Starkle cried in amazement as she circled over the hut and saw more longlegs emerge from their cave. Soon there were eight and four standing outside, staring at Rockeye, Tweaker and Kriki, who continued to slide down the roof and abuse them. Some longlegs began banging together bright objects with their claws, making a sharp, jarring sound which was like nothing Starkle had heard before. It hurt her ears, so she flew to a beech tree where she could be at a safer, more comfortable distance.

Some male longlegs began to throw stones on the roof, but none of the cocks were distracted until Kriki was again hit on the rump and he stopped screeching abruptly, banked away and half fell into the tree beside Starkle. 'Kreeks, that hurt!' he croaked.

'And Rockeye seems to miss them all,' Starkle replied in a tone of mixed wonder and asperity as Tweaker also caught a stone on the wing and Rockeye swooped over the heads of the longlegs with impunity. Tweaker, too, retreated into the trees before Rockeye finally screeched, 'End of demo! End of demo!' when black smoke and sparks suddenly gushed from the chimney into Redeye's face and he clipped a wing on the roof as he flew off in the confusion.

'Who's got dark cheeks, then?' Starkle crowed as Redeye's soot-streaked head appeared through the beech foliage.

'Who's a cheeky kea?' cackled Tweaker. Redeye sneezed and shook himself hard, scattering soot over them all.

Rockeye landed heavily beside Starkle, saying, 'Bloody longlegs! Think they're Ka's gift to the universe! Did yer hear 'em cackling?' He puffed out his breast and began to emit a series of gurgling, hissing, grunting and clucking sounds in imitation of the longlegs, which soon had the other keas chortling and flapping with glee. Starkle warbled with pleasure as one male longleg screamed at them from the cave and threw a stone which fell a long way short of their tree.

When all the longlegs had disappeared inside their cave, Tweaker asked, 'What shall we do now?'

'How about another bit of roofing?' Kriki said. 'That would *really* get up their nostrils.'

'And they would probably get up yours if you tried that a second time,' Starkle retorted.

Rockeye moved along the branch until his wing touched hers. 'Well said, chick, well said,' he commented loudly; and then quietly, so that only she could hear: 'I like a hen with a long beak. Know what I mean?'

Starkle strained and released a dropping. 'Tell me about it sometime,' she said.

Rockeye flew to the topmost branch of the tree and swung expertly as it flexed beneath him. 'Nah. Give the longlegs a rest for a while. Let their feathers settle. Take eight, take a doze. Pick a few berries. Chew a few leaves. See what the sun brings. Eh?' And with that he dropped down through the trees and disappeared.

Starkle was glad of some peace and quiet as the heavy cloud began to break and long plumes of sunlight dappled the forest. Despite all their noise and aggression, Starkle thought the longlegs knew how to pick good perches. Their cave stood on rocks near the top of the forest and, from the overhang at its front, the legs could look out over the edge of a waterfall to a broad and deep valley with wide grassy flats perhaps two hundred metres below. On either wing stood sheltering mountains which would be covered by snow in Grass Time; and the basin above the cave, too, kea-kind with shrubs and bushes, a dark lake and the pass through the mountains which they must have flown through the night before.

Starkle realised with something of a start that she knew nothing of this country — where good feeding places and nest sites were, or good shelter trees — nor how many keas lived in this range. She felt both nervous and excited about the prospect of locals turning up. How would she cope; what would they do? She couldn't put a name to anything in the view. It was her first venture — well, except when *everybody* went down the Kawa Valley during that terrible winter the year before last — but really it was her first time away from Kawa. Momentarily she felt vulnerable, an urge to go home. But then she looked over at Redeye, Tweaker and Kriki, all younger than she. It was normal, the *natural* order of things for young cocks to go off exploring or partying. Well — if they could handle it, she could, too.

She stretched her wings, one at a time. Anyway, she thought, the way back's easy enough. She cocked her head and looked up to the pass. Nothing to it. She shook out her feathers and then, as the clouds lifted and broke further, she caught sight of the distant view towards sunrise. Between the shoulders of the mountains, the valley beneath narrowed into a gorge and then reappeared further, wider, much wider than any valley she had ever seen. And beyond the valley were the brown and black cliffs of strange high mountains, hills without forests and the reflection of much water on the belly of the cloud. It seemed a hard country with nothing kea-kind, and Starkle settled on her perch, thankful for the feel of a beech branch between her claws; even if she could not give this place a name.

Halfway through first beak, Tweaker woke Starkle with the cry, 'The longlegs are going!' She opened one eye to see eight legs climbing slowly up a narrow, rocky track which led through the trees to the high basin above their cave. All had different-coloured humps on their backs and none reacted when Redeye and Tweaker took off and circled over them screeching, 'Faster! Faster! Get a move on! Why don't you open your wings and fly!' At intervals, other longlegs came out from the cave until, towards the end of first beak, Starkle had counted twice times eight plus one, including two fledglings which poked out their tongues at her.

All became still and quiet until Rockeye reappeared and half fell into the tree. 'All gone?' he asked, and seemed to want to say more, but his tongue worked loosely in his half-open beak and no words emerged.

Starkle saw that Rockeye's left eye was half closed and his wings were not firmly folded. 'It looks as if you're half gone, too,' she answered.

Rockeye hopped closer and perched unsteadily on the end of her branch. He flexed and released a dropping which Starkle saw was unusually pale and watery. 'I'm perfeckly allrigh',' he said and then bobbed his head up and down, three times, very fast. 'Ready fer anythin'.'

'Where've you been?' said Starkle.

Rockeye closed his droopy eye and said, 'None o' your business.' He cocked his head towards the other keas and said, 'Isn' tha' righ'?'

'That's his perch,' Redeye said sullenly, avoiding Starkle's sharp eye.

'Yeh. That's between him and the beech tree,' Tweaker said with cocky defensiveness as Starkle climbed higher for a better view of them all.

'You've been on bad grass, haven't you?' she said to Rockeye.

'What do *you* know about grass?' Redeye sneered. 'None's been past your yellow beak.'

'You don't need to drink water to know water's wet, yellow legs,' Starkle retorted. 'By the way you were flying last night, you've been on it, too.'

Redeye hopped through the foliage towards her. 'No hen calls me yellow legs,' he threatened, and lunged at her over a branch; but Starkle smartly, and insultingly, avoided his beak by taking just two short steps sideways.

'Hey hey hey!' croaked Rockeye, seeming to wake up. 'Save it for the longlegs. Save it for local yokels.' He moved closer to Starkle. 'Anyhow. It's about time a chicken like you pulled a bit o' bad grass, eh?' She tried to move away, but Redeye blocked the branch towards the trunk of the tree and Tweaker had moved to perch directly above her. She raised her hackle feathers, but Rockeye began preening her head. No matter how she moved, he pushed her back into the position he demanded, the point of his beak pressing against her ear or the corner of her jaw. As he preened, Rockeye chumbled, 'No harm in a little grass among friends. All the best birds do it. And ain't we saved just the best for you!' He stopped and looked up at Tweaker. Starkle saw that his eyes were now both fully focused. 'Check it out,' he ordered.

Tweaker immediately dropped out of the beech and glided down to the cave. He hopwalked around it and then flew back. 'Check,' he reported.

'Let's go!' cried Rockeye, but none of the cocks left the tree as they waited for Starkle to open her wings. 'Let's go!' Rockeye cried again and bunted her.

'*C'mon*. What're we waiting for?' shrieked Redeye.

'What's all the fuss about?' Kriki asked ingenuously. Tweaker bunted him so hard that he almost fell off the branch.

'Lead the way, Tweaker,' Rockeye said, and when he had begun gliding down to the legs cave again, Rockeye said to Starkle, 'Did you flex yer wings for fun on this trip or did yer just come to be a feather up the arse?'

Starkle stiffened and began to raise her hackle feathers again. But the wry look in Rockeye's eye quelled her anger, and when he and the others flew away to the cave without another word, she felt pathetic and foolish, perched alone in the tree.

For kea curiosity's sake, if nothing else, Starkle flew quietly to the peak of the legs cave and looked down to see what the four cocks were up to. Rockeye's head appeared, poking through a hole in the side. He glanced up at her briefly and then said to the others, 'No legs. It's all ours! Tweaker — you keep a lookout.' He looked at Starkle again and then disappeared. Redeye and Kriki flapped up to the opening, scrabbling with their claws on the ledge beneath it before they disappeared inside, too. Tweaker hopwalked back and forth, opening his wings indecisively, before Rockeye's screech vibrated the roof beneath Starkle's feet: 'Get yer tail up there, Tweaker!' Tweaker flew into the air as if he had been pecked. Flying much too hard, he slewed sideways and upwards to a rock outcrop and there paced around, watching nervously for longlegs.

The cacophony of bangs and clatters increased beneath Starkle and she could not resist for long the urge to see. When she flew to the opening and looked for the first time inside a legs cave, she was struck still by the fantasy of a world she had never imagined; of angles sharper than rock, shadows deeper than those of the forest floor, of strange smells sour and sweet that both repelled and attracted her.

Rockeye and Redeye ignored her, obsessed with a variety of peculiar objects ranged along ledges on the walls of the cave. While Kriki ripped away at something soft in the corner, covering himself with down, the older cocks pushed the objects off the ledges with the precision of a determined search. They bounced and clanged or fell and shattered like ice and when they burst open, liquids, coarse dust and crystals cascaded over the floor. Rockeye and Redeye tasted everything, exchanging only a few terse words — 'Try this. That's blandso. Brill. This has got a peck in it. Yo yo yo!' — in their fanatical absorption with new flavours and sensations.

Starkle remained transfixed in the opening as the beaks of Rockeye and Redeye swung left and right in increasingly reckless destruction. The air in the cave had become laden with dust. Redeye's tailfeathers were stuck together with a substance like honeydew, and his back was flecked with white powder. With a wild shriek, Rockeye reached up for the last object on the highest ledge and wrenched it off with his crystal-studded beak. It smashed on the floor beside Redeye, drenching him with a purple liquid. Its powerful reek was so strong that Starkle almost fell out of the opening. Redeye staggered back, shaking himself and sneezing, and Rockeye flopped down to taste at the widening pool. 'Top claw!' he pronounced, hopping from one foot to the other. 'Top claw! Try a beakful of this!' He imbibed and then hopped around the hut, digging his beak into every pile of dust, every pool of sticky liquid. 'Now you look here, chicken,' he cried, without looking up at Starkle. 'This is what you call grass. Real *bad* grass. The best grass you'll ever see!' He hopped on to a raised platform of wood in the centre of the cave and flapped his wings triumphantly. 'Come and get a bellyful!'

Rockeye's head lurched from side to side and he began a peculiar dance, hopwalking back and forth across the surface of the platform. Kriki now had his head in a broken container, licking at something that consumed his entire attention. Redeye continued to put his beak into the purple puddle, one wing propped against the wall, the other trailing in unidentifiable, strong-smelling mud.

Starkle felt a deep shiver of fear. 'Rockeye,' she cried, 'Rockeye!' But he did not hear her. 'Redeye, Redeye! Get up!' But he could not hear her. 'Kriki, Kriki! For Ka's sake, get out of there!'

Kriki lifted his head at her call. 'You've never tasted *anythin'* like this!' he cried. 'Like rata and honeydew and totara berries all mixed together,' and plunged his head back into the tin.

She twisted her head over her shoulder to peck at her wing in distraction and saw that Tweaker had left his lookout perch. Instinctively she turned and flew out, gaining height quickly for a good view. Tweaker was nowhere to be seen. But there, moving slowly through the last bend of beech forest towards the cave, were four longlegs. She folded her wings and dropped through the air, opening them again so late that she banged against the side of the opening. 'Longlegs!' she screeched. 'Longlegs!' Kriki was quick to respond and squawked through the opening, jarring his shoulder as he flapped through to safety. But Redeye had become absolutely still and Rockeye continued to prance.

Starkle flew inside the cave and landed heavily beside Rockeye, knocking him from the platform. 'Get out! Get out! The longlegs are here!'

Rockeye recovered in a flurry of feathers and raised his wings in threat, shrieking at her, 'No-one does that! No-one does that!'

Starkle cried again, 'The longlegs are here! Do you hear me?' Rockeye froze in mid-flap as her words penetrated his fuddled mind. And then the cave was flooded with light and a male longleg stood silhouetted in the entrance. In confusion, Rockeye flapped around the cave, banging into post and pane until Starkle hurtled past him screeching, 'Follow me!' She flew strongly towards the bright patch of sky above the longleg's shoulder. The longleg fell back as she burst into the open and she caught the rancid smell of its body, a glimpse of enormous brown eyes and pale skin above its multi-coloured breast and back. She heard the longleg cry out and looked back under her wing to see Rockeye disentangle his feet from the longleg's head and waving claws. In a few wingbeats he perched beside her in the secure canopy of the beech trees, his beak half open, his eyes staring in excitement and fear. 'Kreeks,' was all he could say breathlessly. 'Kreeks.'

Kriki climbed through the branches towards them and Starkle asked distractedly, 'Where's Tweaker? Have you seen him?'

'No. But I think I know where he is.' Kriki's reply faded as the noise of longleg talk and cackle became louder inside the cave, and the keas stared in horror as a male longleg came out, holding Redeye in its claws. Redeye's head rolled from side to side and then fell forward as the leg placed him on the stones before the cave. He slumped on his belly, bedraggled wings outstretched, and the other legs came out to watch as the first one poked him with a stick. 'We've got to *do* something,' Starkle said, nervously clasping and unclasping the branch.

Rockeye stared blearily at the inert form of Redeye and chumbled, 'He's my cobber.'

Kriki said, 'But what?'

'He's my cobber,' Rockeye chumbled again.

Redeye came to life as the longleg continued to poke him. He stared up, head over his shoulder, beak open against his tormentor, and then careered over the stones and through the low bushes beyond, one wing flapping, the other trailing loosely. 'His wing's broken!' cried Kriki.

Rockeye croaked, 'He's my cobber,' once more and swooped towards Redeye, reaching him as he scrabbled onto worn rocks near the waterfall. At the edge of streaming bluffs which fell sheer towards the valley, Rockeye confronted Redeye with his wings raised in an effort to turn him to safety. Starkle and Kriki watched in terrified silence as Redeye stopped and lunged at Rockeye like a weakened, blind chick. Rockeye took the blow on his breast, trying to maintain his grip on the slimy rock. But his claws slipped and he fell backwards, opening his wings to catch himself in air full of spray. Redeye followed him, tumbling forward head first, attempting to fly with one wing, and then disappeared from sight.

'What's going on?' Tweaker's voice sounded above Starkle.

She and Kriki both rushed at him through the leaves and Starkle caught him a sharp peck on the back. 'Where have *you* been?' she snapped.

'What have I done, what have I done?' Tweaker said, hunching in defence.

'Left your "cobbers", that's what,' Starkle said.

'He's been on the grass, too,' Kriki said, indicating the red stain across Tweaker's stomach.

'You're not exactly one of Ka's perfect chicks yourself,' said Starkle.

Kriki looked down glumly between his toes. 'Actually, I feel really sick.'

Tweaker said, 'I only went down to the longlegs' hole, to the place where they throw all the grass.'

'And now your cobber's dead,' Starkle said bitterly. 'Because . . .' and she stopped, uncertain of the truth as the longlegs gathered together at the edge of the bluff and began cackling in the way they did when they seemed happy.

Starkle took off and half circled over the waterfall so that she could see beyond the bluffs. More than fifty metres down, over the crown of a small beech tree whose roots ran nakedly across the rocks, Redeye lay spread like a wet shag drying its wings. Rockeye was clinging to a flexing neinei which grew from the face of the bluff, continually flapping his wings to maintain balance.

Starkle glided down and past them, crying, 'Is he alive?' Redeye raised his head and croaked words which were lost in the roar of the waterfall. She landed at the edge of the forest and waited for Rockeye to join her.

'She's jake!' he cried, ebullient again, eyes shining. 'Tough as old lichen. Knew just when to spread the old feathers.' He spoke more loudly so that Tweaker and Kriki could hear as they came spiralling down. 'Landed like down, 'e did. Need more grass than that to fix a true rocker.'

'He could have been killed,' Starkle said.

'Nah. No chance. Legs don't kill. Look at me!' Rockeye bunted Tweaker. ' 'E'll be rockin' again before dark.'

'I feel sick,' said Kriki.

Tweaker cackled at the sight of Redeye shaking his head periodically as water from the falls sprayed over him. Rockeye hopped over to Tweaker, whose cackling stopped abruptly when he began preening him hard. 'Now you get over there and stay there until Redeye's ready to move and if you leave 'im for as much as two wingbeats, I'll pull out your tailfeathers. One by one. Slowly.' Tweaker flew off hurriedly as Rockeye gave him a swift bunt with his wing, and he perched beside Redeye in the shaking crown of the small beech, miserably trying to dodge the spray.

'Look at you, all right,' Starkle said. 'Look at Redeye. Look at Tweaker.

Look at Kriki. You're all sick. You've eaten enough grass to rot your feathers. You're here only by the luck of Krikta. A day, a month . . . it's only a matter of time before you *all* lose your wings.'

Rockeye was silent for a moment and then he leaned forward and ripped a piece of bark from the branch he was perching on. 'Thanks for raising the screams back there, chick. I owe you one. But it doesn't give you the perch to come on with all the strengths about the meaning of life. Me and Redeye have been around in places you-just-couldn'-*imagine*. And you think *this* is bad?' He sidled closer to her. 'But you've got a longer beak than I thought, chicken. Hang around. There are better things to do yet.'

'I feel sick,' Kriki chumbled. 'I want to fly home.'

'And *your* beak's shorter than I thought,' Starkle answered Rockeye. 'Call me if it grows longer. Come on, Kriki. That's not such a bad idea.' She climbed to a rocky ledge, ready to take off, and Kriki followed her, head down, avoiding Rockeye's disparaging look. Starkle watched briefly as Redeye began making his first efforts to perch on the beech tree and Tweaker screeched something none of them could hear. Above, the longlegs turned and disappeared beyond the edge of the bluff.

Studying Redeye, Rockeye said, 'If you don't make Blooming tonight, there's a choice perch at Behind Sunrise. Swing right between the lakes. Halfway up to the first Claw of Ka there's a boulder among the last hakeke. Behind there is the best nest site you've ever seen.'

Starkle did not reply. She took off and flew directly across the face of the bluff, Kriki not far behind. As she sought an updraught to help her gain height, Rockeye's last calls echoed in her ears: 'See you in the springtime! Have fun! Don't do anything I wouldn't do!'

When they cleared the bluff, Starkle and Kriki saw the longlegs gathering outside their cave. One moved a long stick with a tail, pushing grass through the entrance in puffs of white dust. More longlegs descended colourfully through the rocky basin above the cave, and Starkle saw with an uplifting sense of relief that the sun shone over the pass through the mountains.

Bill Manhire

An Amazing Week in New Zealand

So for six days he crusaded
and on the seventh he flew to Australia.

Athletic Park, April 1959:
a southerly straight off Cook Strait,
the microphone bandaged in gauze.

Here in Balclutha there is quiet sunshine
and we sit on the grass,
waiting for the voice over the landline.

Our togs are back on the bus.
We have been promised
a swim afterwards.

Come forward. You come.

*

Thus in the capital
the Christ folk watch and pray,
they have bibles and binoculars

and they shake their hymn sheets
in goodly company
while we sit and listen only

Come, you come

to the tall undeniably handsome man
(who is forty but looks thirty)

with an easy, friendly manner
and a sound-system
flown in from Melbourne.

His face goes by on the tram.

*

His face goes by on the bus
Lord Lord yes
past shops with unrepeatable prices

but I am not
going forward. I am sitting
here on the grass

constructing my hut in the pines,
planks with a sway,
high life on a windy day.

I am sitting here on the grass
watching the old wolf,
Akela, finger his hip-flask

*

and I smile. A scout smiles and whistles
under all difficulty. Wicked Shere Khan!
Stupid Bandar-log! I am pure as the
                                    rustling wind.

But how to read Nature's secrets . . .
The feathers and fur on the ground,
a rabbit lying there like a glove . . .

What is it evidence of?

*

I'm going to ask you to do something hard and
tough. I'm going to ask you to get up out of
your seat, hundreds of you, get up out of your
seat, and come out on this field and stand here
quietly, reverently. God has spoken to you. You
get up and come. I can hear you in your
heart. You want a new life. You want to live
clean and wholesome for Christ. The Lord has
spoken to you . . .

*

But I want to remember
the three hundred things
a bright boy can do . . .

the boy as this or that,
chorister or scientist,
the boy as magician

sweet talking

the girl doomed to cremation
and the cries of spectators
who see flames and smoke

then bones and a skull, then there's
only their own applause

*

for everyone's safe of course
and the boy's busy investigating
more astonishing

things: invisible ink
and a musical ring,
a puzzling and wonderful chicken,

while Christ comes again and again
in the clouds, cumulo
nimbus, the wind and the rain, riding

those parallel lines that end
in a point, in a friendly warning:

'Dear King Prempel. You must give up
human sacrifice and slave-trading.'

*

Lift your eyes from the page.

God's glance is a wind
that goes through you,
mysterious language

that teaches a scout to see sign
in a tangle of stars
or a twig or two

while lipstick on your collar
(your first record)

tells its tale on you, black
with that yellow label

and you follow the narrow trail
through falling leaves,
sign after sign leading

to where the ground is level
at the foot of the cross,
and there is Billy on his knees . . .

You see Billy Graham up here.
But he is not the main actor.
The main actor is the one who comes to hear.

And look! the pickpocket returns the wallet
and Billy gets to his feet,
surprised but friendly.

He has the vigour of three men.
He shakes your hand before he strikes.

A smile and a nod.
A smile and a nod.
He's giving the glory to God.

*

The boom of bronze over the landline.
The West Coast farmer stops milking his cows.
A boy stops making strange noises.

But how do you 'get right' with God?
What is soteriology? All I know is
people are changing their lives today.

We're ending the old life of sin.

*

That's it . . . that's it . . .
come on . . . there are others coming . . .

Just as I am, without one plea
But that Thy blood was shed for me

sing it again softly as others come . . .
say that eternal Yes to the Lord.

*

And Fay the Widgie . . . How is she?
Bright lipstick! My word!

All brazen façade and crazy parties,
leopard skin pants and a pony tail.

But now her parents are puzzled.
Where is their self-centred daughter?
She hasn't gone to town.

Come on. You come down.

*

The publican wants God as a partner,
the businessman, the wife, oh
the girl with scars on her wrists
taking her baby to God

the shiftless drunk no one trusts
who lives in a packing shed
the days are weeks and the weeks are months

Doreen and Fay and Don the borstal-boy

and God is not a clean shirt but a clean body
lifting from the pool
after a width underwater, the dazzle
of water pouring back. So

that after you stop saying No to God
you feel one hundred per cent.
You know you're

in trouble: you know
you need help
from the tender-hearted Lord.

*

The boy as ventriloquist —
the distance and resonance
of approaching noise: man

in the chimney talks
to the man in the roof, both puzzled
by those muffled cries

from the cellar. Then you make a mistake,
then make the effort to make
crowd-pleasing music,

the *pangka-bongka* of the banjo
the *zhing-sching* of the cymbals
the *plim-blim* of the harp

steady *beat* of the heart

or the Jew's-harp: *whanga-*
whonga whee-whaw
whoodle-onga eedle-ongle

whow-zeedle oodle-ee whay-
whonga whaw: almost impossible
to do, like the roar

of an excited crowd, the sound
of winter skaters, a choir singing
as the folk go forward, one

by one, *now come, you come* . . .

*

One thousand miles of miracle
lead to where the ground is level
at the foot of the cross

and here we are on our knees
inspecting the world of loss:
broken twigs, a hair,

a scrap of food,
big sign and small sign, let
nothing escape you,

trampled grass, a drop of blood,
a button, a match, a leaf,
thing like a glove . . .

But God is not here,
not in sunshine, not
in God's open air

but somewhere altogether elsewhere

in dark accumulations
in winter macrocarpa

*

in the needle of sound in a circle
Lipstick on your collar

the nervous current of the tiger's claw
the windy cry from the pack

*

Akela! Akela!

*

who takes another swig
then sucks on his Life Saver

whow-zeedle oodle-ee
whay-whonga
whaw . . . Lord

Lord, I am
not going forward.

Dan Davin

Black Diamond

One of the odd things, though natural I suppose, about war is that because —
or that's how I'd explain it — your future looks somewhat unpromising, you
tend to get sudden shocks of early memory of the times when you were young
and lucky enough to feel secure. I remember how the first time I really noticed,
as distinct from seeing, that the New Zealand Division's special sign in the desert
was the Black Diamond. The Provo blokes always went ahead of the foremost
troops and planted steel or wooden poles with a black diamond-shaped figure
on top and as long as you found your way from one of these to the next you
knew you weren't too far away from your own chaps. But what struck me this
day I'm talking of, when I first really noticed, was how loaded for me personally,
in the rather too extensive and neglected backyard of my mind, and not too full
of blooming lilacs at that, this black diamond sign was. For when I was a kid
Black Diamond was the best coal you could get round Southland. Here we were
in a waste of sterile sand, but the sign evoked at that moment, in a most sovereign
way, memories of a landscape almost unimaginably different in its green, wet
expanses, from the perilous and lethal territory, sown only with mines, over
which we were now travelling.

Though I had left Southland years before my recollection of my early life in
Gore was intense. Sitting beside my driver in late 1942 as we headed towards
Tripoli, in my retrospective musings, I used to revert in a large part of my mind
to early childhood. I remembered how we thought, my brothers and sisters
and I, that grown-ups were a pretty odd lot and it was hard to know what they'd
be up to next. Now, of course, I can see that this was because we didn't spend
much time working out how their minds worked, and why. Anyway, we simply
didn't know enough to understand it all. We did, though, have enough grasp
to stop them from stopping us from whatever it was that we might want to do,
and stopping them from making us do things we certainly didn't want to do.

The old man wasn't too much of a problem for us. He was a railway guard
on small branch lines running out of Gore and he was away most of the
time; and when he was at home he spent most of his time down in the back
paddock planting spuds or digging them up again, according to the time of
year. Come to think of it, that's what we're all doing, one way or another,
but of course I didn't think of it then — just concentrated on keeping out of
the way in case he wanted you to lend a hand.

Driving all those hundreds of miles through the Western Desert and beyond, I began to reflect a lot about those days and about my father. He had what you might call a princely memory, an Irish one: he tended to recall disaster — Cromwell, the great Irish famine, the flooding of the Mataura — but he didn't blame anybody but himself. He won't remember now — over eighty if he were still alive and remembering different things or the same things differently. And I haven't the ghost of an idea whether he'd remember as I do those years, about 1918 or 1919, when we were living in the cack-coloured railway house we'd moved to after the big Mataura flood. Well, the facts — however he might have remembered them or might have come to see them — didn't much matter. After all the past is the creation, or the making up or whatever, of those who survive long enough to be the only witnesses of its future, or of the next generation, inexperienced in the facts, who have to devise a past and a present for themselves.

Anyway, however historians might fiddle around with the plasticine of truth, those were hard times in Gore, at least for some of us. My father and mother, at the time I'm speaking about, had only five kids but my mother had begun to bulge a lot — which puzzled us since she ate the least at meals because she always served herself last — and she'd begun to spend more time in bed than we could remember. Also our Aunty Mollie had come down from where she lived in Auckland on a visit, bringing her daughter Nora, our cousin, whom we boys didn't like much, though our sisters did.

Keeping the home fires burning, an expression the grown-ups seemed to have had a sort of relish for in those years of the Armistice and all that, was a real problem. The way we kids saw it, next to getting enough porridge and sausages and stuff to eat, keeping warm was the worst problem of the lot, that winter. We'd used up the totara logs our old man had spent his fortnight's holiday cutting out of the bush on the hilly side of the Mataura. We were always competing for who could get his feet first in the kitchen oven or get the best place near the fire in the sitting-room. We burnt lignite there mainly, but it needed a bit of decent wood or coal first to get it going and I've never forgotten my fury when I discovered that our Cousin Nora had broken up the wooden chocolate box in which I used to keep my treasures, bits of magazine and *Buffalo Bills* and that sort of thing, and she'd used it to start the fire one morning when I was out milking our half-Jersey half-Shorthorn cow so as to get enough milk for our porridge.

Looking back on it I can't find the heart to blame Nora, however much I remember how I felt. Aunt Mollie was a sort of infatuated mother, having only the one child. Whenever one of us kids looked a bit peaky or went off his food — not often — she'd say to my mother 'Give him malted milk like I gave my Nora.' And when even she was cross with Nora about some awful behaviour she'd say 'Black Man want Nora,' which made us feel at least then on Nora's side since we didn't see much wrong with being wanted by a black man and of course didn't realize that Aunty Mollie was using 'black' as a direct translation for the Irish 'Dhu' which took you into a quite different world, that of the 'black stranger' with which my mother used to threaten us as the representative of the outside world, the world outside the light and the family.

The fact remained, though, that the lignite we were having to rely on for the range and the fire was bloody slow and bloody cold. It especially got on the nerves of Aunty Mollie. She felt the cold more than any of us. Though she'd been born and brought up in Southland, she had got used to the sissy, thin-blooded climate of Auckland where she was always telling us about how you could grow lemons and oranges and grapefruit and how her husband, Andy, never had to wear woollen underpants, and all that sort of thing. So it was she who said to my elder brother, John, that us kids ought to get cracking and do something about the cold. John's own way of dealing with the cold was to play football or go exploring into the hills round Gore. So his first reaction was to say 'Go to Hell,' or 'Go home to Auckland,' except that, being like all of us a well-brought up Catholic child — we went to the Sisters of Mercy School — probably wouldn't have spoken quite like that. As far as I remember, that winter, Hell though didn't seem such a bad sort of place.

On thinking it over though John decided that Aunt Mollie was right. He remembered that, down at the shunting yards where the coal trucks came and went, there were bits of coal on both sides of the rails, stuff that had fallen off in the shunting. Good coal at that: Black Diamond from Nightcaps and places further down south. He was a very determined bloke, my brother John, and the following Sunday after Mass he set off to inspect the site and see what catches there might be, inquisitive policemen or railway inspectors or whatever. That night he told me it was worth giving her a go.

His next thing was to get two pairs of old pram wheels from the town dump and then make a kind of trolley out of old apple and tomato boxes. He had a natural feeling for things like nuts and bolts and sprockets and so on and he even managed to make a steering-wheel with reins of fencing wire to the front wheels. The only thing he couldn't manage was an engine. Only people like Doctor Pottinger could afford to run a car and John had been looking at it closely — it was an Armstrong-Siddley I seem to remember — in the hope of inventing one for himself on the same model. He had some good opportunities for watching it lately because Doctor Pottinger for some reason and to our vague alarm and sense of self-importance had been coming to our house a lot these last few weeks.

Anyhow, it wasn't like nowadays and John's closest inspection of the town dump didn't produce handy wrecks the way it might nowadays or anything you could cannibalize — not like the Western Desert by 1942 — so John was forced to fall back on the other and easier source of energy, me and my young brother Matt. Luckily Gore was so low-lying in the Mataura Valley and the railway yards more or less followed the course of the river so there were no great slopes to climb — and no downward slopes to give us donkey engines relief either. And the railway yards were only a mile away from the house we'd moved to after the big flood.

When he'd at last, like a one-man Swiss Family Robinson, got the damned trolley into a going concern — me and Matt functioning as Man Fridays, if you'll forgive the confusion — we waited under starter's orders for the next Sunday, and then we hauled and pushed our vehicle along to the shunting yards. Because every grown-up was at church, or at home sleeping Saturday night off, we didn't have to worry about nosey-parkers or sticky-beaks. So all we had to look out for was where the blokes who'd been shunting the rakes of coal-trucks had juddered a bit on the rail points and the jolt had made a few chunks fall down on the track. You got quite good at it after a bit, the way you learnt where was the best place for catching eels in the creeks or crawlies in the flooded gravel pits, or in the flood pools round the Mataura. I must admit, though, that I felt a bit queasy once or twice, when I remembered how Sister Mary Benedict had held up poor Tommy Bates as an awful warning to us when he got drowned in the river because he went swimming on a Sunday instead of going to Sunday School and how Billy Dryden had been struck by lightning for the same reason.

Still, that didn't last long and I don't think we wasted much worry about whether the Devil stoked up Hell with the very best Black Diamond on Sundays. We were more interested in keeping warm on week-days than being fried in Hell for what we'd done on Sundays or Holy Days of Obligation. And, anyhow, Tommy Bates had been a bloody fool for taking a swim in the trickiest part of the Mataura just to show off his breast-stroke and Billy Dryden was in for it anyway because he'd stolen a ham from the Presbytery's larder and was scoffing it under a tree when the lightning struck.

It wasn't too hard to spot the places where the biggest chunks of shiny black coal were and John had no great problem manoeuvring our machine into the right bit of territory just alongside a rake of big trucks that, even though they were covered with those large tarpaulins my father used to scrounge sometimes to save himself the trouble of thatching his haystack against the winter, still had a lot of spillage between the lashed-down corners.

It wasn't long before we got the trolley loaded more or less to the top. So then, with John whipping us on, we pushed and pulled her back home. It was a bit tougher, that return trip — it felt like two miles as against the half-mile or so we'd felt it on the way to start with, that morning. We made it all right, though, pretty pleased with ourselves once we'd got there. We dumped the coal behind the wash-house and put a lot of old lignite and other piss-awful scrappy coal in front of our dump, just in case the old man went out there in daylight and happened to notice. We were rather counting on his having been put on night-shift just about that time. He was always going to and fro from places like Waimea and Hedgehope and had to spend most of the daytime having a kip, with Aunt Mollie bringing him a bit of grub at mealtimes. And he spent a lot of his waking-time talking to our mother in a sort of whisper, obviously not wanting us kids to hear whatever it was. Auntie Mollie herself, being from Auckland, didn't have a clue and I suppose Mum, who seemed to have to spend a lot of time lying down, was too busy wondering what would happen next to be able to spot, as she otherwise would have done, that there didn't seem to be any problem about keeping the coal range and the sitting-room fire going.

We thought we'd give it another go the next Sunday but there we made a mistake. The shunters wanted the coal trucks off the track so as to let a big load of gravel get through for a new road they were making towards the Mataura. So the points had been changed and the shunters were working overtime instead of observing the Sabbath. I've an idea that the bloke in the signals box towards the Mataura station had seen what we were up to the previous Sunday and because he was a North of Ireland Proddy Presbyterian dog he was out to spoil our doings. I expect he thought we ought to be at Sunday School. Anyway, there we were, John and the other two of us, scrabbling away under the wheels of the coal trucks, going like hell as if it were real diamonds we were after, when, bang, and the whole rake of trucks was suddenly on the move — not very fast, luckily, to start with, but too bloody fast for safety, or at least our safety.

The sort of coal we were getting was nothing to the real coal under the tarpaulins which bulged. The coal these trucks had in them was your real diamond coal, not just black but Ethiopian, glinting and sparkling at every edge and angle. It was real dinkum coal, with corners on it. In fact it was rather queer, now that I look back on it, because it made you want to touch it and yet it wasn't like skin, the way you got the feel of someone else's skin, a good many years later.

This was still in 1919, though, and none of us was old enough to be puzzling about skins except our own and how to save them. And the first forward jolt of the shunting-engine at the corner end — a cobber of my old man's was driving, I found out later — brought down a huge chunk of Black Diamond, bigger and heavier than a camel's hump, and right on top of John's back as he was grubbing for the smaller lumps underneath.

John was pretty strong for his age, luckily, but it was a heavy wallop he had to take. I was watching from the next track, because I had that awful instinct for seeing when something terrible was about to happen and was always, as I see it now, both an accomplice, or accessory, and witness for the defence. The way it seemed, that moment, he looked as if he was up the creek for good, and I was somehow responsible. Still, people who expect the worst aren't always right, can be feeling disappointed even, and after I'd gaped at him for a bit, useless bastard that I felt, I saw him do a sideways roll. The great hunk of Black Diamond came off his back. He wriggled clear of the moving trucks, back to where the points were.

My next brother, Matt, by this time had seen what was going on from the other siding where the bits of coal weren't too heavy for him. Our eyes met across the sidings, the middle rake of trucks having gone, and his were even more frightened than mine. How would we explain it all to our mother, if he'd been killed, and how would we get on without him? And, anyway, we were completely bushed, not having him to tell us what to do next.

We didn't have to worry for long. The trucks were out of the way and the line was clear, the shunter not seeming to have noticed anything. There was John, on his feet, as good as gold, and carrying in his arms that bloody great chunk of Black Diamond I'd have sworn would have killed anyone else.

'You silly little sod,' he said to me, 'why didn't you tell me the bloody engine was starting up?'

I said nothing back because there didn't seem anything much worth saying. He knew it wasn't my fault and he was only saying what he felt which doesn't necessarily have anything to do with logic or things like that. When you've made a mistake it's natural to try to put the blame on someone else. Young Matt must have felt the way I did, because he just peeled off a few of the smaller lumps from our trolley, to make room for John's huge Black Diamond.

Down south, it got dark very quickly in the winter. By the time we'd sweated the bloody trolley out of the yard and on the way home, there was something nice about seeing the gas lamps lit in our house, at a distance that didn't seem all that impossible. We'd tried to make John lie down on the top of our load and take it easy but of course he wouldn't have any of that and insisted on dragging instead of pushing the way we were doing.

We did manage, though, to talk him into nipping round the back of the house especially as we could see Dr Pottinger's Buick pull up just after us and him get out carrying a black Gladstone bag. It didn't seem a good idea for us to show ourselves just then, whatever he might be up to.

Cousin Nora spotted us, though, and she said Dr Pottinger had a baby in the Gladstone bag. We weren't much impressed by that story but when I went to the front of the house to make excuses for being so late back, as soon as I got into the front hall I could hear awful noises, moaning and that, and it was my mother's sound I could recognize, and yet the sound of an animal being hurt. So I ran towards the kitchen — we never went into our parents' front bedroom except sometimes exploring when they were both out — and there I found Aunt Mollie with great pots and pans of water boiling on the range and herself running around like a scalded cat.

Just as Matt came in through the back door she seemed to get the idea that we existed and had to be coped with.

'Your mother has just given you a little brother,' she said.

We weren't much worried about little brothers as long as Mum was all right and Aunt Mollie said she was fine now. Then she noticed that John was missing and wanted to know where he was.

'He's out bringing in a bucket of coal,' I explained. Then, to distract her, I said, 'What's our new little brother like?'

'He's the jewel of a boy,' Aunt Mollie said. 'Very dark hair, and a lot of it, like your father. Your mother wants to call him Donal Dhu.'

'What's that mean?' I asked her.

'Daniel the black,' she said. 'Like a black diamond.'

Ruth Dallas

Early Memories
from *Curved Horizon: An Autobiography*

When I first looked out of the front windows of the house in Dee Street, I saw a bitumened street where electric tramcars rumbled and clanged, motor cars and cyclists passed and people walked to and from town. Once a year, at the time of the Southland Agricultural and Pastoral Summer Show, herds of farm animals from the surrounding countryside rattled by on foot. Alarming bulls were led past, cattle-herds were hustled on by drovers with stock-whips and dogs, flocks of sheep flowed by like a river, and horses walked, clip-clop on the hard road, all on their way to the Invercargill Showgrounds, which lay only a few blocks distant between the railway line and the Waihopai river. The time of the Summer Show was a time to press your nose against the window or to stand out on the footpath if you dared.

I still like corner houses, with their freedom of access, their front gates and back gates, though at first nothing more important happened at our back gate than the arrival of the ash-man on Wednesdays, with his covered cart and sleepy draught-horse. The way the old horse stood on three legs and rested one leg was something I admired and copied, as best I could, with a mere two legs. The ash-man was ash-coloured from his boots and tied trouser-legs to his cone-shaped felt hat: a fire-resistant, solitary figure as he dumped the hot ashes from our tins into his cart, where the ever-blowing south-west wind found them and whirled them out again, enveloping him and his cart and driving them in clouds along Lowe Street. It was not garbage the ash-man collected then, but ashes; garbage was burnt in the fires that kept our houses warm, large fires of coal from the mines at Ohai, and wood from some of the last remnants of forest and scrub-land: red pine, black pine, broadleaf and manuka.

Sometimes my father and I shared an hour together in the warmth of the kitchen fire in the early morning before the rest of the family were awake. In winter the night still lingered outside, silent with frost or murmurous with rain. The blinds were still drawn and the solitary suspended electric light illumined a deserted kitchen. My father made a quick fire from kindling that had been split the evening before and spread on the rack or in the oven to dry. The fire burned in a black, cast-iron coal range that was kept gleaming by the application of black-lead and vigorous daily polishing. He set the kettle over the flame to boil while he went outside for the milk and the morning newspaper. I sat in my grandmother's creaking wicker chair, which he had drawn up to the fire for me, warming my toes and watching the bright, crackling flames, never tiring of staring at the hinges of the oven door, which seemed to me like three dragons, two swimming in one direction, a third passing between them. Who knew where they were swimming, or where they had been in the night? They were as mysterious as the figures of Darby and Joan in the weather-clock, out of reach on the mantelpiece, who appeared at the door of their little house only one at a time. As soon as I was old enough I spelt out the word *Orion* on the shelf below the oven. How was it pronounced, I wondered, and what could it mean? On the chimney-flue I read: 'H. E. Shacklock Ltd., Maker'. These words, all equally meaningless, passed into my brain forever, like a brand.

Our kitchen was an old-fashioned family living-room, quickly warmed, with windows facing north and east, containing a large solid table, a sofa, six bent-wood chairs which had been made in Austria and bought at the Christchurch Exhibition, and a mellow old dresser for the storing of food and cutlery. The sink and cupboards were in an adjoining scullery or kitchenette which led to the back door. The small bedroom opening off the kitchen was mine. My father returned with the billy of milk and the morning paper, followed by the cat, who liked to sit with his two front paws on the steel fender. On a fine morning my father might be heard singing one of the Irish songs he had learnt from his half-Irish mother, or, on a frosty morning, his step might be accompanied by the slight chink of ice which had formed on top of the milk. I used to listen for this sound, always hoping the frozen milk would taste like ice-cream, which it never did, its flavour being indistinguishable from the pieces of ice we licked on frosty mornings wherever we could find them.

When the kettle boiled he made tea and took a cup to my mother and grandmother, then filled his shaving mug with hot water. My father's morning shave was a routine which fascinated me even more than the dragons on the kitchen range. He brought out his shaving mirror and hung it on the wall by the east window. When the mirror was in place, a hinged shelf opened below it. On the table he spread a towel, a stick of shaving soap like a fat candle, a soft lathering brush, his shaving mug, his sharp, untouchable, winking, blade-razor, and neat squares of paper on which he wiped his razor and which he afterwards burnt. His razor-strop hung from a hook on the wall. Up and down the leather-strop, up and down, flashed the shining blade as he stropped it. How I should have loved to do that! But it was as well to keep quiet while the shave was in progress. With his face lathered white from ear to ear, my father peered into the mirror with such fierce concentration as he wielded the blade that only an idiot would have tried to interrupt him. From this operation he emerged looking pink and clean and in high good humour.

My mother and grandmother got up and resumed control of the kitchen and family. My two sisters appeared. Our space of quiet was over. The room began to hum with activity like a beehive. A starched and ironed large white cloth was shaken out of its folds and spread over the table; plates and cutlery rattled; bacon and eggs sizzled. Outside the day dawned, the blinds were drawn up, the windows became steamed-over, and being small and unimportant in the midst of the family bustle I would climb on the sofa under the window and rub holes in the steam on the glass so that I could peer out at the rigidly white or saturated back garden.

Beyond one kitchen window grew an ancient umbrella-shaped apple tree, twice as tall as the house and pressing some of its branches so close against the walls and windows that you might think it would like to come in. But that was not true; it lived out its own rhythm, indifferent to the coming and going of the people within the rooms. Like a calendar, it kept the seasons, gnarled and bony in winter, on sunny spring days casting the shine from its white and red blossoms over our faces as we sat round the table; in summer flooding the room with green light reflected from its leaves, and in autumn causing us all to abandon for a day our usual pastimes so that we might join in with the excitement of picking the apples. On that day, very long ladders were brought from my father's store of equipment, rakes, buckets, baskets and boxes. When the tree was relieved of its burden it seemed glad, a bit dishevelled where we had disturbed its leaves, but light and airy. So closely did I keep a watch on this tree from day to day, I could not have known it more intimately if our house had been built in its branches.

My first clear visual memory of my mother is associated with an experience of terror. I was four. I had been left in the kitchen; something was happening in the front rooms of the house where Mother was ill and in bed. Although it was still quite early in the morning, a strange man had come, 'The doctor', Grandmother told me, 'stay here, in the kitchen, and keep warm'. Outside, a white frost, like snow, glittered on the garden. I could hear increasing muffled noises in the front of the house, male voices, heavy footsteps. I opened the kitchen door, ran up the passage to the front door, which stood wide open, and saw some men carrying a stretcher out of the house. They had passed through the door and were going down the steps. On the stretcher, wrapped to the chin in coarse yellow blankets that I had never seen before, and appearing strangely helpless, lay my mother, her dark hair sharply black against the pallor of her face. Cold air rushed through the open door; the white frost on the ground was hateful; I detested the yellow blankets and the strange men; they were carrying my mother away; I opened my mouth and roared. Grandmother caught me into her arms. To the sound of my bawling, my poor mother, who had pneumonia and was dangerously ill, was carried to a waiting ambulance and thence to hospital. Such was my terror, every detail of that scene remained with me for life. I have never ceased to feel relieved that this was not my last memory of my mother, who was always passionately dear to me, both then and in later life. The post-war influenza epidemic, know as 'the big 'flu', lingered in the community for a few years and many died of pneumonia.

Now the sun was shining through the open back door and Grandmother was standing at the bench beating eggs in a bowl.

'What are you making, Granny?'

'Just a pikelet to take to your mother in hospital, and you are to come with me.'

At this prospect I was flooded with blissful happiness. Grandmother lifted me to the kitchen table, where my face, hands and knees were scrubbed till I was as clean as a new pin. I was dressed in my best clothes. How strange to visit hospital and find your mother there, smiling; to be upstairs, looking down on the hospital lawn and Liffey Street, to be among so many white beds, and most strange of all, so remarkable that you would never forget seeing it, the ornamental iron-work that railed the hospital veranda. Dee Street Hospital, which was at that time known as Queen Victoria Hospital, served as the Invercargill General Hospital till Kew hospital was built in 1937.

At last, Mother was home in her own bed, and a large coke fire glowed in the fireplace in her room. I had not seen a coke fire before. I danced on the fender — suddenly I was falling forward into the fire. The nearness of the coke shocked me. I put out my hands to save myself. Mother cried out from the bed and Joan grabbed me so quickly that only my hands reached the fire and struck coke that was not yet red hot.

In the summer I climbed one day with Mother up Bluff Hill, travelling the eighteen miles by train to Bluff where, at the top of the hill, at the flagstaff, some friends of Grandmother's lived, Mr and Mrs Burrage. A road to the top had not yet been built. With the aid of telescopes and binoculars, approaching visitors were observed by Mr Burrage and identified early on the long slow climb. Calculations were made about the time of arrival at a point which was considered a place of rest, and where the mistress of the lonely and solitary house liked to meet her visitors with fresh scones and a pot of tea.

On the wild, green, manuka-scented slopes of Bluff Hill a herd of cattle grazed, indifferent to the sea far below and the sky above, and only mildly interested in the black-frocked, snow-haired lady with her round basket, who came down to meet her visitors well-armed against the cattle with a large black umbrella with which she threatened them and which she intended to open and fling in their path if they charged. How memorable, to eat fresh scones and drink tea on a summer's day on the slopes of the hill, with the sea distant and motionless below, while we rested on our long climb. There, on a lichened boulder, I saw for the first time a grasshopper. Later, a kind man with whiskers let me peer through his telescope at Dog Island lighthouse, like a white, unlit, daylight candle on the sea, and at the bare block-like buildings of Quarantine Island. This was the first time I became aware of the largeness of space and the smallness of a grasshopper, and came home with my head full of a feeling for size and distance, an experience that permanently altered my view of the world. It was a perfect day, a memory to treasure, like a milky pearl.

That year my parents took me with them by car on a visit to Christchurch. I was very car-sick and had fallen asleep before we reached Dunedin. I was surprised on waking to see the numerous lighted three-storied windows of the City Hotel, where we were to stay overnight in Dunedin. I was sick again on the rest of the journey, but remember seeing some of the many windmills that stood on the Canterbury plains. In Christchurch we stayed at Sockburn with one of my father's sisters, whose husband, Charlie Horwell, owned a butcher shop there. I was fascinated by my uncle's hand-operated sausage-machine, and by his large grindstone, which I enjoyed turning.

Back home, in the last term of 1924, before I had turned five, I began to attend Waihopai School in Herbert Street, in the company of my nine-year-old sister at first, then with classmates from the neighbourhood. The school, of about five hundred pupils then, was within walking distance; we would cut across the Queen's Park golf links on a track in the grass made by children's feet from the Kelvin Street stile to the school stile. The track had two or three good mud slides in wet weather, which caused our mothers to wonder at the amount of mud on our shoes. Few golfers were on the links during working hours and the park provided an attractive route, with its open spaces and groups of trees, oak, bluegum, fir and pine, and a small reedy pond. Between the park and school grew a beautiful stand of silver poplars whose leaves turned a clear canary colour in autumn. We crossed the park four times a day, because we came home for mid-day dinner, but in my last years at Waihopai that route was closed off and we were thus compelled to keep to the streets and footpaths, which were not so interesting.

I admired my infant teacher, Miss Salmond, who asked us to stand in our places and sway with our arms raised as though we were trees in the wind, and who distributed gaily coloured squares of glossy new paper to fold into shapes and take home. I picked the first daffodil that bloomed in our garden and carried it to school as a gift, where it was received absently and placed in a green vase on the classroom windowsill and died. I felt sad, believing I had caused its death by picking it.

Towards Christmas Mother managed, not without difficulty, to collect her daughters together for a studio photograph, an undertaking which can't have been easy for the photographer either, since there was a great disparity in the size of the three girls aged fifteen, ten and five. Joan refused to have her hair trimmed for the occasion and I followed suit. The photographer had distinct ideas of his own and made Ada furious by insisting that she retire behind a screen and change into fancy shoes and stockings of a style that she would not normally wear, and, what is more, 'They did not fit!' I don't know whether the three long strings of beads that linked the figures together were ours or the photographer's, probably the latter's since we were all different in character and Mother would not have made the mistake of giving us similar possessions, but our dresses must have been her handiwork, since she made all our clothes. The photographer asked us to 'Watch for the little birdie in the camera' and crouched behind it with a black cloth over his head, and that was the only time we three girls were photographed together. The photo might have been commissioned to send to Mother's sisters at Christmas, as Aunt Johana had moved to Dunedin with her husband and family, and Aunt Agnes Goodlet and family were living in Hamilton.

The following year, 1925, was the year of the South Seas Exhibition in Dunedin and Johana invited our family to stay with her to attend. My parents and grandmother and sisters visited the Exhibition in relay, but I was 'too small', Mother told me. I made a great fuss about being 'the only member of the family not allowed to go', but my parents took no notice and I had to be content with several mementoes, including a green and gold glass mug with my name engraved on it, which I treasured.

If the day often began for me in my father's company, it usually ended in my grandmother's. In the evening the family migrated to the sitting room in the front of the house, where there was an open fire, a piano, a gramophone, and from the time a neighbour first brought in a crystal set, a radio. The first radio I saw had all its parts set out on a board on our front room table and we listened through earphones. My grandmother was in her seventies and dressed in a manner then considered fitting for old ladies, in black, as a matter of course. She wore a long black frock reaching almost to her ankles, black stockings and black shoes. I don't know why older women were always expected to wear black, unless it was a heritage from their much-loved Queen Victoria, who had died a quarter of a century earlier. Her build was slight; she had 'shrunk' she told us, and this we could see for ourselves from photographs taken when she was a nurse in the full bloom of middle life, with her strong, proud lift of shoulders and high cheek-bones. Her hair, which she wore long and twisted into a soft little bun with the aid of a 'switch' (which was a length of hair of her own colour given to her by a friend), kept its colour, brown, and her eyes when I knew them had the tranquillity of age. For me, there could be no face in the world more beautiful; it was equalled only by my mother's.

As my grandmother was the oldest member of our family and I was the youngest we sometimes found ourselves in each other's company at the fringe of more central activities. I had to leave the gathering in the front room and go to bed early and Grandmother retired at the same time. Sometimes we shared a supper in the kitchen which the front room folk knew nothing about. She might fancy old-fashioned Scotch porridge for supper, which was a little unusual and not likely to be relished by the others, so we did not tell the others. I, too, liked porridge for supper. I used to tell her that our picture was on the mantelpiece on the Mazawattee tea tin, where a grandmother and her grand-daughter were shown drinking tea together. I sat at the table in the tidied and deserted kitchen making a canal through the oatmeal in my plate to uncover the picture of the Invercargill Water Tower printed on the china and postponing bed as long as possible by asking her about her Scottish childhood, but she lived in the present, not the past, and was not easily drawn. When tired of my questions she would say to me, 'Whist! You'd speer the leg off an iron pot'. She also used to say, to an adult, and over my head, when she thought I was paying too much attention to adult conversation, 'There's a chiel amang ye taking' notes, and i'faith he'll print them'.

'Tell me about the time you saw the man hanged, Granny.'

'I didn't see the man hanged. I mind I was sent for a billy of milk. I saw this great crowd of folk gathering in the square and I had a peek to see what was going on. I was small, but I saw the man up on the gallows. They fastened the rope round his neck. Then someone behind me put his two hands round my throat. I was so taken up with watching the man that I thought it was the rope round my neck. I thought I was hanged. I heard someone say, "What are you doing here?" It was my uncle who had come up behind me and grabbed me. I never again followed after a crowd.'

Sometimes Grandmother took me visiting, or to see Charlie Chaplin at the 'pictures', and when she met an old friend up town who had not seen her for many years and I heard the friend exclaim, 'I thought you were dead!', I would be stiff with indignation at the friend's even suggesting that my grandmother might be dead. Once when we were walking through town she misjudged a step and fell on the footpath. I could not have been more shocked if the sun had fallen from the sky. She rose quickly, unhurt, and brushing the dust from her black silk coat, said, 'Say nothing about this at home. It would only worry your mother.' For Grandmother, life began and ended with my mother, as it did for my father. When I was older I, too, felt protective towards my gentle mother. Occasionally, though not often, Grandmother sang as she worked about the house. I could feel the hair rise on my scalp when I heard her clear, melancholy mourning for Bonnie Charlie. 'Better lo'ed ye canna be. Will ye no' come back again?' Mother did not sing, but often played on the piano, 'by ear'. When coaxed, she could recite long dramatic poems that she had learnt by heart at school; 'Beside the ungathered rice he lay / His sickle in his hand', or, 'She's somebody's mother, boys, he said / Who hurts a hair of yon grey head / Dies like a dog.' She was to remember these Longfellow poems all her life, but did not think of them at all seriously.

When I was about seven she sometimes had difficulty in getting me to go to school, the novelty of school having worn off for me. I was happy at home and wanted to stay there. One morning I refused to go at all and kicked up such a fuss that nine o'clock came and passed and it was too late to go, or so I imagined. My father and sisters had long departed; only Mother and Grandmother remained. The house contained that hollow, after-breakfast silence when all family activity seems to have ceased forever. If my father had still been in the house it is unlikely that I should have attempted this performance; I should have known from the beginning that it would have been useless. He was a man of very strong character who could use words effectively and his eyes alone could speak for him. There was no reason why I should not go to school. I was simply being naughty and Mother knew it. She threatened to take me herself if I did not obey her, but this I could not believe. The ground was cut from under my feet when she put on her coat and bustled me off taking no notice of my wails and protests.

I remember, as I was hurried along in childish misery, the strangeness of the deserted golf-links where only a few sheep grazed in one corner, deserted because all the children were now in school, and how the dewy, silver-white grass, glittering in the morning sun, tried to break in upon my darkness. As we drew near the school, which was the bare, bleak, brick building with a small belfry that has since been demolished and replaced by new buildings, a shocking thought struck me. Supposing I should be seen? I imagined mocking voices. 'Her mother had to bring her!' To be brought to school by a parent, or met after school, was considered babyish. How could I face up to such a disgrace? It was not to be borne. So I said very meekly that I would now go on alone. When she won this victory about whether or not I should go to school she won them all and I gave no further trouble in that direction.

In the summer Mother took me with her on a trip to Dunedin to visit Aunt Johana, and pointed out to me, as we passed in the train, the house at Longbush where she was born. As a child she had often watched the trains passing and thought that the people she saw in the carriages looked 'so comfortable', never dreaming that one day she too would look from the windows of the Invercargill to Lyttelton express. In Dunedin my aunt lived at number 96 Queen Street in a house that I have since wished I could use in fiction, but have thought that it was too unusual to be credible. It was a tall, narrow, double-storied wooden house with bay windows that looked out towards the harbour and peninsula and was built on a steep hill. The front door was approached by means of a path with a hand-rail, but when you wanted to go out the back door it was first necessary to go upstairs. In addition to the front staircase in the hall, a flight of steep stairs led up through the downstairs kitchen. The back door opened on to a small yard and gate leading to native bush scented by fuchsia, moss and ferns, preserved to form part of the green Town Belt. George Street was only one block down the hill. We went to town in the tram and had afternoon tea with my aunt at the Savoy Restaurant, which was decorated with palms in pots, ornamental light-shades and elaborate flower displays like a romantic stage-setting, and where a violinist and pianist played subdued music and a three-tiered cake-stand was placed in the centre of each table. One day we drove to Brighton, where my grown-up cousins hired rowing boats and tried to row us up-river, but the boats stuck fast on the shallow river bottom every few yards and the excursion turned out to be strenuous as well as hilarious, since determined physical effort was required to push the boats clear. A long tram ride took us from town to St Clair Beach, where I thought it disappointing to see the remains of the early salt-water baths, which had fallen into disrepair.

In Invercargill, in 1927, Mother opened a small fruit and sweet shop in Dee Street close to the hospital after noticing that there was a place for such a shop. My parents were now buying the house at 297 Dee Street, which they at first rented. A valuer from the Southland Building Society jumped on the floors to test the piles and pronounced the house sound enough for a mortgage; my father removed the front verandah and built a small porch, installed a hotwater system and made improvements in the bathroom and elsewhere and was planning to build a petrol station in front of the house. He withdrew from the taxi rank and was then working as barman for Dick Harris at the well-known hotel called 'The White House', situated on Bay Road outside the city boundary — the nearest licensed premises to Invercargill in those days of prohibition (1906–1943). He travelled there and back by train and I went with him one day to play with Marjorie Harris, who was about my own age, spending a happy day on a swing and sliding down hay in a barn. The Harrises were generous people and gave Joan a memorable holiday one summer when they took her with them to their holiday house at Riverton Rocks.

My father discussed his plans for a petrol station with the proprietor of a petrol station in South Invercargill, Mick O'Neill, a very large black-haired Irishman whom I thought a giant when I went with my father in his car to call on him. I usually went wherever the car was going. Mick O'Neill's service station, and Russell's in town, on the corner of Gala Street, were the only two petrol stations in Invercargill in those early days of motoring. Petrol delivery tankers had not yet come into use; petrol was delivered in four-gallon tins, tipped by hand into underground tanks through a funnel and pumped up by hand, gallon by gallon, as required. Mick O'Neill had a large advertising sign on the roof of his premises which announced in red letters, 'HELL'. The letter 'S' had blown away from an advertisement for SHELL and not been replaced.

Notes on Contributors

ROB ALLAN. Lives in Port Chalmers; a poet and teacher of the deaf. He won the PEN First Book of Poetry Award in 1992 for *Karitane Postcards* (1991). At present he is working on a sequence of post-modern sonnets on Dunedin.

GRAHAM BILLING. Poet and novelist, b. 1936, Billing has lived mainly in Dunedin and Christchurch. Winner of numerous awards; his topic is chiefly the sea. His sixth novel is *The Chambered Nautilus* (1993).

ALISTAIR CAMPBELL. Born in Rarotonga in 1925, Campbell spent years in Dunedin at school and university. His poetry has appeared in seven collections and *Collected Poems, 1947–1981* (1981). *Stone Rain: The Polynesian Strain* was published in 1992. *Island to Island* (1984) is an autobiographical account of his return as an adult to the Cook Islands in search of his forebears.

JOY COWLEY. Born in Levin in 1936. Cowley wrote several adult novels in the 1970s but most recently has concentrated on children's books and religious works.

ALLEN CURNOW. New Zealand's greatest poet, most prolific critic and editor was born in 1911 in Timaru and lived in the South Island until 1930. In 1988 he published *Continuum: New and Later Poems 1972–1988*, and in 1990, *Selected Poems 1940–1989*.

RUTH DALLAS. Dallas was born in Invercargill in 1919 and lives in Dunedin. She has described growing up in the south in her autobiography, *Curved Horizon* (1991). A poet and children's author, Dallas has won many awards. She has been a Burns Fellow, has an honorary doctorate from Otago University, and was awarded a CBE in 1989. Her *Collected Poems* appeared in 1987.

DAN DAVIN. Born in rural Southland in 1913. Although Davin lived most of his adult life in England, the inspiration for his seven novels and four collections of short fiction was largely his early life in Southland and Otago. He died in 1990.

KIM EGGLESTON. Born in 1960 on the West Coast, poet Eggleston has published *25 Poems: The Mist Will Rise and the World Will Drip With Gold* (1985) and *The Whole Crack* (1987).

DAVID EGGLETON. Born in 1952, Eggleton has close ties with Dunedin, where he has been a Burns Fellow. He is widely known as a performance poet, and is respected as a critic and commentator on society. Collections of his work are: *South Pacific Sunrise* (1987), *After Tokyo* (1987) and *People of the Land* (1988).

STEVAN ELDRED-GRIGG. Historian and novelist Eldred-Grigg spent his youth on the West Coast, but he has strong family links with Canterbury, where he now lives. Recent novels are *Oracles & Miracles* (1987), *Siren Celia* (1989,) *The Shining City* (1991), and *Gardens of Fire* (1993). He writes something of his own life in *My History, I Think* (1994)

FIONA FARRELL. Poet, novelist and playwright, Farrell was born in Oamaru in 1947. As Farrell Poole she published poetry, *Cutting Out* (1987), stories, *The Rock Garden* (1989). As Farrell she won the New Zealand Book Award for Fiction in 1993 for *The Skinny Louie Book* (1993).

KATE FLANNERY. A Christchurch fiction writer who first came to attention in 1991 when her story 'A Girl's Best Friend' won the Bank of New Zealand Katherine Mansfield Award. This story and others were published in *Like You, Really* (1994).

JANET FRAME. Novelist, short fiction writer, autobiographer and poet, Frame (b. 1924) has been closely associated with Oamaru and Dunedin. Author of eleven novels, Frame's most recent title is *The Carpathians* (1988); *The Envoy from Mirror City* (1985) is the third volume of autobiography.

MAURICE GEE. Born in 1931, in the North Island, but he spent time in Nelson. One of the country's best novelists (both for children and adults), Gee has won numerous awards and fellowships. His most recent works are *Prowlers* (1987), *The Burning Boy* (1990), *Going West* (1992) and *Crime Story* (1994)

BERNADETTE HALL. Christchurch poet, playwright and teacher; b. 1945. Hall has published three collections of poetry: *Heartwood* (1989), *Of Elephants etc* (1990), and *The Persistent Levitator* (1994).

MICHAEL HARLOW. Born 1938 in USA, Harlow has lived in New Zealand, mostly in Dunedin and Christchurch. A poet, editor, teacher and, most recently, a Jungian analyst, Harlow is a former Katherine Mansfield Fellow (1986). His most recent collections are *Vlaminck's Tie* (1985) and *Giotto's Elephant* (1991).

MICHAEL HENDERSON. Born in 1942 in Nelson, novelist and short fiction writer Henderson's most recent work was the short fiction collection *The Lie of the Land* (1991).

KERI HULME. Born in 1947, Hulme draws inspiration from the coastal areas of Okarito and Moeraki. Since her Booker Prize-winning novel, *the bone people* (1983), she has published short fiction, *Te Kaihau/The Windeater* (1986), poetry, *Strands* (1992), and an appreciation of the South, *Home Places: Three Coasts of the South Island of New Zealand* (1989).

ROB JACKAMAN. Born in England in 1945, now living and lecturing in Christchurch, Jackaman began publishing prolifically in the 1970s. His later work is to be found in *Palimpsest* (1989) and *Triptych* (1989).

CHRISTINE JOHNSTON. Born in Dunedin in 1950, Johnston trained as a teacher of languages. She was Burns Fellow at Otago University in 1994. Her first novel, *Blessed Art Thou Among Women* (1991), won the Reed First Fiction Prize in 1990. Her short fiction has appeared in *Landfall* and *Sport*, and been broadcast on radio. A novel for teenagers, *Goodbye Molly McGuire*, was published in 1994 and another, *The Haunting of Molly McGuire*, is forthcoming.

MARION E. JONES. Born in Los Angeles in 1934, Jones now lives in Brighton, near Dunedin. She has had short fiction published in *Landfall*, *Islands*, *Sport* and *Takahe*.

GRAHAM LINDSAY. Born in 1952, this widely published Dunedin poet now lives in Christchurch. He is editor of a post-modern poetry journal *Morepork* (1979–80). His collections include *Big Boy* (1986), *Return to Earth* (1991) and *The Subject* (1994), his fifth book.

IAIN LONIE. Iain Lonie was born in 1932. He was editor at the University of Otago Press at the time of his death in 1988. He published seven collections of verse from 1967, *Winter Walk at Morning* appearing posthumously in 1991.

RACHEL McALPINE. Born in 1940 in South Canterbury, poet and novelist McAlpine has published *Selected Poems* (1988), *Running Away from Home* (1987), and *Farewell Speech* (1990), a novel based on the life of the feminist Kate Sheppard.

CILLA McQUEEN. Born in England in 1949, McQueen has written most of her poetry from Carey's Bay, near Port Chalmers, and Dunedin. Three collections have won the New Zealand Book Award for Poetry; she is a former Burns Fellow (1985, 1986). Recent collections are *Benzina* (1988), and

Crik'ey: New and Selected Poems 1978–1994 (1994). *Berlin Diary* (1990) combines poetry and prose.

MARGARET MAHY. Best known as a prize-winning children's writer, Mahy (b. 1936) has lived in Canterbury since the 1950s. Among her novels for teenagers are *The Catalogue of the Universe* (1985), *The Tricksters* (1986) and *Memory* (1987).

BILL MANHIRE. Manhire was born (1946) and spent his youth in the south. Poet, short fiction writer, editor of poetry and short fiction anthologies, and teacher of creative writing, Manhire has published most recently *The Brain of Katherine Mansfield* (1988), *The New Land: A Picture Book* (1990), *Milky Way Bar* (1991), which won the 1992 New Zealand Book Award for Poetry, and *An Amazing Week in New Zealand* (1993).

OWEN MARSHALL. Born in 1941, Marshall has been most closely associated with Blenheim, Timaru and South Canterbury. One of New Zealand's most distinguished short fiction writers, Marshall has published six collections since 1979, the most recent being *The Divided World: Selected Stories* (1989), *Tomorrow We Save the Orphans* (1990), and *The Ace of Diamonds Gang and Other Stories* (1993). He was Burns Fellow at Otago University in 1992.

JOHN NEWTON. Born in 1959. Newton's only collection of poetry, *Tales of the Angler's Eldorado* (1985), is influenced by his early life in the Marlborough region. Recent poems have appeared in *Sport.*

NEVILLE PEAT. Born in 1947, Peat currently lives and works in Dunedin, where he is a conservationist and writer. Since 1983 he has published sixteen titles, the most recent being *The Falcon and the Lark* (1992).

BILL SEWELL. Formerly editor at the University of Otago Press, Sewell (b. 1951) now lives in Wellington, where he works as a poet and legal researcher. His most recent collection are *Making the Fair Land Glow* (1986) and *Balancing on Blue* (1991).

PHILIP TEMPLE. Born in 1939 in England, Temple has lived in New Zealand since 1957, mostly near Dunedin. A former Katherine Mansfield Fellow and Robert Burns Fellow, he published *Dark of the Moon* as well as a reprint of *Beak of the Moon* in 1993. Both are fantasies set in a bird world.

BRIAN TURNER. Turner was born in Dunedin in 1944 and has lived there ever since. His poetry is strongly tied to the Otago region. Recent collections are *Bones* (1985), written largely while he was Burns Fellow at Otago University in 1984, *All That Blue Can Be* (1989) and *Beyond* (1992).

HONE TUWHARE. Born in Northland in 1922, poet Tuwhare has lived for long periods in Dunedin (where he was Burns Fellow in 1969, 1974) and Balclutha. One of New Zealand's most popular poets, his volume of poetry *No Ordinary Sun* (1964) has been reprinted ten times. *Mihi: Collected Poems* (1987) was illustrated by Ralph Hotere. *Deep River Talk: Collected Poems* (1993) presents poems from all his collections, and nine new poems.

IAN WEDDE. Born in Blenheim in 1946, Wedde is a widely published poet, novelist, short fiction writer and commentator on the arts. Recent poetry includes *Driving into the Storm: Selected Poems* (1987) and *Tendering* (1988). Fiction includes *Symmes Hole* (1986) and *Survival Arts* (1988).

FORBES WILLIAMS. Born in Melbourne in 1960, Williams has lived in New Zealand, mostly in Dunedin, where he lectures at the Medical School, since the mid-1970s. His first collection of short fiction is *Motel View* (1992).

TOSS WOOLLASTON. Born 1910 in Taranaki, artist Woollaston has painted chiefly in the Nelson area. The story in this anthology appeared in *Landfall* and is from a second volume of autobiography (following on from the 1982 *Sage Tea*), as yet unpublished.

Acknowledgements

Godwit Publishing gratefully acknowledges the following authors and publishers for permission to include material in this anthology: Rob Allan and Hazard Press for '9' and '10' from *Karitane Postcards* (1991); Graham Billing and University of Canterbury Press for pp. 102–14 of *The Chambered Nautilus* (1993); Alistair Campbell and Penguin Books for 'Growing Pains in the War Years' from *Island to Island* (Whitcoulls, 1984); Joy Cowley and Penguin Books for 'The Cleaning of Windows' from *Zigzag: New Zealand Stories* (1993); Allen Curnow for 'A Busy Port' (*Sport 7*, 1991); Allen Curnow and Auckland University Press for 'A Time of Day' from *Continuum: New and Later Poems, 1972–1988* (1988); Ruth Dallas and University of Otago Press for 'Early Memories' from *Curved Horizons: An Autobiography* (1991); Winnie Davin for 'Black Diamond' by Dan Davin (*Islands 37*, 1986); Kim Eggleston for 'Wednesday Afternoon in June' from *25 Poems: The Mist Will Rise and the World Will Drip With Gold* (Strong John Press, 1985); David Eggleton and Penguin Books for 'Postcard' from *People of the Land* (1988); Stevan Eldred-Grigg and Penguin Books for 'Cinderellas Waiting for the Ball' from *Oracles and Miracles* (1987); Fiona Farrell and Penguin Books for 'A Story about Skinny Louie' from *The Skinny Louie Book* (1992); Fiona Farrell Poole and Auckland University Press for 'Cemetery, Oamaru' from *Cutting Out* (1987); Kate Flannery and Penguin Books for 'A Girl's Best Friend' from *Like You, Really* (1994); Janet Frame and Random House for pp. 165–173 of *The Envoy from Mirror City: An Autobiography: Volume Three* (Hutchinson, 1985); Maurice Gee and Penguin Books for pp. 109–12 of *The Burning Boy* (Viking, 1990); Bernadette Hall for 'Miriama' (*Vital Writing 3: New Zealand Stories and Poems, 1991–92*, Godwit Press, 1992); Michael Harlow and McIndoe Publishers for 'Stop-time: Galata Kebabci/Dunedin' from *Giotto's Elephant* (1991); Michael Henderson for 'The Two-Tooth in the Thicket' (*Dominion Sunday Times*, 20 October 1991); Keri Hulme and Auckland University Press for extract from 'Fishing the Olearia Tree' from *Strands* (1992); Keri Hulme for 'Slipping Away from the Gaze of the Past' from *Home Places: Three Coasts of the South Island of New Zealand* (Hodder & Stoughton, 1989); Rob Jackaman and Caxton Press for 'Palimpsest: I', 'White-Robed Lady' and 'Leviathan' from *Palimpsest: An Historical Sequence of Poems* (1988); Christine Johnston and Reed Publishing for pp. 3–19 of *Blessed Art Thou Among Women* (1991); Marion E. Jones for 'Shadow' (*Sport 2*, 1989); Graham Lindsay and Auckland University Press for 'Maiorum Institutis Utendo' and 'Green Island' from *Big Boy* (1986); The estate of Iain Lonie and Victoria University Press for 'A Summer at Purakanui' from *Winter Walk at Morning* (1991); Margaret Mahy and J.M. Dent & Sons for pp. 18–28 of *The Tricksters* (1986); Bill Manhire for *An Amazing Week in New Zealand* (Just As I Am Press, 1993); Owen Marshall and McIndoe Publishers for 'A Day With Yesterman' from *The Lynx Hunter and Other Stories* (1987); Rachel McAlpine and Penguin Books for pp. 46–53 of *Farewell Speech* (1990); Cilla McQueen for 'Map' (*Sport 8*, 1992); Cilla McQueen and McIndoe Publishers for 'Recipe for One' from *Benzina* (1988) and pp. 34–35 of *Berlin Diary* (1990); John Newton and Untold Press for 'Sparrowhawk' and 'Taylor Domain' from *Tales From the Angler's Eldorado* (1985); Neville Peat and McIndoe Publishers for pp. 11–17 of *The Falcon and the Lark: A New Zealand High Country Journal* (1992); Bill Sewell and McIndoe Publishers for 'Sutton' from *Making the Far Land Glow* (1986); Philip Temple and Penguin Books for 'Rocking' from *Dark of the Moon* (1991); Brian Turner and McIndoe Publishers for 'Lawrence Cemetery' from *Bones* (1985) and 'In the Nineties' from *Beyond* (1992); Hone Tuwhare for 'Snowfall' from *Deep River Talk* (Godwit Press, 1993); Ian Wedde and Penguin Books for pp. 209–13 of *Symmes Hole* (1986); Forbes Williams and Victoria University Press for 'from Dunedin' from *Motel View* (1992); Toss Woollaston for 'The Twenty-seventh Nun' (*Landfall 174*, June 1990).